T0285070

Praise for

EXECUTIVE PRESENCE

THE MISSING LINK BETWEEN MERIT AND SUCCESS

"With clarity and honesty, Sylvia Ann Hewlett shines a light on a central truth: if we fail to master the 'intangibles' of leadership we're in danger of missing the mark. Sylvia's impeccable research and guidance prepares us to crack the Executive Presence code."

> —Ann Beynon, commissioner, UK Equality and Human Rights Commission; director for Wales, BT

"In today's business world, authenticity is the new currency of leadership. In Sylvia Ann Hewlett's valuable book, she demonstrates how you can crack the code of Executive Presence by embracing what differentiates you from the pack."

> —Mark T. Bertolini, chairman, CEO, and president of Aetna

"Sylvia Ann Hewlett's book is essential reading for anyone striving to minimize the gap between how others perceive you and how you want to be seen. It arms you with the skills to create, curate, and manage your personal brand and convince people they are in the presence of someone going places."

> —Joanna Coles, editor in chief of *Cosmopolitan*

"Clear and compassionate, Hewlett explains what it means to have Executive Presence and why it's essential for anyone who wishes to lead in today's uncertain and fast-paced work environment. With memorable stories and examples—including the author's firsthand experiences of getting it wrong as a young woman just starting her career—*Executive Presence* is both practical and compelling."

> —Amy C. Edmondson, Novartis Professor of Leadership and Management, Harvard Business School

"This is a powerful and urgent book for young professionals climbing the ladder. Credentials alone will not get you the next big opportunity. You also need Executive Presence—the ability to signal confidence and credibility. In this immensely readable study, replete with vivid stories as well as hard data, Sylvia Ann Hewlett tells us how to ace EP."

> —Sallie Krawcheck, CEO and cofounder of Ellevest and former head of Bank of America's Global Wealth and Investment Management division

"Sylvia Ann Hewlett has taken some of the mystery out of the claim that 'you just don't have what it takes' in this groundbreaking book on Executive Presence. Combining story after story with well-grounded research, this book provides a simple guide that will help you crack the code to career success."

—Katherine W. Phillips, Paul Calello Professor of Leadership and Ethics, Columbia Business School

"Whether you are an aspiring corporate star or a seasoned veteran, Sylvia Ann Hewlett's *Executive Presence* will captivate you—pithily written, laden with stories, and grounded in the latest research. You will find a lesson that you can't wait to adopt on every page. It is the modern handbook on the art of visible leadership for which many of us have been waiting."

—Sir Trevor Phillips, chair of the Equality and Human Rights Commission and producer of the BBC series *Windrush*

"In *Executive Presence*, Sylvia Ann Hewlett forges into that murky gray zone between how women look and how they perform. With wit and aplomb, Hewlett convincingly shows why presence matters and how women (and men) can achieve it without compromising their values or their careers. Her advice is well-researched, heartfelt, and always on the mark."

—Debora Spar, senior associate dean of Harvard Business School Online and former president of Barnard College

"Sylvia Ann Hewlett is again leading the way by examining a critical component of business success, Executive Presence. She is a master at making a vague topic clear. She demystifies the meaning of Executive Presence and provides tangible, practical advice that readers can easily use to lift their game."

—Anré Williams, president of Global Merchant Services American Express

"In this significant book, Sylvia Ann Hewlett challenges the conventional wisdom that Executive Presence is an innate quality that can barely be defined, much less developed. Anyone seeking to close the gap between their merit and their success could benefit from her practical, engaging, and human advice."

—Kenji Yoshino, Chief Justice Earl Warren Professor of Constitutional Law, NYU School of Law

E

EXECUTIVE PRESENCE 2.0

P

LEADERSHIP IN AN AGE OF INCLUSION

EXECUTIVE PRESENCE 2.0

SYLVIA ANN HEWLETT

HARPER
BUSINESS
An Imprint of HarperCollinsPublishers

HarperCollins books may be purchased for educational, business, or sales promotional use. For information, please email the Special Markets Department at SPsales@harpercollins.com.

Originally published as *Executive Presence* in 2014 by Harper Business, an imprint of HarperCollins Publishers.

REVISED AND UPDATED EDITION PUBLISHED 2023

Library of Congress Cataloging-in-Publication Data

Names: Hewlett, Sylvia Ann, 1946- author.
Title: Executive presence 2.0 : leadership in an age of inclusion / Sylvia Ann Hewlett.
Description: Second edition. | New York, NY : Harper Business, 2023. | Revised edition of the author's Executive presence, [2014] | Includes bibliographical references and index.
Identifiers: LCCN 2023021880 (print) | LCCN 2023021881 (ebook) | ISBN 9780063270558 (hardcover) | ISBN 9780063270565 (epub)
Subjects: LCSH: Executive ability—Psychological aspects. | Leadership—Psychological aspects. | Self-presentation. | Influence (Psychology) | Interpersonal relations.
Classification: LCC HD38.2 .H49 2023 (print) | LCC HD38.2 (ebook) | DDC 658.4/09—dc23/eng/20230720
LC record available at https://lccn.loc.gov/2023021880
LC ebook record available at https://lccn.loc.gov/2023021881

23 24 25 26 27 LBC 5 4 3 2 1

To the amazing young adults at the center of my life:
Shira, Alex, Lisa, Barry, David, Luana, Adam, RB,
and Emma. You've taught me most of what I know about
authenticity, inclusivity, and how to show up in this world
in 2023.

CONTENTS

Contents

PART II: EXECUTIVE PRESENCE 2.0

ACKNOWLEDGMENTS

This book and these themes have been close to my heart for more than ten years, and it gives me great pleasure to acknowledge the extensive help I've received from scholars and corporate executives but also leaders in the world of culture and the arts. Many of these remarkable individuals plunged in not once (in 2012) but twice (in 2022), with precious insights and vivid stories that allowed me to attach voices to my new data and crack the EP code in a post-pandemic world that is still wrestling with #MeToo and Black Lives Matter.

The scholars I have talked to and leaned on for wisdom include: Victoria Bateman (Cambridge), Peter Cappelli (Wharton), John Eatwell (Cambridge), Amy Edmondson (Harvard), Eddie Glaude (Princeton), Allan Krueger (Princeton), Katherine Phillips (Columbia), Debora Spar (Harvard), and Kenji Yoshino (NYU Law School).

The corporate and nonprofit leaders I had the privilege of talking with and learning from include: Mercedes Abramo (Cartier), DeAnne Aguirre (Hercules Capital), Jameel Anz (Arab Bank), Tanya Bannister (CAG), Lydia Bottegoni (Blizzard Entertainment), Erika Irish Brown (Citi), Jyloti Chopra (MGM Resorts), Suzi Digby (ORA), Bob Dudley (Axio Global), Marisa Ferrara (Google), Cassandra Frangos (Spencer Stuart), Trevor Gandy (Merkel), Rosa Gudmundsdottir

Acknowledgments

(Reginn HF), Lorraine Hariton (Catalyst), Roz Hudnell (Intel), Kennedy Ihezie (AIG), Sylvia James (Winston & Strawn), Barbara Jones (Bracewell LLP), Andrés Jónsson (Gód Samskipti), Megan Knight (Google), Logan Kruger (Limon Dance Company), Darin Latimore (Yale School of Medicine), David Miliband (IRC), Andrea Turner Moffitt (Plum Alley Investments), Annmarie Neal (Hellman & Friedman), Elizabeth Nieto (Spotify), Emma Petersson (Ogilvy), Marylin Prince (Prince Houston Group), Scott Rothkopf (Whitney Museum of American Art), Ivan Sacks (Withersworldwide), Todd Sears (Out Leadership), Deborah Rosado Shaw (PepsiCo), Shari Slate (Cisco), Virgil L. Smith (Smith Edwards Group LLC), Keisha Smith-Jeremie (Tory Burch), Vanessa Spatafora (DraftKings), Brande Stellings (Vestry Laight), Tiger Tyagarajan (Genpact), Cornel West (Union Theological Seminary), Anré Williams (American Express), Tai Green Wingfield (Unity), and Kevin Witcher (SWBC).

I owe particular gratitude to the leaders who participated in the survey research and sat down for extended conversations. This was a big ask in 2022 as many organizations were stretched thin dealing with disruptions wrought by Covid and a European war.

I am enormously grateful to Jonathan Burnham and Hollis Heimbouch at HarperCollins. This is the fourth book we have done together, and I'm both in awe of their commitment to my work and their willingness to dig deep into my manuscripts and provide unvarnished feedback. My drafts are always more elegant and spare after Hollis's close attention. I'm also greatly indebted to my literary agent, Molly Friedrich, who has always encouraged me to intermingle data and analysis with storytelling. I think I've finally nailed it.

When it comes to my own "team," I'm immensely appreciative

of the skill sets, empathy, and 360-degree support provided by Melissa Milsten (my project manager), Lance Chantiles-Wertz (my "tech star"), and the staff at Knowledge Networks and NORC, who were invaluable in the data-gathering phases of the research.

A final word on Richard Weinert, my husband of forty-six years. He has become my superpower. The pandemic hit everyone hard, and in my case, social and professional isolation was compounded by major spinal surgery that kept me immobilized for several months. Richard's tender, loving care and buoyant can-do attitude gave me the courage and discipline to finish this important book. These days I call him my "trophy husband."

My first run-in with executive presence (EP) occurred when I was seventeen. I was in the second year of the sixth form at my grammar school in the UK and applying for the ultimate "reach" schools—Oxford and Cambridge. I'd gotten a certain distance, having passed the rigorous entrance examinations, but was now facing a round of interviews. I anticipated a rough time. I knew enough about the world to understand that I came from the "wrong" background (Welsh, working-class), and my knees knocked and I broke out in a cold sweat at the mere thought of facing the scrutiny of Oxbridge dons. I feared they would size me up and decide I did not have "it," which of course they had in spades.

Seeing my distress and eager to be helpful, my mum volunteered to "dress" me for my first interview at St. Anne's College, Oxford. She'd read a ton of Nancy Mitford novels and thought she knew what kind of clothes the "upper crust" wore. I didn't push back—I knew I was clueless. I'd grown up in a backwater coal mining community and had few clothes and no social graces. I was eager for help. Having battled huge odds to pass the entrance tests, I knew that this interview was the only thing standing between me and a coveted place at one of the most distinguished universities in Europe. And I had a good shot—half of those interviewed got a place. I just had to figure out how to look the part of someone who moved in the right circles.

So early one December morning we hit the winter clearance sales—rising at the crack of dawn so that we would be at the head of the herd storming C&A (a department store in Cardiff, Wales). And did we score! In the sales racks of the ladies' suits department my mum found exactly what she was looking for: a nubby tweed suit with a fox collar. And I don't mean the collar was made out of fox fur. I mean the collar was a fox—or most of a fox. The tail was a big feature (you were supposed to fling it around your neck as extra protection against the winter cold), and then there were two beady eyes and two sets of claws.

As might be expected, my Oxford interview was a disaster. The admissions committee was gobsmacked. I literally took their breath away. They simply did not know what to make of a seventeen-year-old who wore a fox and seemed to be trying to look like the Queen Mother—especially since this particular seventeen-year-old spoke English with a thick working-class Welsh accent (more on that in chapter 3). I did not get in . . . and was devastated. But it was hard to blame my mum. She had tried so hard.

To my great relief I got a second shot at my dream. A month later I learned that I'd also passed the Cambridge entrance examinations (in those days the two top universities in the UK crafted their own rigorous tests). I was invited to go for an interview. I told my mother that she was off the case—this time I was dressing myself. Remembering "the look" of the other female candidates at Oxford, I borrowed a pleated skirt and a simple sweater from a friend and ironed my unruly hair so it fell in the shining sheets that seemed to be in vogue. Despite an acute attack of nerves, I did well enough in the interview. Three weeks later I learned that I had won a place. I was over the moon. I knew that a Cambridge education would transform my life prospects.

Looking back, I realize that I didn't need to do brilliantly in those interviews. I merely needed not to stick out like a sore thumb.

Introduction

The fact is, back then, Oxford and Cambridge universities were under pressure from the British government to diversify and had committed to increasing the number of female and working-class individuals in the student body. Unbeknownst to me, I was a prime candidate, and those admissions committees were leaning over backward to give me a place. But the fox collar *and* the Welsh accent were just too much for class-conscious Oxbridge dons. I just stuck in their craw. Losing the fox was a winning idea.

Given the travails of Oxbridge entrance, you would have thought I'd learned a thing or two about the power of appearance. Perhaps I did, but it was hard to hang on to. Time and time again I made costly mistakes.

Take my hippie professor phase. My first job was in academia, and when I joined the Barnard College faculty as assistant professor of economics, I assumed that since I was working on a college campus, and not on Wall Street, it was okay to be young and fun. So I wore my hair waist-long and I specialized in flowing ethnic skirts—my favorite was hand-stitched and had a rather loud patchwork quilt pattern. I failed to understand that looking as though I was on my way to Woodstock got in the way of establishing authority on the job. I was facing a tough sell even without the hippie skirts. I was twenty-seven when I started this job, and it was a stretch to convince anyone I was a professor and not just another student. The last thing I needed was to compound the challenges I faced as the youngest faculty member—and one of the few females in the economics department. Looking back, I now understand that my early struggles to command attention and respect in lecture halls and faculty meetings did not center on content or delivery (I was a clear, crisp speaker and knew my material cold), but rather on the way I presented myself.

Time passed and after some painful experimentation, I eventually fixed the way I looked, evolving a signature style that combined

3

elegance and professionalism with a "safe" amount of idiosyncratic flair (more on this in chapter 4). But I wasn't out of the woods on the EP front. Twenty years later I hit another—and much more serious—brand problem. It turns out that EP is a fragile thing: It needs to be nurtured, invested in, and curated. I failed to do this and fell flat on my face—necessitating an EP makeover.

Here is what happened.

In 2002, Tina Brown (who, at that point, headed up Talk Miramax Books) published my book *Creating a Life*. It launched on April 7. The weekend before, *Time* magazine ran a cover story on the book and the CBS News show *60 Minutes* aired a feature. This coverage triggered a maelstrom of media attention. The *New York Times* and *BusinessWeek* did feature pieces on the book; so did *People* and *Parade* magazines. I appeared on the *Today* show as well as on *Oprah* and *The View*. The coup de grâce: In late April I was lampooned on *Saturday Night Live*, confirming the fact that my book had briefly entered the zeitgeist.

Alas, the good news did not last.

On May 20 I picked up the *New York Times* and glimpsed on the front page a noisy headline that blared "The Talk of the Book World Still Can't Sell." Halfway through the first sentence my blood ran cold—the subject of the article was *my* book. In gleeful tones the reporter, Warren St. John (a young, male, hotshot business writer), walked the reader through how *Creating a Life* was shaping up to be a total bust on the sales front. He found the explanation all too simple: "Women are just not interested in shelling out $22 for a load of depressing news about their biological clock," he opined smugly and snarkily. I was stunned. These dismissive words did not describe the book I had written.

I didn't even need to finish the article to understand the damage it would do—which was swift and devastating. In a matter of weeks, *Creating a Life* was DOA—and, figuratively speaking, so was I. I went from being a much-feted author to a pariah, since one of the results of being trashed on the front page of the *Times* is that everyone knows. It's like being stripped in public. My entire circle of friends and colleagues read this piece. In fact, one reason I felt so bad was that I knew that many more people would read the alpha-male spin of Warren St. John on page A1 of the *Times* than would ever read *Creating a Life*. That article effectively buried what was my most deeply felt and pain-filled book.

I tried to rebound, of course. Over that summer I threw myself into a new book project. In early September I met with Molly Friedrich, my longtime literary agent, to pitch my new idea. "It's something more fine-grained, more academic," I offered. Looking me in the eye, Molly let me have it. "Sylvia," she said, "there's not going to be a next book. Given your recent track record, you're not going to get a decent publisher or a decent advance. You need to get a day job."

I was stunned. How had this happened? How could my livelihood be in jeopardy and my reputation—carefully built over years—be in tatters? The explanation dawned painfully and slowly: I had constructed, but hadn't protected, my personal brand. I'd invested in it—establishing myself in both academia and public policy circles as an intellectual heavyweight with the chops to take on the really thorny questions of our time—but I hadn't proactively looked after it. I might have realized, when the *Time* story broke, that I was seriously out of my depth. Although I'd written high-profile books before (*When the Bough Breaks* had received a Robert F. Kennedy Book Award), it didn't occur to me to arm myself with a PR professional, someone who could craft a media campaign that would amplify, rather than distort, my message. Instead I reveled in the immediate impact of *Creating a Life* and had plunged in with naïve delight, doing every radio show and print interview that came my way. Quite quickly the content of the book was dumbed down, making me vulnerable to attack. It's one thing to be thoughtfully critiqued by the *New York Review of Books*, and quite another to be bent out of shape by the *National Enquirer*.

So, having squandered my hard-won gravitas, I had little choice but to start over, building my credibility and authority brick by heavy brick. As a woman north of fifty, I did not have time on my side. But decades spent doing good work in both academia and the public sector had given me a network and at least a few sponsors that I could turn to for a fresh start. That fall I applied for, and got, two adjunct teaching positions—one at Columbia and one at Princeton. I poured immense energy into these gigs and by the spring was able to convert the Columbia position into a continuing part-time job—as director of the Gender and Policy Program at the School of International and Public Affairs. With my brand refurbished, I had fresh currency in the very circles I wanted to reengage with: professional women and their employers. Because, of course, I hadn't changed my focus: I still wanted to make a difference, to transform the lives and career prospects of women and other underrepresented groups. This time around I decided to focus on changing the face of leadership, to help create the conditions that empower many more women, people of color, and LGBTQ+ employees and others to sit at decision-making tables. In 2004 I founded a think tank (the Center for Talent Innovation, now called Coqual) that has become an influential research organization globally and done much to accelerate the progress of women and other previously excluded groups around the world. In driving this tranche of work I've written four books and twenty-seven articles—for Harvard Business Review Press. I've learned my lesson. Nowadays I proactively curate where I publish and avoid the popular media. I want to be seen as an intellectual heavyweight, not as tabloid fodder.

My bumpy ride on the EP journey has contributed special energy as well as important perspectives to this book. To flag two of the more significant:

Appearance challenges are not trivial, but they do tend to be easily fixed and pale in comparison to other, more profound EP problems. Remember that fox collar? Although it blew my chances at St. Anne's College, I was able to quickly ditch that look and improve my chances when I got a second shot.

Reputational glitches are much more serious—and immensely difficult to recover from. Resurrecting my brand after the disastrous launch of *Creating a Life* took about six years. I didn't breathe easy until my body of new work had spawned a fifth *Harvard Business Review* article. At that point I knew I had reestablished my gravitas.

The irony, of course, is that this entire discussion centers on image, not substance. Whether we're talking about appearance or gravitas, we're focusing on what we're signaling to the world rather than what we're really accomplishing. What kind of outfit I wore to my Oxford interview had no bearing on my intelligence or my preparedness for an Oxford education. Seen from that vantage point, it should not have mattered. But it did. Enormously. Similarly, the fact that *Creating a Life* was dragged into the gutter by the tabloid press (and talk radio) had no bearing on the intrinsic value of the book. After all, it made it onto the *BusinessWeek* list of the ten most important books of 2002 and I still meet women whose lives were transformed by its content. But messaging matters. Enormously. The wrong message and the wrong messenger can destroy careers, whatever the substantive reality.

So read this book. Understanding EP and cracking its code will do wonders for your ability to achieve success and do something wonderful with your life.

PART I

1

Steve Jobs had it and Michelle Obama has it. It's embodied by people as varied as Volodymyr Zelenskyy, the much admired president of Ukraine who's leading the heroic resistance to the Russian invasion, and former prime minister Margaret Thatcher, known by the moniker the Iron Lady, who led the rebirth of free-market conservatism in late twentieth-century Britain. The legendary leader Nelson Mandela exuded it—when he donned the Springboks' jersey and shook the hand of the captain of the winning all-white national rugby team, the world knew that South Africa had found a leader intent on reconciliation.

It is executive presence—and no man or woman attains a top job, lands an extraordinary deal, or develops a significant following without this heady combination of confidence, poise, and authenticity that convinces the rest of us we're in the presence of someone who's the real deal. It's an amalgam of qualities that telegraphs that you are in charge or deserve to be.

And here I want to underscore the word *telegraph*. Executive presence is not a measure of performance: whether, indeed, you hit the numbers, attain the ratings, or increase market share. Rather, it's a measure of image: whether you signal to others that you have what it takes, that you're star material. If you're able to crack the EP code you'll be first in line for the next plum assignment and be given a chance of doing something extraordinary with your life.

The amazing thing about EP is that it's a precondition for success whether you're a management consultant, a Wall Street banker—or a cellist.

Every October, a distinguished jury assembles at Merkin Concert Hall in New York City to judge the finalists in the Concert Artists Guild's international competition. Several weeks of rigorous auditions have already taken place, and an applicant pool of 350 instrumentalists and singers from all over the world has been whittled down to 12 extraordinary young musicians. Last fall, I attended the final auditions.

A twenty-three-year-old Korean violinist was first up.[1] He entered the auditorium from stage left and after taking a detour behind the Steinway piano, sidled onto the apron of the stage looking painfully ill at ease. Head bowed, violin dangling, he stared at the floor, doing his best to avoid eye contact with the jurors as he waited for his accompanist to get settled. Unfortunately, it took a while, since she had trouble adjusting the piano stool to the right height. The violinist shifted his weight awkwardly from side to side. I could feel restlessness rising in the audience. One juror blew his nose; another started tapping her foot.

Finally the accompanist struck the first chords of a glorious—and immensely difficult—Beethoven sonata, and the violinist raised his instrument and started playing. But it took a while for the audience to be drawn in—to give this musician a chance.

An Irish mezzo-soprano had slot number two. The energy was very different from the get-go. She walked confidently onto the stage, shoulders squared, head held high. Her dress was perfectly chosen, a simple navy blue sheath that conveyed elegance and seriousness of purpose. I spent a moment silently applauding her choice, but my attention was quickly drawn to her face, which was adorned with a radiant, joyous smile. She seemed to be telling me that something immensely pleasurable and exciting was about to begin. The jury caught the vibe and leaned forward in anticipation, lips parted, wanting and expecting to be impressed.

The other finalist who stood out was number seven—a twenty-year-old cellist who had just received an outstanding review for a recording she'd done of the Dvořák cello concerto. As she started playing, I sensed trouble. It was her arms. They flapped. Every time she tackled her cello with a vigorous down-bow, the flesh bounced up and down. I was mesmerized—and so were the jurors. The problem was not excessive weight (she was of medium build) but her choice of clothing. Her dress was a disaster—a black silk number with a skimpy, ill-fitting halter top. No wonder her arms flapped—anyone's would in such a getup.

My heart went out to this young musician. A distracted jury is never a good idea. Throughout her twenty-minute program the judges failed to focus their full attention on her music, and her powerful playing did not get its due.

These are the finalists that stand out in my memory: Musicians number one and seven did not receive prizes. The mezzo-soprano did.

I've gone to these auditions several times over the years and am always impressed by the number of seemingly peripheral factors that feed into the judging process. For sure, each finalist in this international competition clears a high bar of excellence. All of the young musicians I heard at Merkin Hall last fall were enormously skilled. They wouldn't have gotten through the early rounds of the competition if they weren't outstanding practitioners of their musical craft.

But in the finals what distinguished one musician from another was all the nonmusic stuff. The way they walked onto the stage, the cut of their clothes, the set of their shoulders, the spark in their eyes, and the emotion that played on their faces. All of these things established a mood either of tedium and awkwardness or of excited anticipation.

Richard Weinert, who was president of the Concert Artists Guild between 2001 and 2019, marvels at the importance of what he calls presence. "As we've grappled with launching the careers of these extraordinarily talented artists, we've learned that how they present themselves matters enormously. Yet oftentimes they don't see it as being part of what they need to do. Graduates of the top conservatories—Juilliard, Curtis, and the like—have had little training in it and haven't given it much thought. It often comes as a shock when we explain that how they move on stage and what they wear—how they establish rapport with the audience—is as important as their musical skills."

A recent study underscores the importance of image (or EP, to use the language of this book) for classical musicians. In a piece published in the *Proceedings of the National Academy of Sciences*, University of London researcher Chia-Jung Tsay, working with a sample audience of one thousand, reports that people shown silent videos of pianists performing in international competitions picked out the winners more often than those who could also hear the sound track.[2] The study concludes that the best predictor of success on the competition circuit was whether a pianist could communicate passion through body language and facial expression.

This evidence from the world of music underscores the tremendous power of EP: How musicians present themselves creates an indelible impression. We might like to think that we're evaluating a performance of Bach or Shostakovich based solely on what we hear, but in reality we're profoundly conditioned by the visuals. Judgments are made before the first note sounds in the concert hall.

It's no different in the workplace.

CRACKING THE EP CODE

So how do we figure out this image thing?

One financial sector CEO told me in an interview, "I can't describe it, but I sure know it when I see it." The fact is, many of us find EP a woolly and elusive concept. We can't define it, and we have a hard time putting our arms around it.

Which is why I wrote this book.

Ten years ago, my research team at the Center for Talent Innovation (now Coqual) set out to crack the code, fielding a national survey that involved nearly 4,000 college-educated professionals—including 268 senior executives—to find out what coworkers and bosses look for when they evaluate an employee's EP. In addition to this survey research, I conducted a number of focus groups and interviewed some forty executives.

As we shall see in chapters 8 through 10, I went back into the field a decade later, using the same questionnaire and similar protocols. This new work, which I carried out in 2022 and early 2023, allowed me to lay out in rich detail, using both qualitative and quantitative data, precisely how EP has evolved over the last decade, pointing in particular to what has changed and what has stayed the same. We shall explore this material in Part II. For the moment, suffice it to say that, despite seismic shifts wrought by a global pandemic, the #MeToo and the Black Lives Matter movements, and a European war, the core principles of Executive Presence laid out ten years ago remain remarkably constant.

EXECUTIVE PRESENCE 2.0

In both 2012 and 2022, I found that EP rests on three pillars and comprises a dynamic mix of:

- How you act (gravitas)
- How you speak (communication)
- How you look (appearance)

While the specifics vary depending on context (what works on Wall Street doesn't necessarily work in Silicon Valley), these three pillars of EP are universal. They are also somewhat interactive. For example, if your communication skills ensure you can "command a room," your gravitas grows exponentially; conversely, if your presentation is rambling and your manner timid, your gravitas suffers a blow.

One thing to note at the start is that these pillars are not equally important—not by a long shot. Gravitas is the core characteristic. Some 67 percent of the 268 senior executives we surveyed said that gravitas is what really matters. Signaling that "you know your stuff cold," that you can go "six questions deep" in your domains of knowledge, is more salient than either communication (which got 28 percent of the senior executive vote) or appearance (which got a mere 5 percent).

Projecting intellectual horsepower underpins gravitas, but there's more to this attribute than being the smartest person in the room. It's about signaling that you have not only depth and heft but also the confidence and credibility to get your vision across and create buy-in when the going gets rough—when your enterprise or venture is under extreme pressure. In fact, projecting confidence and "grace under fire" was the number one pick of senior executives asked to identify what constitutes EP.

Fifteen years ago, another trait might have been the top pick. In the years before the 2008 global financial crisis, CEOs were

Three universal dimensions

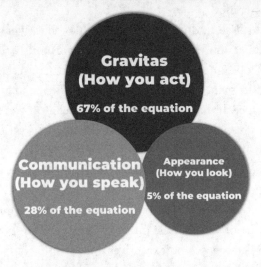

Figure 1. EP: Three universal dimensions

treated like demigods—rock stars in wing-tipped shoes—and charisma was a much-sought-after attribute. A huge personality and forceful presence marked a person as a leader. Think of GE's Jack Welch or Virgin's Richard Branson. But in the wake of the Great Recession and the Covid-19 pandemic, the ability to appear calm, confident, and steady in the face of an economic storm has become far more important.

How do people know you have gravitas? You *communicate* the authority of a leader—through your speaking skills and ability to command a room. Indeed these two communications traits are the top picks (one and two) of the senior executives who participated in the surveys and interviews. Tone of voice, bearing, and body language can also add to—or detract from—your ability to hold your audience's attention, whether you're presenting to a small team or addressing a plenary session at a global conference.

One surprise finding of our research is that, when it comes to communication, eye contact matters enormously. Being able to look a colleague in the eye when making a presentation, or being able to make eye contact with an audience member when making a speech, has a transformative effect—on your ability to connect, to inspire, to create buy-in. This fact has serious consequences. It means that you need to lose your glasses, your notes (and oftentimes your PowerPoint), and just wing it. This is not easy. It requires a huge commitment of time since you need to prepare and practice so thoroughly that the arc of your remarks becomes part of your muscle memory. There are no shortcuts.

In our survey senior executives told us that appearance is inconsequential—only 5 percent identified it as the most important aspect of EP. This is deceptive. The fact is, appearance (as we saw in the musical competition) is a critical first filter. While senior executives (and coworkers) see it as unimportant in the long run, it constitutes an initial hurdle. If a young female associate turns up at a client meeting wearing a tight blouse and a miniskirt, or a young male associate turns up with breakfast on his tie, she/he may not be invited back—no matter how impressive her qualifications or how well prepared she is. The fact is, blunders on the appearance front can get you into serious trouble—and get you knocked off the list of those in contention for stretch roles or plum assignments—no matter how brilliant you are. It's sobering to understand how quickly this happens. As we shall see in chapter 4, research conducted by Harvard Medical School and Massachusetts General Hospital suggests that colleagues size up your competence, likability, and trustworthiness in 250 milliseconds—based solely on your appearance.

The only good news in my data on appearance is that "grooming and polish" was chosen by more respondents than "physical attractiveness" or "body type" (whether you are slim or well-endowed, tall or short) as key contributors to EP. The comfort here of course is that grooming and polish can be learned and acquired. It's a huge relief to know that cracking the code on the appearance front isn't a function of what you were born with; rather, it's a function of what you do with what you've got.

Part I of this book lays out the key components of gravitas, communication, and appearance. It tells us what our bosses and coworkers are looking for and gives us the wherewithal to deliver the most sought-after qualities. Fully three chapters in Part I are devoted to describing pitfalls and trip wires, because it's not a simple matter, this cracking of the EP code. Most complicated of all is the fundamental tension between conformity and authenticity. How much should you fit in? How much should you stand out? How much of the "real you" are you prepared to sacrifice on the altar of success?

While every professional we interviewed told us he or she wrestles with this tension, the struggle is particularly painful for women and people of color. These historically underrepresented groups are dealing with a double whammy. Not only do they need to shape and mold their identities to fit an organizational culture (something every professional faces), but they're required to "pass" as straight white men. Why? Because this continues to be the dominant leadership model. According to a 2021 McKinsey & Company study, 64 percent of financial-services C-suite executives are still Caucasian men, and 23 percent are Caucasian women; only 9 percent of C-suite positions are held by men of color and 4 percent by women of color.[3]

One comforting finding is that over time, the authenticity struggle gets easier. With age and experience, those who truly do have the right stuff on the gravitas front earn the right to be more authentic, to bring more of themselves to work.

Michelle Gadsden-Williams, global head of Diversity, Equity, and Inclusion at BlackRock, recalls the moment when she realized that the ways in which she was different didn't constitute the bar keeping her from moving up, but rather a powerful lever that might propel her progress. Early on in her career as a young manager in a global pharmaceutical firm, she plucked up her courage and delivered some bad news contained in a new in-house survey to the executive committee of the firm. The data in this report showed that among Black employees, attrition was high and morale low because these individuals struggled against subtle (and not-so-subtle) bias in the organizational culture. When the CEO, mystified and perplexed, asked why, Gadsden-Williams described three instances of bias she had personally experienced at the firm, and then suggested some solutions. Walking out of the room that day, she says, she was filled with anxiety: Had she stepped over the line? Would her outspokenness cost her? But to the contrary, the courage she exhibited brought her leadership potential into sharper focus for the firm's executive committee. Not only were her recommendations adopted, but Gadsden-Williams was promptly promoted.

When it comes to bringing one's full self to work, no one inhabits their authenticity better than my friend Cornel West, civil rights crusader and professor of philosophy at Union Theological Seminary. With his distinctive Afro, black three-piece suits, and fearsome oratory, West never fails to make a powerful and lasting impression. Yet despite his intellectual heft and formidable presence, he has experienced soul-crushing pressure to conform to the expectations of a white establishment threaded through with racial bias. In 2016 West returned to Harvard as a Professor of Practice in Public Philosophy. Five years later, he was denied consideration for tenure despite rave reviews and the fact that he had held a tenured professorship at Harvard earlier on in his career. West claimed he had been denied consideration for tenure because of his advancing age and his support for the Palestinian cause. This viewpoint didn't sit well with Harvard's top administration and benefactors. West was hurt and angry. "What's so controversial and fraught about giving tenure to someone you gave a University Professorship to at twentysomething years old?" he asked rhetorically. The upshot? West decided it was time to leave the Ivy League behind and take an appointment at Union Theological Seminary, an institution that offered him the recognition and status he deserved.

In an interview, West told me that it is precisely in the crucible of these punishing experiences that he's learned (and relearned) the imperative of lifting rather than hiding all aspects of his identity. The reason he brings such moral and intellectual force to the table when dealing with inequality, gun control, or the unmet needs of "the 99 percent" is that he connects viscerally with those who are on the receiving end of discrimination, injustice, and violence. He's been there, and walked that walk.

So take heart: While wrestling with the EP code is hard and can sometimes eat into your soul, these struggles create the conditions that allow you to flower and flourish. Once you've demonstrated that you know how to stand with the crowd, you get to strut your stuff and stand apart. It turns out that becoming a leader and doing something amazing with your life hinge on what makes you different, not on what makes you the same as everyone else.

2

In May 2010, as a torrent of crude oil spewed from the ocean floor into Gulf of Mexico waters, ABC News anchor Jake Tapper drilled into Bob Dudley, then BP's managing director, for an explanation.

"So 'topkill' failed," Tapper opened, referring to BP's attempt to plug the well by pumping heavyweight drilling mud into it. "Should the American people prepare themselves for an uncomfortable fact—that this hole will not be plugged until August, at the earliest?"[4]

Dudley—features composed, collar unbuttoned—affirmed that, while August was a possibility, BP was working around the clock and would contain the spill as soon as was humanly possible.

Tapper turned up the heat. "As you know there are serious questions as to whether or not there have been corners cut— safety corners—that resulted in this accident," he said. Why, for instance, did BP use "the risky option" of a metal casing known to buckle under high pressure?

Dudley calmly countered that no corners had been cut, no risky options pursued.

"But why were operations not shut down immediately until well control could be restored?" Tapper persisted, his tone ever more accusatory.

"That is another issue the investigation is going to look at very,

very carefully," Dudley responded evenly, never breaking eye contact with the camera lens. He then went on to say that getting to the bottom of this tragedy was BP's top priority. The company owed that to the people of the Gulf.

Two months later, Dudley again sat in the hot seat—this time, on *PBS NewsHour*, where he answered questions put to him by hard-hitting host Ray Suarez about the catastrophic consequences of the spill.[5] Dudley, his voice steady but charged with empathy, stepped in with his first response. "I've seen the devastation," he began. "I went down to Grand Isle two weeks ago and I saw the oil on the beaches. . . . I traveled out to Grand Pass and saw the oil in the marshes and talked to the local people." He then leaned forward and looked Suarez in the eye. "You know," he said, "we're going to make good on the claims from individuals and businesses down there." And he methodically laid out the steps BP was taking to do just that. Suarez then made a reference to the *Exxon Valdez* incident—a very badly handled oil spill. Dudley didn't shy away from the implied comparison; instead he explained that BP wouldn't "hide" behind a declaration of bankruptcy or some legal processes, as Exxon had done. Suarez continued to press, but during the entire grilling there wasn't a single question Dudley avoided or refused to answer and he came over as a compassionate and highly competent leader who knows how to handle a crisis, and that indeed is his image.

Bob Dudley is not a leader who gets hot under the collar, but it's not because he's stayed out of the kitchen. On the contrary, as he detailed in an interview with me, his career in Big Oil, which began at Amoco at the height of the OPEC crisis, has put him at the epicenter of the industry's worst nightmares. As CEO of TNK-BP, he battled a group of Russian oligarchs intent on squeezing him out. He dealt with various kinds of harassment, including, some say, threats to his life, and, when his visa was denied, proceeded to run the company from an undisclosed remote location. Fresh from that challenging set of experiences, he was put in charge of BP's operations in Asia and the Americas, reporting to CEO Tony Hayward. Then the Deepwater Horizon exploded, Hayward imploded (more on that later), and BP stock tumbled to half its value. In July, the firm tapped Dudley, who was heading up the Gulf Coast Restoration Organization, to take over from Hayward. Such was Dudley's credibility that before the well was even capped, BP's share price took an upturn.

When I attempted during our interview to credit him with BP's recovery, Dudley demurred with characteristic humility. "There were a lot of people who performed unbelievably well," he said. But nothing, he agreed, is more important in troubled times than a leader who projects calm and confidence. "I want people around me who can be clear-thinking and calm in a crisis," he emphasized. "I don't believe I've ever been able to judge or trust a person unless I can see what they're like under pressure."

Virginia Rometty is another corporate leader who is greatly admired for her extraordinary ability to weather a crisis with confidence, decisiveness, and grace under fire. As we shall see in chapter 8, two-thirds of executives I talked to in 2022 singled her out as their number one pick in the "gravitas-in-action" bucket. When elevated to the CEO slot at IBM she took on the herculean challenge of transforming an ailing hundred-year-old behemoth with an outdated product line and close to half a million employees. She tackled the challenge head-on and, starting in 2013, drove radical change, selling off legacy product lines and investing in next-generation technology. After facing down twenty-two quarters of revenue decline she emerged triumphant. When she departed the company in 2020, BIG BLUE was back. How did Rometty do it? Confidence was a big part of it. She totally believed in her vision and communicated it brilliantly. But steely resolve was also crucial. When IBM's biggest shareholder Warren Buffett dumped his stock in 2017, she didn't blink. Instead, she rallied her board and doubled down on her mission. No wonder she's seen as an exemplar of "grace under fire."

In the academic world, Katherine Phillips, a professor at the Columbia Business School, modeled a particularly courageous brand of gravitas. Early in her career when she was a junior faculty member at Northwestern's Kellogg School of Management, Phillips told her colleagues at a succession-planning meeting that it was "a waste of energy" to discuss replacing Max Bazerman, a world-renowned faculty member who'd recently left, because none of them was willing to allocate the necessary resources to lure in an equally towering intellect.

"You guys have already taken his office, his courses, and his grant monies and divvied them up among yourselves," she pointed out, referring to the fact that Bazerman's empire had already been picked over. "What's left? What are you willing to give back? X, y, or z? No one top-notch will consider coming to Kellogg without an amazing package that needs to include x, y, and z." She let that sink in, then added, "Let's not waste time talking about it anymore, because what I'm seeing is, Max has already been replaced"—she raised an index finger and jabbed it—"by you . . . and you . . . and you."

"Well, they were stunned," Phillips told me, marveling at her own youthful bravado. "But after the meeting two senior faculty members thanked me for saying what I did. And it sparked a much more honest discussion in the department."

This incident established Phillips as someone others could count on to speak the truth when no one else dared, which is one of the reasons she was appointed the Paul Calello Professor of Leadership and Ethics at Columbia Business School—the first African-

American woman to hold a chair at this prestigious school. "You could say that 'speaking truth to power' has become part of my personal brand," she observes. "I've never been afraid to say what others won't—and people have come to count on me for that."

A few years back, a newly appointed CEO of a medical device manufacturer faced a difficult challenge. Recently enacted U.S. healthcare rules meant the firm would be hit with a 2.3 percent excise tax—an unforecasted loss equivalent to $75–$100 million in reduced profits. This new leader knew he needed to move quickly and cut expenses across the board—including (most painfully) head count. By strategically reallocating resources from poorly performing units to more promising divisions, he could probably save hundreds of jobs. Still, there would be layoffs. More than two hundred, in fact.

The CEO delivered the bad news himself. "I pulled the group together, stood in front of them, and walked them through why the company needed to make these cuts and answered their questions," he told me in an interview. "Obviously I couldn't get rid of their pain—and I didn't try to. But I did want them to know that it wasn't a personal thing (these were hardworking, loyal employees) but a structural thing (the company needed to downsize in order to survive and thrive going forward). I also wanted them to know that there would be a 'package' and we would do our utmost to help them find a way forward." He paused. "Still, it was a pretty tough two hours. They were surprised and distressed, and felt blindsided—even betrayed. They let me know it in no uncertain terms. But one thing was clear to me. I needed to be there. I wasn't about to hide in my office and expect a junior colleague to deal with the tough stuff."

Lots of leaders do precisely that, I pointed out. "Have you seen *Up in the Air*, where George Clooney plays the professional ax man, flying around the country doing the dirty work for leaders lacking the courage to fire employees themselves?" I asked him. He had.

"You have to be there in bad times as well as good, to show you lead from the heart as well as from the head," this CEO observed. "This emotional intelligence thing is important. If you don't reach out personally, if you don't show empathy, if you don't speak from your heart, you lose the trust and respect of not only your employees but also your investors. And then you're truly powerless."

THE RIGHT STUFF

We all know a real leader when we see one. Like Bob Dudley and Virginia Rometty, he or she projects an aura of calm and competence that instills faith even in—*especially* in—the white-hot center of a crisis. Like Kathy Phillips, he or she reveals integrity and demonstrates courage by uttering truths when they are inconvenient or most unwelcome. And like our medical-device firm CEO, he or she demonstrates courage and emotional intelligence that secures followership even in the wake of news that would seemingly destroy it.

These qualities connote gravitas, that weightiness or heft that marks you as worth following into the fire. Gravitas is the very essence of EP. Without it, you simply won't be perceived as a leader, no matter what your title or level of authority, no matter how well you dress or speak. Gravitas, according to 62 percent of the leaders we surveyed, is what signals to the world you're made of the right stuff and can be entrusted with serious responsibility.

But what is it, really? What makes up gravitas—this elusive but all-important piece of executive presence? How do you come by it, and how might you telegraph it?

According to Senior Leaders

Gravitas Top Traits, 2012

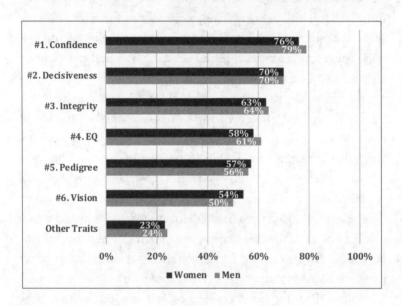

Figure 2. Top aspects of gravitas

CTI research reveals gravitas to consist of six key behaviors and traits.

What strikes me about this list is how timeless it is. It makes perfect sense, in troubled as well as calmer times, all the senior executives I interviewed prize "grace under fire" (76 percent concur it's critical for women's EP, and 79 percent concur it's critical for men's EP). Just consider what we've been through over the last twenty-odd years in terms of unprecedented events. The century opened with a bang: not Y2K, but the bursting of the dot-com bubble, wiping out billions. In 2001, the unthinkable occurred with the September 11 terrorist attacks, driving us to war in both Afghanistan and, by 2003, Iraq.[6] Before the year 2001 was out, the economy took another major blow when it was revealed that accounting fraud and corporate malfeasance had bankrupted Enron, the $100 billion energy and commodities firm. In 2008, the subprime mortgage crisis robbed Americans of their jobs and savings, triggering a recession in the United States and touching off a global financial meltdown.

But these shocks to the system, which seemed massive at the time, pale in comparison with what has happened in the recent past. As we shall explore in chapters 8 through 10, the culture and value shifts plus the Covid-19 pandemic disrupted business models the world over, and companies, large and small, are still reeling. Every day, it seems, leaders are confronted by problems they've never tangled with before: How to manage a hybrid workforce? How to deal with energy costs driven sky-high by a European war? How to embed "zero-tolerance" for sexual misconduct in your leadership ranks so as to risk-proof your corporate culture? Given this daunting list of challenges, is it any wonder that we're drawn to leaders who project confidence and credibility and keep their promises, keep their cool, and show compassion when making the truly hard choices?

Gravitas alone won't secure you the corner office, of course: You've got to have the skill sets, the experience, and the innate talent to qualify for the job. As Linda Huber, chief financial officer at Moody's, observes, "Substance must be the bedrock in order for someone to be taken seriously." But if you have depth of experience and those vital skills, gravitas is all that's between you and that top job. It can't be faked, but it can be cultivated.

GRACE UNDER FIRE

How *exactly* do you come by composure in a crisis?

You've got to reach inside yourself to that place where you believe, you absolutely *know*, you're eminently qualified to do the job at hand.

"Self-confidence is your iron core," says Anne Erni, former head of human resources at Bloomberg LP, now chief people officer at Audible. "To lean into the wind when your heart is pounding, you have to believe in yourself, deep down. It's not something you can fake."

Steeliness is forged, history shows us, in the crucible of crisis—and it may take a crisis for you to discover your core of confidence. Angela Merkel, Germany's chancellor from 2005 to 2021, may not have aced the euro crisis, but no one contested her competency or credibility as a leader, in large part because she never lost her composure. Christine Lagarde, president of the European Bank since 2019 and before that head of the International Monetary Fund, likewise enjoys universal respect for her poise and levelheadedness in helping steer Europe and the world through Brexit and the Covid-19 crisis. Margaret Thatcher, Britain's former prime minister, will forever be known as the Iron Lady for having weathered, with nary a hair out of place, protracted crises at home (double-digit unemployment, a national coal miners' strike), a lingering cold war with the Soviets, and a Falkland Islands showdown with Argentina. Most of us are like teabags, to borrow Eleanor Roosevelt's shrewd words: We don't know how strong we are until we're in hot water.

That you may have boiled the water in which you steep doesn't necessarily undermine your opportunity to acquire gravitas. Look at headline makers who've proven their mettle not by averting mistakes, but by owning up to them. For example, Jamie Dimon, CEO of JPMorgan Chase, failed to forestall some $5.8 billion in trading losses in 2011—which is not much of a testament to his leadership prowess! Dragged before Congress to explain why, he might well have joined the infamous ranks of dissemblers like WorldCom chief Bernard Ebbers. But instead, Dimon accepted responsibility and equably answered questions, maintaining his composure and exuding confidence without coming off as arrogant. Far from gutting his gravitas, this public flogging actually seemed to bolster it. Jack Welch, the former CEO of General Electric, observed in *Fortune* that Dimon would be remembered as a man who "dusted himself off, got back on his horse and rode on—stronger and a whole lot wiser."[7] In early 2023, Dimon got on his horse again, first organizing a consortium of banks to stabilize First Republic Bank, then working with regulators to stabilize markets, then winning the auction to buy it. The business press has been admiring. Bloomberg ran several pieces giving Dimon credit for being a calming force who displayed leadership chops in this crisis.[8]

So while avoiding catastrophe may demonstrate competence, it is handling catastrophe that confers gravitas. Recall Captain Chesley "Sully" Sullenberger, the US Airways pilot who landed in the Hudson River after striking a flock of Canada geese. Avoiding the geese was not an option; what *was* an option for this leader was not succumbing to the "worst sickening, pit-of-your-stomach falling-through-the-floor" feeling he suffered moments before the crash.[9] As a result of Sully's extraordinary poise and control, every passenger and crew member survived that forced landing unharmed.

You will make mistakes. You will suffer the mistakes of others. Accidents completely out of your control will befall you. Each of these represents, however, a monumental opportunity to acquire and exude gravitas: to reach within yourself, at the height of the storm, for that eye of calm, and to speak and act from that place of clarity. Because when you demonstrate that your confidence cannot be shaken, you inspire confidence in others. At worst, you'll win their forgiveness and forbearance. Very possibly, you'll win their trust and loyalty.

Tim Melville-Ross tells of just such a watershed moment in his career, when a mistake he made might have cost him his job, his career, and his reputation—but instead provided him occasion to man up and show the public what he was really made of. Back when he was CEO of Nationwide, the United Kingdom's biggest building society (equivalent to a savings and loan in the United States), Melville-Ross acceded to pressure from one of his top directors to adopt a questionable accounting practice, one that would help the firm hold its margins in a shrinking economy. "To my undying shame, we tried to screw the customer," he admits. "A good building society simply doesn't do that. I made the wrong decision." But then he made the right one: He sacked that director and made a very public apology. He wrote a letter to the London *Times*, one that he closed by inviting readers to write to him personally. Many did write, Melville-Ross told me, and took him to task for his blunder. The larger result of his falling on his sword, however, was restored faith in Nationwide—and, interestingly, in him personally. "It established me as a leader of integrity," he says, "a reputation which has carried me through many a storm since." Melville-Ross went on to chair the Higher Education Funding Council in the UK and head up the Institute of Business Ethics.

You have this same choice. In a crisis, you can lean into the wind, acknowledge your shortcomings, and rise above them; or you can take cover. You can acquire gravitas, the cornerstone of a real leader. Or you can demonstrate that, no matter what your actual title, you really don't deserve to be in charge.

Tony Hayward is a case in point. When the BP oil spill first made the news, Hayward seemed to have the public's trust because he'd shown himself to be "frightfully" candid about BP's previous stumbles and "dreadful" performance. But the minute he attempted to distance himself and the company from blame—the infamous "What the hell did we do to deserve this?" comment to BP executives, and then, two weeks later, observing to the *Guardian* that "the amount of volume of oil and dispersant we are putting into [the Gulf] is tiny in relation to the total water volume"—the public turned on him.[10] His comments were seen as peevish and arrogant rather than confident. Any chance he may have had to restore public opinion—by apologizing, for instance—he squandered with ever more stunning displays of insensitivity, the most memorable being his infamous remark "I'd like my life back."[11] These petulant words provoked a savage reaction. News commentators couldn't believe that he was complaining about his schedule—missing a few summer weekends on his yacht seemed a paltry sacrifice in the context of this catastrophic spill that had wreaked havoc in the Gulf. So many residents had lost their livelihoods—and eleven oil rig workers lost their lives. So instead of calming the waters, Tony set fire to them. It was a blunder that cost him his job.

SHOWING TEETH

Lynn Utter, former chief operating officer of Knoll Inc., now a partner at Atlas Holdings, recalls the moment in her career when she first showed teeth. She'd just been named head of the container unit at Coors Brewing Company, replacing a thirty-year company veteran to become the company's first female senior leader. Just a few months into the role, Utter sat in a meeting with half a dozen male board members who were debating whether to invest millions of dollars to fund a start-up as part of a joint venture. Having done her homework, she was utterly clear on how and why Coors should do the deal. Still, she listened to others, hoping for insights outside her own, until finally, fed up with the equivocation, she stood and addressed the room. "If we do not invest," she said with calm, sturdy authority, "we are not living up to the fundamental philosophy of our partnership. If we do nothing, the fact is, the entity is doomed. Either we step up, or we call it off."

With her strong endorsement, the investment went forward. "I do not think they expected me to have that kind of backbone," Utter says. "But I'd done my homework and knew the numbers cold. I knew what we needed to do and felt it was up to me to show strength and point the way forward."

Making difficult decisions is what we look to leaders to do. It is not so much about rendering the right decision, but about rendering a decision at a time when no one else dares, that confers gravitas, because it telegraphs that you have the courage, as well as the confidence, to impose a direction and take responsibility for it. Yahoo CEO Marissa Mayer showed she had the chops when she announced that all employees, starting in June 2013, would need to be working out of Yahoo's offices.[12] For the survival of the company, whose share price was tanking, she was revoking telecommuting privileges. "Speed and quality are often sacrificed when we work from home," read the memo that employees received from HR head Jackie Reses. "We need to be one Yahoo!, and that starts with physically being together."[13] The move sparked a firestorm: Some leaders (Jack Welch among them) applauded the move as an appropriate piece of discipline for the ailing firm; others (Richard Branson was one) condemned it as "a backwards step."[14] But Mayer had the courage to recognize that business as usual was not going to bootstrap Yahoo out of its death spiral.

She made a bold, if unpopular, decision. She showed teeth. That display of confidence and courage boosted her gravitas and, consequently, her shareholders' faith in her ability to turn the tide.

CTI research finds that 70 percent of leaders consider decisiveness to be a component of EP for both men and women, second only to confidence in a crisis, making it a core aspect of gravitas. Being able to make decisions isn't so much the issue as needing to appear decisive in public—the difference, again, between doing the job of a leader and *looking* like one as you're doing it, between demonstrating competence and exuding *presence*. George W. Bush clearly recognized this imperative when he zeroed in on being "the Decider" and built this as a central part of his brand. Mitt Romney similarly trumpeted his assertiveness on the presidential campaign trail; in his view leadership and "showing teeth" were synonymous. Better to get a reputation, as president, for being a hard-ass than a wuss—"soft" on terrorists, or illegal drugs. In August 2021, Joe Biden played the decider, tough-guy card when he abruptly pulled American troops out of Afghanistan after twenty years of war. Although there was much criticism of how he got out, he was given great credit for having the guts to face the fact that the US had lost, and it was time to get out of this war.

Given that showing teeth draws on so many stereotypically male attributes—aggression, assertiveness, toughness, dominance—it's ostensibly easier for males to appear decisive. Yet if the emergence of testosterone clinics is any indication, men aren't necessarily naturals at showing teeth. The *Financial Times* reported that, in search of "the positive side of aggression," men are dosing up on testosterone, convinced the hormone will confer the "alpha male personality" of a bona fide Wall Street mover and shaker.[15] One clinic, located steps away from the New York Stock Exchange,[16] offers twice-weekly treatments as part of a $1,000-and-up monthly regimen.[17] The injections aren't without risk: Side effects include sleep apnea, increased risk of heart disease, growth of latent tumors, and testicular shrinkage.[18] But the results, to hear the clinic's Wall Street clientele describe them, more than justify the risks. Testosterone makes them feel bolder, louder, and more assertive, they say; as a result, they're more comfortable showing teeth and taking risks. "It's important to project an aura of invincibility," one trader confided to me. The way he sees it, he's buying job security.

Women, however, definitely have a harder row to hoe—not in *being* decisive, it bears repeating, but in *appearing* to be. Women like Hillary Clinton or Marissa Mayer who've made more than their fair share of tough decisions are often described as "unfeminine"—aka unlikable—in the eyes of their peers and subordinates, a phenomenon we'll explore at much greater length in chapter 6. It's the classic double bind: If you're tough, you're a bitch and no one wants to work for you, but if you're not tough, you're not perceived as leadership material and you won't have anyone working for you. It's a high-wire act that every capable woman has had to perform, and the higher she goes, the more perilous the act.

Executives of color, too, need to find balance in their stride. Take Roger W. Ferguson, the African-American leader who was president and chief executive officer of TIAA (Teacher's Insurance and Annuity Association of America) from 2008 to 2021. Like many female leaders, he needed to walk a fine line between being seen (particularly by his board of directors) as a forceful, effective leader, and a disruptive troublemaker. Ferguson tested those waters when, on the brink of retirement, he threw his weight behind another African-American executive as a potential successor. TIAA's board of directors was not ready for what they saw as a radical move. Nevertheless, in chapter 8, we will learn more about how Ferguson successfully lobbied for Thasunda Duckett to follow in his footsteps and faced down a great deal of opposition to become the first Black CEO of a Fortune 500 company to install a Black CEO as a successor.

Whether you are a female or a Black leader, the way to walk this tightrope between being seen as tough or a troublemaker may be, as Lynn Utter demonstrates, to dish out the toughness very discriminately—to hide your teeth more often than you bare them. Real leaders don't issue edicts just to look and sound like they're in charge. Real leaders listen, gather critical information, weigh the options carefully, look for a timely opening (typically when everyone else is writhing in indecision), and *then* demand and drive action.

"Oftentimes it is just as important to know when being decisive is *not* the thing to do—to let events play out in a certain way and bide your time," cautions Bob Dudley. "I see a lot of people trying to be too decisive too quickly."

When the moment demands a decision that you're prepared to render, step forth and render it. Just choose those moments with care.

SPEAKING TRUTH TO POWER

In the aftermath of Superstorm Sandy, Governor Chris Christie of New Jersey shocked his fellow Republicans by publicly heaping praise on Barack Obama just days before the 2012 presidential election. Speaking live on Fox News, with images of his ravaged state playing over the airwaves, Christie told viewers that he'd had three conversations in the last twenty-four hours with the president, asking that his state be declared a federal disaster to expedite funds, and that that morning Obama had signed the paperwork. "I have to give the president great credit," Christie concluded. "He's been very attentive and anything I've asked for, he's gotten to me. He's done, as far as I'm concerned, a great job for New Jersey." When asked if he'd be touring the state later by helicopter with Governor Romney, Christie, a vocal supporter of the Republican candidate just days before, told the correspondents he didn't know and wasn't interested. "If you think right now I give a damn about presidential politics," he said heatedly, "then you don't know me."[19]

Those who know Christie weren't, in fact, shocked by his behavior. Mike DuHaime, an advisor to the governor, observed he was acting true to form. "He calls 'em as he sees 'em," he told the *New York Times*.[20] That's what Christie does: When homeowners refused to evacuate from New Jersey's barrier islands, Christie called them "both stupid and selfish."[21] Prior to Sandy, he called President Obama "the most ill-prepared person to assume the presidency in my lifetime."[22]

Christie doesn't hesitate, that is, to speak his truth—however impolitic it may be, however mighty the audience he offends with it. And that candor marks him, paradoxically, as a presidential contender.

Speaking truth to power, as more than 60 percent of our respondents affirm, is a potent affirmation of leaderlike courage. The higher you go in an organization, the more impressive you are when you demonstrate you have the spine to share your true convictions. "I want people who will walk into my office and say, 'Here's where I differ, I want to talk to you about it,'" Tiger Tyagarajan, CEO of Genpact, told me in a 2023 interview. "I love that! This is the kind of courage I'm looking for, in addition to the given of stellar performance."

Make sure, however, that when you challenge authority, you're coming from a place of integrity and leaning on a store of knowledge. Anything less and your actions will be perceived as insubordination and/or arrogance—the opposites of gravitas.

And then prepare to be truly tested.

Financial powerhouse Sallie Krawcheck established early on in her career a penchant for telling it like it is. As a research analyst on Wall Street, she downgraded Travelers for its acquisition of brokerage firm Salomon Brothers, a move that earned her the fury of Citicorp's Sandy Weill (Citicorp would acquire Travelers to form Citigroup). Impressed with her intellectual integrity as well as her analysis skills, however, Weill eventually hired her to head up Citigroup's Smith Barney unit, promoting her within two years to be CFO of Citigroup. Krawcheck continued to tell it like it was, suggesting, at the height of the 2008 financial crisis, that the company partially refund its clients for investments positioned by Citi as low risk that had taken a nosedive during the downturn. CEO Vikram Pandit wasn't appreciative of this piece of advice and fired her.

The story doesn't end there. In 2011, the integrity and courage Krawcheck exhibited at Citi won her the top job at Merrill Lynch, which had recently been taken over by Bank of America. Her brief: to make this much-revered wealth management house profitable again. Despite huge success on the financial front (revenues rose by 54 percent in her second quarter on the job), she found herself in the crosshairs of new CEO Brian Moynihan, whose leadership had resulted in losses of $8.8 billion across Bank of America during that same quarter.[23] By September of that year, Krawcheck was out.

"I've found that speaking truth has not always stood me in good stead in terms of my career progression," Krawcheck told me when we discussed her extraordinary journey. "But it always, always, always stood me in good stead in terms of managing businesses." She added, with heartfelt pride, "Had I to do it over again, I wouldn't do it any differently. Not one thing."

DEMONSTRATING EMOTIONAL INTELLIGENCE

Mitt Romney's compulsion to show teeth—to remind us at every turn that his tough leadership style had made him a phenomenally successful CEO—might have garnered him more votes in the 2012 presidential election had he not, at the same time, demonstrated at every turn his utter insensitivity toward half the electorate. Like Tony Hayward, Romney was tone-deaf when it came to tuning his remarks for constituencies outside his war room. Comments such as noting that his wife had "a couple of Cadillacs" didn't persuade voters of his love for American cars, but rather that he lived in a rich man's bubble and was insulated from working people's reality. In a similar vein, his comment that he had consulted "binders full of women" to fill his cabinet as governor but didn't find any who were qualified failed to impress anyone. Rather, this remark served to underscore how out of touch he was with the times and the sensibilities of workingwomen. The final blow, delivered at a private fund-raiser and captured on a video that quickly went viral on the Web, was his sweeping condemnation of 47 percent of the electorate as freeloaders who pay no income tax! (Freeloaders, it turned out, included not-yet-employed returning veterans and the disabled.)

Romney's 47 percent comment "did real damage" to his campaign, as he himself conceded, underscoring just how important emotional intelligence—or EQ, as psychologist Daniel Goleman calls it—has become for leaders.[24] A hefty majority of our respondents see EQ as very important, with 58 percent noting its importance for women's executive presence, and 61 percent noting its importance for men's. And here's why: While decisiveness and toughness in a leader signal conviction, courage, and resolve, when these qualities are not tempered by empathy or compassion they come off as egotism, arrogance, and insensitivity.

Look at Marissa Mayer's decision to force Yahoo's staff to return to their desks on campus. Issuing this edict showed teeth, as we've discussed, but regrettably, it also showed a leader out of touch with the realities other working parents contend with. Mayer drew fire not for being tough but for being hypocritical, having solved her own child-care issues by building a separate cubicle next to her office for her infant son and nanny. "I wonder what would happen if my wife brought our kids and nanny to work and set 'em up in the cube next door?" joked the husband of one Yahoo mom.[25] His voice was tinged with bitterness.

Making and enforcing unpopular decisions is indeed part of showing you've got the chops to be put in charge. It's just that in today's ever-flatter organizations, acting insensitively seriously compromises your ability to create buy-in among employees and realize optimal outcomes for the firm. This was the conclusion two researchers from Harvard and Stanford reached after spending weeks on two offshore oil rigs studying the culture changes management had initiated to improve safety and performance. The research team expected that, in this most dangerous and macho of work environments, aggression, bravado, and toughness not only would be on display but would be embraced and rewarded. But as a result of management's stated goals—bringing down work-site injuries and bringing up capacity—they witnessed a remarkable shift in attitudes and behaviors among the crews on oil rigs. Workers confirmed that, previously, the culture discouraged asking for help, admitting mistakes, or building community. The crew, in prior years, had been "like a pack of lions," with the guy in charge being the one who could "out-shout, out-intimidate, and out-perform all the others." Once the emphasis shifted to safety, however, the company stopped rewarding "the biggest baddest roughnecks" in favor of men who could admit to mistakes, seek help when they needed it, and look out for each other. Over a period of fifteen years, shifting in values and norms helped the oil company achieve its goals: Accident rates fell by 84 percent and production hit an all-time high.[26]

Even on an oil rig, that is, demonstrating emotional intelligence (EQ) is a key leader trait because it builds trust—essential in conditions where bravado could get you killed and a lack of concern for the team might cause others to wonder if you were cutting corners and compromising their safety. In less life-threatening conditions, however, EQ is just as important for building trust because demonstrating it shows you have not only self-awareness but also situational awareness. It's absolutely vital in white-collar worlds such as finance, law, and medicine to show you're capable of reading a situation, and the people in it, correctly. Standout leaders who can be trusted to pick up on all relevant cues win fellowship and are able to steer organizations through uncertain times.

My interviewees also spoke of the importance of EQ in "reading a room"—the room being a metaphor for your immediate audience, in person or virtual. *What's the vibe, or unarticulated emotion you need to address or temper? What do people need from you in order to move forward?* Leaders who pick up on these cues know when to be decisive and when to hold back; when to show teeth, and when to retract their claws. "It may be more important to comfort a room than command it," points out Kent A. Gardiner, a senior partner at Crowell & Moring LLP, "because at times comfort can further consensus-building and problem-solving." Gardiner, whose career has encompassed RICO prosecutions and major civil and criminal antitrust litigation, describes how he cooled one particularly heated mediation session. "Everybody was unhappy, everybody was antagonistic, so getting up and pounding away was only going to increase the gulf," he says. "I let a little venting occur, and then I got up and said, 'Let's think about it this way,' and then went on to lay out the financial realities of both sides and moved the discussion away from a litigation resolution toward a business resolution. And people listened. People felt like it was a new discussion, not just a fight."

It's not simply managing your own feelings, although restraint on that front, as Gardiner shows, makes an enormous difference. Rather, it's recognizing what the other side has at stake and standing in their shoes.

"Not showing that you have an understanding for people's feelings is absolutely a no-no," says the CEO of the medical device firm. "It does not negate your ability to make tough decisions, or prevent you from calling it out when employees fail to do their jobs. *But* you do need to do all of that with compassion."

When considering the importance of EQ, it's critical to understand that you can acquire these sensitivities and skill sets. Emotional Intelligence and an ability to stand in the shoes of others are not inborn, rather, they are behavioral muscles you build through trial and error, through experience. Recall Michelle Obama's misstep in 2010 when she whisked her daughter and some forty friends off to Spain for a glitzy summer vacation. It was something Jackie O might have been celebrated for, but then, Jackie's husband hadn't gotten voted into office to fix a global financial crisis. To be spending lavishly on a European holiday when her fellow Americans were grappling with unemployment, protracted recession, and gutted retirement plans was a Romneyesque blunder, one that got her dubbed "a modern-day Marie Antoinette."[27] That was the last time the first lady acted so heedlessly; indeed, as we will explore in chapter 10, over the last several years Michelle Obama has acquired perfect pitch. For example, when Hadiya Pendleton, a fifteen-year-old honor student who'd performed at the 2012 inauguration, was killed in a random shooting just a week later, Michelle attended her funeral and met with her family. Several times over the next ten years she returned to Chicago to meet with other high schoolers terrorized by gang shootings and make an impassioned plea for tighter gun control laws nationwide. No one who saw her deliver that speech could doubt the first lady felt our pain.[28] Indeed in January 2022, Michelle Obama was back in Chicago keeping Hadiya's legacy alive by naming the winter garden at the Obama Presidential Center in her honor.[29] The gaffes of her first years in the White House have been forgotten.

RIGHT-SIZING YOUR REPUTATION

Make no mistake: Your reputation does precede you, either bestowing gravitas or bleeding you of it. Before you enter a room or open your mouth, your reputation speaks for you—never more so than today, when word of your latest blunder or scandal races at lightning speed around the globe in 140 characters or less. As we shall see in chapter 9, with the growing power of social media, people will form an opinion of you before you're in a position to help them form it. Managing your personal brand has become almost a job unto itself, lest it be managed for you by people who don't hold your best interests at heart. Increasingly, you've got to be proactive in asserting who you are, and what you stand for, so that you can shape how you are perceived.

Even in Hollywood, where celebrities are fixated on honing their image, Angelina Jolie is seen to have done an excellent job creating and controlling her image. She's clearly a standout beauty and accomplished actress, but she's also a universally admired public figure with depth, heft, and clout. How did this happen?

First off, she's distinguished herself among movie stars by her dedication to underprivileged children the world over, several of whom she's adopted. Her efforts seem to come from a deep place, and far exceed the photo-op moments that characterize celebrity "involvement" in good causes. After filming *Lara Croft: Tomb Raider* in Cambodia, she started traveling with UNHCR, the United Nations' refugee agency, as a goodwill ambassador, a commitment that's taken her on forty-some field missions since 2001 and won her a special envoy appointment. She started the Maddox Jolie-Pitt Foundation to address conservation in Cambodia and the National Center for Refugee and Immigrant Children to provide free legal aid to young asylum seekers, work that earned her membership in the Council on Foreign Relations.[30] She does much of this work under the radar of the press, and yet the gravitas it has conferred is palpable.

Many a sterling reputation is forged in the crucible of scandal. Recall Magic Johnson, the all-star basketball player who contracted HIV/AIDS. When news of his illness broke back in the early 1990s, AIDS was a scourge associated with homosexuality and intravenous drug use, yet Johnson made a courageous choice: He made himself very publicly an example of the dire consequences of unprotected sexual activity and in so doing transformed the behavior of homosexuals and heterosexuals alike, tamping down the spread of AIDS. Today, Johnson is known as a former basketball megastar, but also as a successful businessman, philanthropist, author, and inspirational speaker.

Bear in mind that your reputation is not a function simply of your deeds and actions: Social media and the ubiquity of smartphones—with their handy-dandy cameras—conspire to make your reputation a function of what people see, including your attire, office decor, automobile, vacation home, and collectibles. This visibility makes it imperative you style your environment as carefully as you style yourself—a point we'll take up at length in chapters 4 and 10. Even the photos on your desk or office wall say something about you, so make sure they communicate a message that's in keeping with your mission. One senior executive learned this the hard way: She featured on her office wall a photograph taken of herself emerging from a limo clad in a very short black dress that revealed a stunning length of well-toned thigh. The image, which had appeared in a national glossy magazine, was accompanied by an article trumpeting her rapid ascendance in an almost exclusively male culture—a triumph she felt warranted exposure on her wall. But her colleagues felt otherwise. One of them insisted she take it down. "Is this what you want people to focus on? Is this your leading edge?" he asked her angrily. "It's critical to the success of this firm that shareholders feel confident in your judgment. Anyone seeing this photo would have to question it."

VISION AND CHARISMA

One doesn't become the wealthiest person in the world for even a minute without being a visionary. Elon Musk is a case in point. In 1999, at the age of twenty-eight, he made his first $300 million when he sold his first start-up, a software company, to Compaq. That same year, he cofounded an online bank which, through a merger, ultimately became PayPal. Within less than two years, PayPal was acquired by eBay for $1.5 billion. Less than two years after, he founded SpaceX, an aerospace manufacturer, and signed on as an early investor in electronic vehicle manufacturer Tesla. In the years since, he has founded three additional companies in sectors as varied as solar energy, artificial intelligence, and construction. In 2022, he bought the social networking platform Twitter. After first trying to back out, he sealed the deal and proceeded to gut the company, laying off hundreds of key personnel and abandoning many. He's now mired in a protracted and public struggle to save some version of the values and commitments that had made the platform successful. These massive missteps have tarnished his brand, tanked Tesla's price, and outed him as hotheaded and reckless.

At the opposite end of the spectrum is Mark Benioff. His star is only rising. As I'll lay out in chapter 8, he is the visionary behind Salesforce, the philanthropic venture with an employee culture that is as much about giving back as it is about getting ahead. Over the last twenty-odd years, Benioff has built an organization that gives 1 percent of employee hours, 1 percent of equity, and 1 percent of product to the community it services. Since its founding in 1999, Salesforce has donated more than $500 million to causes and become a model for how to build a successful company with a compassionate corporate culture.

Exceedingly few of us will conjure up or drive a vision as powerfully as Musk or Benioff. Yet, to project gravitas, it's critical for an up-and-coming executive to have an inspiring take on where he or she wants to take a team or business. Over half of the leaders we surveyed believe it matters a lot for both men and women.

Joanna Coles, editor of *Cosmopolitan*, had long had a vision of spearheading a different kind of women's magazine, one that has its fair share of fashion and fun but also encourages women to use their new clout to make a difference in this world. She has always believed that such a magazine could be enormously commercially successful. She finally got a chance to realize her vision when she was appointed editor of *Marie Claire*—a fashion magazine that focuses on thirtysomething-year-old professional women. During her five-year tenure at *Marie Claire*, she shifted its editorial content so as to include important pieces of investigative journalism that targeted women's issues. One of the first pieces she commissioned in this space was a story on women's rape kits getting tossed to one side (shelved, filed, or just plain lost) instead of being tested and used in criminal prosecutions. This article proved riveting to readers—and drove circulation to a new high. It zeroed in on a young woman whose rapist was out there in the community raping other women because no one had bothered to log into a national database the DNA sample collected from her. But this piece, besides driving sales, also vaulted the magazine into a more serious realm, short-listing *Marie Claire* for a prestigious journalism award. With that success, Coles had license to embark on a socially conscious editorial agenda, one that helped shine a spotlight on women such as Angelina Jolie for their humanitarian achievements, and not just their beauty or fashion sense. She then went on to bring the same sensibilities to *Cosmopolitan*, inspiring a whole new generation of women to take themselves seriously. Coles's social conscience hasn't always earned her praise or popularity: Coles is hard-driving and famously demanding of her staff—there is a whiff of *The Devil Wears Prada* about her. But this doesn't concern her in the least. "I won't be one of those people who lies on her deathbed thinking, 'I wish I had spent less time in the office,'" she muses. "I will lie on my deathbed thinking, I wish I'd given everything one hundred and fifty percent instead of the occasional one hundred percent."

Indeed, as Mellody Hobson, president of Ariel Investments, pointed out in an interview, likability is what women need to sacrifice. Leadership cannot be a popularity contest, she affirms.

"There are people who absolutely don't like me," Hobson told me. "I'm a fierce Black woman and I make them uncomfortable. But I also know they respect me. I'm someone with whom they'd want to be in a foxhole. That's how we talk about leadership at this firm: *Who do you take into the foxhole?* You don't take people you like, you take someone who is going to save your life in a really bad situation. You don't want a whiner. You don't want someone who panics. And you certainly don't want fake optimism. What you want is brutal optimism. Great leaders are *brutally* optimistic."

BLUNDERS

In focus groups and interviews I asked senior executives (and white-collar employees across the board), Tell me about your mistakes. What behaviors get you in real trouble on the gravitas front?

The blunders shown below trigger a wide range of consequences. While an up-and-comer can recover from a lack of depth on some technical issue, it would be a whole different story if he or she used a racial slur or cooked the end-of-year figures. Lack of integrity and sexual impropriety call into question a person's

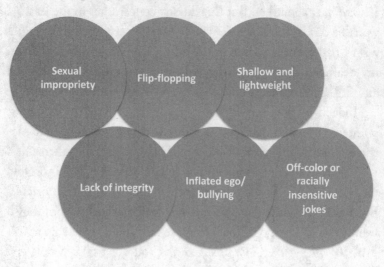

Gravitas Blunders 2012
From focus groups and interviews

- Sexual impropriety
- Flip-flopping
- Shallow and lightweight
- Lack of integrity
- Inflated ego/ bullying
- Off-color or racially insensitive jokes

Figure 3. Gravitas blunders

judgment and values on such a fundamental level that they are fired from their job and oftentimes, shown the door.

Sexual impropriety is a particularly damaging gravitas blunder. Examples include former congressman Anthony Weiner, former International Monetary Fund chief Dominique Strauss-Kahn, former four-star general and CIA director David Petraeus, and former Hewlett-Packard CEO Mark Hurd. A quick Google search turns up a raft of other C-suite-ers who all recently became "formers" as a result of sexual shenanigans: CEO Brian Dunn of Best Buy, CEO Gary Friedman of Restoration Hardware, and CFO Christopher Kubasik of Lockheed Martin among them.

As we shall see in chapter 8, in the wake of the #MeToo movement, a credible charge of sexual harassment or assault became even more damaging. McDonald's CEO, Steve Easterbrook, faced two rounds of investigation and in the end both lost his job and was forced to pay $104 million in a clawback settlement.

Interestingly, while sexual impropriety can knock the powerful off the top perch, there's usually a chance at recovery or some sort of consolation prize cushioning the fall—for men, at least. After being forced to resign when his extramarital affair with his biographer Paula Broadwell came to light in the course of an FBI investigation, David Petraeus was quickly snapped up by investment firm Kohlberg Kravis Roberts & Company to become chairman of the firm's newly created KKR Global Institute. He also landed faculty positions at the City University of New York and the University of California, Los Angeles, where he was given a named chair. Mark Hurd engineered a similar comeback. Six weeks after he was shot down from the top perch of HP as a result of a sexual peccadillo, Hurd became co-president of Oracle—thanks to his close friendship with Larry Ellison.

The women involved in these sexual transgressions fare much less well. One reason is that many of these relationships involve a senior male leader and a female subordinate who has neither the power nor the prestige to help her recover. For example, in the wake of her affair with Petraeus, Paula Broadwell was disciplined by the military and lost both her commission in the reserves and part of her retirement benefits. The female contractor who allegedly carried on that affair with Mark Hurd has not been able to find work since the scandal broke and is currently living in a trailer park in New Jersey. Sad to relate, gravitas blunders are steeped in bias and inequity.

If sexual misconduct is often a career-ender, so is lack of integrity, especially when it's mixed with venality. Martin Shkreli, founder of Turing Pharmaceuticals, is a case in point. In 2015 he hiked the price of antiparasitic drug Daraprim by over 5,000 percent, leaving thousands of patients in the lurch. Hit by waves of public criticism, his company tanked, and two years later Shkreli was convicted in federal court on an unrelated matter: two counts of securities fraud. Ethics seems not to be his strong suit.

As will be explored in chapter 9, Elizabeth Holmes is another powerful example of a leader who, for twenty years, displayed a stunning lack of integrity and buried herself and her company under a pile of egregious lies. In January 2022 she was found guilty on four counts of fraud and conspiracy and sentenced to eleven years in prison.

HOW TO DEEPEN YOUR GRAVITAS

Gravitas is that je ne sais quoi quality that some people have that makes other people judge them born leaders.

But born leaders are made, oftentimes through their own systematic efforts. They live intentionally, guided by a set of values or a vision for their lives that compels them to seize every chance to put their convictions into practice. We gravitate to them because they telegraph that they know where they're going—a rare and intoxicating certainty that most of us lack. That is the genesis of their gravitas.

So consider what larger vision you're here to fulfill, and make sure it informs each of your everyday actions. If you can articulate it, you're well on your way to achieving it. People with a clear goal who show they are determined to achieve it exude gravitas, which in turn bolsters their chances of securing the support they'll need to achieve their goals.

THREE PIECES OF ADVICE FROM EXECUTIVES WHO HAVE TANGLED WITH GRAVITAS CHALLENGES

✓ *Surround yourself with people who are better than you.* "Best piece of advice I ever got," says James Charrington, chairman of Europe, Middle East, and Africa (EMEA) at BlackRock. "Recognize your own weaknesses, and hire people who will complement your strengths by shoring up what you're not good at. Invariably those I've seen struggle to move forward are those who have trouble recognizing their shortcomings. When you talk about your flaws, it's disarming, and it helps others see what you really are good at— and your gravitas grows because you're seen as confident enough to admit weakness."

✓ *Stick to what you know.* Do not shoot from the hip; do not claim to know more than you do or possibly could know. Michelle Gadsden-Williams, the executive we met earlier, learned an important lesson when she asserted to the executive committee of the company she worked for that the playing field for Black employees wasn't level. As she told me in our interview, "It was tempting to play up the drama and claim that there was a great deal of disaffection and disengagement among my colleagues. But the fact is, I didn't know that, I hadn't done those interviews. What I did know was how I myself had been hit by bias and discrimination. So in the end, I decided to back up my assertions by offering concrete examples culled strictly from my own experience and I was careful to frame them that way." Looking back, Gadsden-Williams is glad she made that judgment call. "The fact that I stuck to firsthand testimony and didn't confront them with a generalized indictment allowed them to listen. It turned the tide."

✓ Mellody Hobson, the longtime president of Ariel Investments, has a simple piece of guidance: *smile more.* She received this advice thirty years ago from her mentor, one of Motorola's most senior women. At that time, Hobson, eager to demonstrate her seriousness of purpose as a female climbing the ladder, was focused on cultivating a stern, no-nonsense demeanor. As she told me in an intervivew, "I was flabbergasted by her suggestion, it seemed so lighthearted." But this experienced executive was very persuasive, telling Hobson, "Smiling a lot projects happiness and likability, and people want to work with those they like and those who are happy. In this world, there are energy givers, and energy takers. Who do you want to spend time with? Who are the people you pick up immediately when they call and who are the people whose call you let go to voice mail? You want people to want to take your call."

3

My first term as a student at Cambridge University was rough. As mentioned in an earlier chapter, I grew up in the coal mining valleys of South Wales and spoke English with a thick Welsh accent, whereas the vast majority of my classmates at Cambridge had attended elite public schools (Eton, Harrow, Cheltenham Ladies) and spoke impeccable "Queen's" English.

In class-conscious England, my South Wales accent was bad news. I dropped my aitches, talked about "our mam," and said "ta" instead of "thank you." Back in the 1970s these colloquialisms were not regarded as charming or cute. Indeed, my first week at Cambridge I overheard my tutor describe me to a colleague as "uncouth"—a memory that still makes me wince.

At bottom my accent signaled that I was uneducated or "ill-bred" (to use a particularly demeaning English term). And in a sense I was. I had very little knowledge of the world. My father occasionally brought home a local tabloid called the *Western Mail* but didn't see the point in buying a national newspaper, so I knew next to nothing about current affairs. Our household boasted a motley collection of nineteenth-century novels, courtesy of my mother, who loved the Brontë sisters, but outside of that I was not well-read. At eighteen I'd never been to the theater, shopped at a high-end store, or traveled abroad. We spent family vacations in a trailer park in West Wales. As a result I had no small talk or cocktail patter. It wasn't a personality thing—I was friendly and outgoing. I was tongue-tied because I didn't have anything to talk about that suited my new milieu. I had no way of joining in conversations about, for instance, the Tory leadership struggle, the skiing season in Austria, or the latest in bell-bottom jeans.

My fellow students weren't openly rude or hostile—after all, they were "well-bred" young people—but they kept their distance. I wasn't on invitation lists for sought-after freshman parties, and I found it impossible to penetrate the cozy circles that dominated the interesting clubs. I remember being the awkward, ignored outsider at the Cambridge Union (the university-wide debating society).

I soon realized that to survive and thrive I needed to strip myself of my accent and lose the most obvious of the class markers that set me apart from my peers. By January of that first year I was on the case and set about a transformation. I started with voice and speech—which were, after all, how I "betrayed" myself. I couldn't afford elocution lessons or a voice coach, so I bought a tape recorder and spent long hours listening to, and then attempting to copy, the cut-glass voices on BBC Radio. I sought out the newscasters on the BBC World Service since they spoke a particularly clear and neutral form of Queen's English. It took close to two years, but I nailed it.

Concurrently I set about elevating my conversation so that it reflected the caliber of my thinking rather than the limitations of my background. I subscribed to the *Guardian* and the *Times Literary Supplement*, bought cheap tickets to the Arts Cinema, and plunged into the literature on African liberation movements. I had gotten a grant to spend the summer in Ghana assisting a professor with her research project, so why not develop some well-informed opinions about this intriguing continent? Africa was very "in." By the middle of my second year, I was trying out my newfound verbal and cultural fluency on my slowly expanding circle of sophisticated friends.

My makeover well underway, it was simply a matter of time before these improvements took and I could carry on conversations about a variety of topics without giving away my social class origins. This is not to say my struggle was over: My family saw my new accent as some kind of betrayal, as did I. Was my new way of speaking something fake because it did not reflect the real me? (More on questions of authenticity in chapter 7.) At the time, I tamped down my concerns and focused on the success I was beginning to enjoy at Cambridge as a result of my transformation. I felt I had learned a valuable lesson: Communication is not so much *what* you say but rather *how* you say it. And this you can condition and control. The tone and timbre of your voice; your choice and use of words; your inflection, articulation, and delivery; and even your body language determine what and how much your listeners take in—and what impression of you they will form and retain as a result. Other people's perceptions of you are very much yours to shape.

ALWAYS ON

Most of us tend to think of communication skills in terms of formal presentation skills. But when are you not onstage? When are you not being judged? No matter what your job title or how junior or senior you are, you are always presenting. Whether it's a quick email to your boss, or a casual comment you make to colleagues in the hallway, every written or verbal encounter is a vital opportunity to create and nurture a positive impression.

According to Senior Leaders

Communication Top Traits, 2012

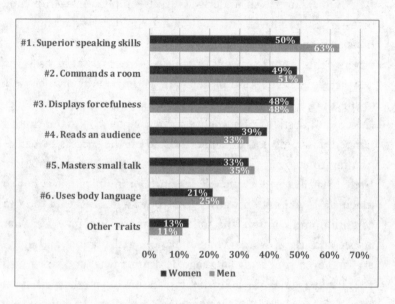

Figure 4. Top communication traits

What are the most effective communication tools and tactics? The traits listed in the graphic above were chosen from twenty-five traits by the senior executives who participated in CTI's nationally representative survey. They include obvious things such as superior speaking skills and the ability to command a room, but also less obvious things such as the ability to banter and use hand gestures to emphasize an important point. All six contribute to an up-and-comer or a seasoned leader engaging and keeping the attention of an audience. Effective communication is all about engagement. Research studies show that, among the tools you bring to this task, content is the least important aspect. An analysis of 120 financial spokespersons found that what makes a speaker persuasive are elements such as passion (27 percent), voice quality (23 percent), and presence (15 percent). Content matters a measly 15 percent.[31]

Engaging and keeping the attention of your boss, your team, or a client turns out to be about the medium and not the message. Your topic may be of intrinsic interest, but unless you minimize distractions for your audience—no easy feat in this age of the omnipresent smartphones—you'll never manage to convey that interest. Look at the phenomenal popularity of TED talks, which spotlight some pretty arcane subjects. What makes a talk TED-worthy is not merely the topic but also the speaker's ability to engage the audience, in person and online, for eighteen minutes without the benefit of notes, PowerPoint, music, or lectern. It's no coincidence that what makes a great TED talk is a speaker who happens to deploy masterfully many of the core communication traits highlighted above. To be heard above the din, to be seen despite the glitz, to be accorded authority and credibility, and to be remembered and heeded, you will need to master at least two of them.

SUPERIOR SPEAKING SKILLS

Fundamentally, communication is about speech—a point made rather poignantly by Tom Hooper's Oscar-winning 2010 film, *The King's Speech*, which dramatizes the real-life transformation of Bertie (Albert), the stammering son of King George V, into an eloquent King George VI after his older brother Edward abdicated the throne in 1936. Wife Elizabeth, keenly conscious of how her husband's speech disability undermines England's confidence in him as a leader, arranges for Bertie to work with a speech therapist whose tactics are decidedly unconventional. It's an agonizing and humiliating process, but one that ends in triumph: Bertie overcomes his stammer to deliver the radio address that galvanizes the nation to take on Hitler.

Most of us, thankfully, don't have to contend with a crippling stammer, but most of us do suffer from verbal shortcomings that turn out to be almost as damaging to our EP. Executives I interviewed cited inarticulateness, poor grammar, and an off-putting tone or accent as examples of verbal tics that undermine EP. Other executives objected to "uptalk," the tendency of young managers, some men, but mostly women, to end declarative statements on a high note, as if they were asking a question rather than stating a point. Still others complained of people who punctuated every sentence with "like" or "you know." Everybody, it seems, recalled an annoying voice, one that was too high-pitched or too husky, too breathy or too raspy. In particular, those we interviewed mentioned "shrill" women: women who, whenever they become emotional or defensive, raise the timbre of their voice, turning off coworkers and clients, and losing out on leadership opportunities.

These are verbal cues that can be adjusted. The painful part is that you'll probably need to be told you've got a problem before you can begin to address it.

ACCENT

Kent Gardiner, a senior partner at the Washington, D.C.–based law firm Crowell & Moring, recalls how, when he left his native Long Island to work for a federal prosecutor in Texas, his mentor took him aside to share some hard-hitting advice. "You have to change how you speak," he told Gardiner. "You have to flatten your accent. Videotape yourself and work on it because you have to change, or you will not succeed in this state." For Gardiner, hiring a voice coach wasn't a possibility. "I didn't have that kind of money, and my employer didn't have a program for rehabilitating New York accents." But he did work on modulating his Long Island accent, and in doing so developed the habit of listening to his own voice as he spoke, which has stayed with him to this day. "Every time I present to my partners, I think about what I'm going to say but also how I'm going to say it before I get up," he explains. "And as soon as I sit down, I rewind the talk. I just replay it mentally. It's very conscious. I do this constantly, because nothing is more important in this profession than oral communication skills."

Sounding provincial can "destabilize your authority," says Gardiner. A British accent, on the other hand, does wonders for your gravitas, according to our focus groups, perhaps because speaking the King's English automatically sets you apart in global commerce. In the words of a Standard Chartered executive based in Singapore: "Maybe it's the weight of history or the depth of ancestry, but a British accent adds to the impression of heft." Before you rush out to acquire one, however, let me reference my own experience and point out that a British accent is complicated. There are good ones and bad ones, and even the good ones can get you into trouble, making you seem snobbish and out of touch. And then there's the question of authenticity. As we shall find out in chapter 7, appropriating someone else's identity is not seen as a good idea in 2023. Elizabeth Holmes, the convicted fraudster who founded and led Theranos, a now defunct health technology company, compounded her many problems by affecting a deep baritone voice and lacing her speech with expletives. These attempts to mimic the alpha bros of Silicon got her into further trouble as she was increasingly seen as "fake and phony" in her personal style as well as her business dealings.

GRAMMAR

Using language incorrectly marks you as uneducated and signals you are someone who should not be admitted to the inner circle. This is what undermined me at Cambridge. I am not alone in this circumstance. Fully 55 percent of respondents in our survey identified grammatical errors as a top communication blunder. And yet it's the rare person who will risk correcting word usage, as such correction calls attention to chasms of socioeconomic class, education, and ethnicity. Katherine Phillips, the Columbia Business School professor we met in the last chapter, describes how thankful she was to have found a sponsor who, early in her academic career, stepped in to correct her improper English. "You're saying the word wrong, Kathy," Margaret Neale, a Stanford professor and Phillips's thesis advisor, told her. "It's 'ask.' Not 'aks.'" Reflecting back on this pivotal moment, Phillips expressed appreciation for Neale's courage in one of our many conversations—"A lot of white people would be concerned they'd sound racist if they pointed these things out to an African-American colleague, but Margaret realized the deleterious impact of how I spoke on my career. To this day, I am grateful to her."

TIMBRE AND PITCH

The research is overwhelming. Not only does the sound of your voice matter twice as much as what you're talking about,[32] but a deep voice in the lower-frequency range will encourage others to see you as successful, sociable, and smart, according to an article in the *Journal of Voice*.[33] My research confirms that a high-pitched voice, particularly for women, is a career-stunting attribute. Indeed, to hear interviewees and focus group participants tell it, nothing is more destructive of a woman's EP than shrillness. Crowell & Moring's senior partner Kent Gardiner told me of his travails with a female litigator whose tone was so strident and shrill that a client demanded she be taken off his case. Lynn Utter of Knoll described the "fingernails on a chalkboard" effect of a senior female leader who was well-spoken and effective until emotion got the better of her, causing her voice to rise to a shriek—"and then everybody tuned her out." And here's why: "Shrill voices have that hint of hysteria that drives men into a panic," says Suzi Digby, a British choral conductor and music educator. "Women with a high-pitched tone will be perceived as not only unleaderlike but out of control."

Margaret Thatcher was fortunate to grasp and act upon this insight early in her political career. As a new appointee to Edward Heath's cabinet in 1970, she was pilloried for having, as one journalist put it, the "hectoring shrill tones of the housewife."[34] When the BBC dropped her from a political spot because her voice was too high-pitched and harsh, Thatcher got the message that her career might depend on fixing that voice. So she turned to Hollywood voice coach Kate Fleming, who'd given Laurence Olivier the lower-register tones that established his gravitas in *Othello*. From 1972 through 1976, Fleming worked with her, transforming what biographer Charles Moore called "her annoying shrieking" into the voice that helped her win the general election in 1979 and established her as Britain's Iron Lady, a woman renowned for "a smoothness of tone that seldom cracked."[35]

Modulating a shrill voice is not a matter of learning to sound more like a man, but rather of achieving what scientists at Duke University have discovered to be an optimally pleasing sound frequency of around 125 Hz.[36] Human beings are apparently wired to like lower frequencies; and of course, we tend to pay attention longer to voices we don't find irritating. Consider whom you'd rather hear speak at your son or daughter's commencement: James Earl Jones (85 Hz)[37] or Roseanne Barr (377 Hz)?[38]

And if that doesn't incentivize you to bring down your pitch, this should: Optimally pleasing voices win the biggest leadership roles and earn the biggest salaries. Duke University's Fuqua School of Business and the University of California, San Diego's Rady School of Management analyzed recordings of 792 U.S. chief executives at public companies as they made investor presentations or earnings calls. They also gathered data on their salaries, length of tenure, and company size. After controlling for experience, education, and other influential factors, the scientists found that a drop of 22 Hz in voice frequency correlated with a $187,000 bump in compensation and larger company size ($440 million larger, in fact). The implication? The lower your voice, the greater your leadership presence, which correlates to an increased likelihood of running a large company and making a substantial salary.[39]

You may think your voice isn't very mutable. But as Thatcher's experience demonstrates, with the right help you can modify it so that, at the very least, you don't turn colleagues off or drive people from the room. Speech training and coaching can make a difference, often because experts can provide what your colleagues or superiors just won't dare to give: honest feedback on how you sound. You may think you know how you sound, but you're not the best person to judge, as a thoughtful piece in the *Wall Street Journal* article pointed out, because you hear your voice only after it's traveled through the bones of your head.[40] You may also imagine there's nothing wrong with your voice because no one's told you there is. As we'll explore in chapter 5, unvarnished feedback is hard to give and harder to receive. Indeed, consulting companies have sprung up in response to client demand for feedback on just these sorts of matters; confronting a coworker or subordinate about speech issues is so fraught that few actually take this on, and fewer still manage to be constructive in their criticism.

So ask for honest feedback. When given a green light from

you, a sponsor or mentor should be able to walk you through what you need to work on. Then get to work—because a lot is at stake.

COMMAND A ROOM

Say what you will about Arianna Huffington's politics, but she's always known how to command attention—whether her audience is a room full of left-leaning movie moguls or a voting bloc of religious conservatives. In the years she led the *Huffington Post* (a company she founded), she commanded a readership of some 5.7 million.[41] Powerful people as well as the hoi polloi hung on her every word. What exactly is it about Arianna that has made her such a commanding presence?

Erik Hedegaard, who profiled Huffington for a *Rolling Stone* article, suggests it's her "capacity for intimacy." Other profilers have stressed her seductive charm, a Bill Clinton–like capacity for making the listener feel as though he or she is the most interesting person in the room. And then there's her voice and accent—that mesmerizing mix of erudition, honed during her student days at Cambridge, commingled with Greek sensuality.[42]

But perhaps it comes down to this: Arianna is never boring. And if you aspire to lead, you, too, must fascinate your audience—or, to use the language of our survey research, "command a room," whether that room be a shareholder's meeting or the team hang-out space. Nearly half of our respondents said it enhances a woman's executive presence, and more than half said it enhances a man's. Nowadays of course, up-and-coming as well as established leaders need to grab and keep an audience on Zoom and Webex as well as face-to-face in a room. Chapter 9 contains vivid word portraits of leaders who have mastered the art of virtual communication. Eddie Glaude, chair of the Department of African American Studies at Princeton University, is a personal favorite. He was chosen by a majority of the seventy-three executives I interviewed in 2022 as an exemplar of communication in action. I particularly appreciate that the backdrops to Glaude's Zooms and video clips are always thoughtfully put together and splendidly lit.

ESTABLISH CONNECTION

According to British choral conductor Suzi Digby, you've got all of five seconds to "touch the audience," or get them to invest in your message. It's all about making yourself human, she says: not oversharing, not indulging in self-revelation, but unveiling just enough of your inner core that your listeners feel connected to you and start rooting for you. Ironically, this can prove difficult for women, who, as Digby points out, oftentimes find it easy to be forthcoming in private but are often self-conscious and withholding in public settings. But getting an audience to like you, to root for you, while at the same time giving the impression that you don't *need* to be liked—this is the wire you want to walk.

I can speak to the power of this. At a large conference in Los Angeles sponsored by GE's Hispanic leaders, I delivered a keynote that presented CTI's cutting-edge findings about the challenges confronting Latinas in the U.S. labor market. While I was confident the research could withstand scrutiny, I was conscious that I might not: Here I was, an elite-sounding white woman—with an English accent—appearing before them as an authority on Hispanic issues. So I didn't launch right into the research when I took the stage. Instead I shared my own story: how I struggled to overcome my Welsh accent and the issues I faced as someone born a girl child on the wrong side of the tracks. The effect was quite magical. In minutes I felt a palpable dissolution of tension as my audience put aside any reservations they may have had to join me in better understanding the research I wanted to bring to their attention.

DELIVER YOUR WORDS AS A MUSICIAN DELIVERS NOTES

Phrasing, inflection, and pace are what distinguish you as a person worth listening to, says Digby. As in music, it's important to deliver your words conscious of your narrative arc, lifting and dropping your cadence to emphasize key passages or points, paying particular attention to how you end a phrase—what musicians call "phrasing off"—so that your listener senses closure and consequently hangs on to the last word and retains it before making room for the next. The uplift that some younger speakers impose on the ends of their sentences, she observes, "undermines their whole message" by denying this closure.

The speed with which you deliver words impacts, in turn, the effectiveness of your phrasing. Digby, who in addition to leading the Queens' College choir coaches those selected to read passages from the Bible, says she's always amazed at how often even experienced speakers rush their delivery. "Ninety-eight percent of the time even a good speaker will go way too fast trying to cram things in," she says. She coaches them to slow down, but also to surround the text with pauses and silences to enhance its power—again, a tactic composers employ to heighten drama and emphasize preludes and codas. "A musician's impact lies in the rests," she explains. "It's the moment where you establish the tension and the seduction. Don't be afraid of silence."

I've seen this advice put to powerful effect by Sallie Krawcheck, who has learned to command the room by *not* speaking as well as speaking. "There is nothing so powerful as silence to make people sit up in their seats," Krawcheck told me. "It's loud. It's unexpected. It's dramatic. And it's confident." Then to demonstrate the effect, she paused a full second before adding, *"Very* confident." Deliberate silence is a trick she learned sitting at boardroom tables with titans like Sanford "Sandy" Weill, Vikram Pandit, Dick Parsons, and Robert Rubin, where men, she says, were accustomed to getting heard by being the loudest, most profanity-laced voice in the room. To stand out as a woman, and to give heft to her thoughts, she started to punctuate her weightiest words with silence. "Those spaces give gravity to your most important pieces of advice, your most important insights, your most important messages," she explains. "It heightens drama because people are literally hanging on your words."

USE NARRATIVE

Stories, not bullet points, are what grab and hold an audience. Ronald Reagan, an actor by training, earned the sobriquet "the Great Communicator" because he was a colorful storyteller and natural entertainer, not because he wielded facts like a policy wonk. Unfortunately, most newcomers to the stage attempt to establish their gravitas by aping the policy wonk rather than the actor. It's a common mistake among both men and women, particularly young professionals, to assume that an exhaustive and fact-laden presentation will bolster their gravitas, when in fact it does just the opposite: Clinging to stats and charts underscores a lack of self-confidence and highlights an absence of confidence and courage. Remember, it's the TED talk, and not an MIT nuclear physics seminar, that you're trying to replicate.

BE SELECTIVE AND STRATEGIC IN USE OF DATA

Though she holds a PhD in Asian studies, Rohini Anand, Sodexo's global chief diversity officer, has learned to be highly intentional about how she delivers her messages, especially the positioning of facts and figures when presenting to global audiences.

Oftentimes she mixes up the game. In some parts of the world, including her native India, she says, "you build up to your conclusion with at least some hard data," whereas in the United States, "people just want your conclusion, the bottom line." So rather than build to the point, she gets to it quickly and limits herself to just a few data points that support what she's saying. Getting to the Q&A quicker, she finds, boosts interaction and ultimately provides her the platform to share her data.

Coming from academia myself, I experienced a learning curve similar to Anand's. My communication style after seven years teaching at Barnard College and Columbia University was to present lengthy, nuanced arguments supported by a ton of compelling facts in fifty-minute chunks of time. Unfortunately, that style, which had won me a Teacher of the Year award at Barnard, went over like a lead balloon in corporate America. Business executives, I belatedly understood, have short attention spans: It's imperative you cut to the chase, be highly selective with your data, and whenever possible share an illustrative story.

GET RID OF PROPS

Last year, less than a month after my friend Elaine was passed over for a C-suite promotion, I had a conversation with her firm's chief financial officer, an acquaintance of mine. We happened to be seated next to one another at an awards dinner. He knew that Elaine and I had worked together, so I asked him why she hadn't made the cut. After all, she'd been with the company twenty-five years and had an incredibly impressive track record.

He nodded, not in the least surprised by my inquiry. "She was one of the top three contenders for the job; indeed, in some ways, she was the most qualified," he affirmed.

Emboldened, I persisted. "So why didn't she get it?"

He sighed. "You're not going to believe the real sticking point,

Sylvia, but you and I have known each other awhile and I'll come clean—the poor woman just makes too many lists."

I was bewildered—what was he talking about? Seeing the puzzled expression on my face, he tried to explain:

"Picture this," he said. "At our monthly executive committee briefing Elaine would always whip out a long list and meticulously consult it. Instead of looking me in the eye and talking compellingly about her team's wins and losses, she'd have her head in her lists and notes. It's as though she didn't command the material—or trust herself to remember the thrust of her presentation. Now, you and I know she's as sharp as a razor and knows her stuff cold, but she doesn't present that way. She comes across as some kind of glorified executive assistant."

My eyes must have widened, because he added, "We can't put her in front of the board. We can't trust her with our important clients. Don't you see? It's about her ability to impress as well as perform."

As our focus groups affirm, constantly referring to lists, reading from notes, using eighty-seven PowerPoint slides, shuffling papers or flip charts, and putting on eyeglasses the better to see what you're reading are all actions that detract from your gravitas because they focus attention on your lack of confidence. If you cannot command your subject matter, you certainly won't be able to command the room. Know your material cold so that you needn't rely on notes, and needn't rely on your glasses to read notes. This will free you up to establish eye contact with the audience. And nothing is more important than eye contact, says former CEO of Credit Suisse, now CEO of Exos, Brady Dougan, because it telegraphs to your audience that you're utterly in the moment. "There are such multiple tugs on people's attention that distraction is the norm," he observes. "Eye contact shows I have your complete attention, which I deeply appreciate because it's so very rare. In an important meeting, nothing boosts your leadership presence more than signaling that you're totally present."

BE SUCCINCT

"Executive presence is not necessarily about being formal or abundant in your communication, but rather straightforward and brief," says Kerrie Peraino, head of international HR for American Express. "The more you keep speaking, or explaining yourself, the more you cloud or dilute your core message." Women seem especially prone to this blunder, she observes, perhaps because they're less sure of how they're perceived and seek to prove their expertise by overselling their case. According to Moody's Linda Huber, women also feel compelled to validate what they have to say by invoking all the people they consulted. "They go through five conditional clauses before they get to the point," she observes. "It's okay to say, 'I have a different point of view,' and then back it up with two or three reasons you can support with data. Don't start with, 'I've spent hours staying awake thinking about this and talked to thirty-seven people.' Get to the point, and then people will give you their attention."

ASSERTIVENESS

When Barbara Adachi was promoted to regional head of Human Capital Consulting at Deloitte—the first woman to win such a position at the accounting/consultancy firm—she asked a partner we'll call Doug if she could sit on the firm's management committee with the other business leaders of audit and tax. He told her the seat was occupied by the regional director she used to report to, who wasn't about to give it up. "We can't have two people from Human Capital at the table," he added. Adachi persisted. "But

I'm a *partner* and now leading this region," she said. The other partner shook his head. "But people just don't see you as a leader, Barbara."

It was like a punch to the gut, Adachi recalls. A million responses came to mind, she says, including just storming out of the room. Instead, she managed to retort, "That's because I'm not on the management committee!" Doug laughed, and conceded she had a point. "That broke the ice with him," she related to me. "But I could see his point, too: I wasn't viewed as someone who was well connected with other leaders in my region and office. I didn't have a powerful circle of sponsors, either. I may have been a partner, but nobody perceived me as one because I did not project power or presence."

So Adachi, a Japanese-American woman who was raised to listen, not talk, made a decision that would change her life. She went back to Doug and delivered an ultimatum. "If the regional director won't step down from the management committee, then I don't want to be the leader in Northern California, because I'd have all the responsibility and none of the authority. To do this job well, I need to be respected as a leader. And if I can't be on the committee, then I won't be viewed as a peer by the other leaders."

Ultimately Doug put her on the committee.

Being forceful and assertive is a core executive trait, for both men and women (according to 48 percent of our survey respondents). But for women, it's a decidedly more difficult trait to embody, as assertiveness in a woman often makes her unlikable (the B-word is rolled out and she's seen as overly aggressive). We'll explore this tightrope walk in chapter 6; meanwhile, let's review some of the strategies that apply to both men and women in terms of being successfully forceful.

Adachi feels in that moment of confrontation she proved herself a leader by arriving at a bold decision and showing she was ready to act on it. "I wasn't making an idle threat," she explains. "I was willing to walk away from the leadership role because having the responsibility without the authority would be comparable to being asked to hit a home run without a bat. And Doug saw and heard my resolve."

But she may also have prevailed because she framed her demand in the context of the good it would do the company, observes Rosalind Hudnell, vice president of human resources at Intel. "Push back," she counsels, "but try and avoid the I-word. Come from a position that's not about you, but about what's best for the company. Don't yell, and be careful about your tone. Because when you're working for a company, you need to be respectful of that company." The challenge is to keep that in mind while finding a strong voice that reflects your authentic leadership style.

The executives I interviewed uniformly suggest you resist the urge to charge in and make known your demands. "You're not going to get anything done by asserting, 'This is what I want and I want it now,'" cautions a former Lehman Brothers executive who had worked with the company's first female CFO. "[The CFO] was never one to lack voice: She was brilliant on so many topics, and she enjoyed letting others know it," he recalls. "But in her new role, which she knew others begrudged her because she wasn't an investment banker, she overplayed her hand. She came on like gangbusters, shouting and swearing. Maybe she wanted to prove she could be as tough as the boys, but she showed no respect, and given that these guys had built the firm, that was more than a little unseemly. I told her, 'If you want to be heard, you've got to be a little more deferential to those sitting around the table with you.'"

Sensitivity can spell the difference between sounding like a leader and actually succeeding as one, as one female executive discovered when confronted with a labor crisis that threatened to go nuclear. Some four hundred of her employees didn't get their correct biweekly salary because of a payroll glitch. With her firm in the midst of union negotiations, she knew that this vendor mishap could trigger an employee action or a work stoppage, or, at the very least, devolve into a PR nightmare. So she got on the phone with the business leader, his team, and the local HR leader, and listened as they laid out the scope of the problem. She then proposed a two-part solution: laying out a modest, non-negotiable goal and assuring the team she would support them in reaching it. "I am committed to seeing this through with you," she told the team on the phone. But after the call, in a one-on-one conversation with her colleague in charge of the vendor relationship, she made clear that his job was on the line, as his and her reputations were at stake. "I knew that demolishing this guy in front of everybody would not get me the cooperation I needed to resolve the crisis quickly," she observed. "So I allowed him to save face with his team, and then, behind the scenes, let him know that he was totally accountable." Her approach succeeded. The employee pay issue was resolved.

The best strategy for women may be what Linda Huber of Moody's describes as "leading from behind." In a room full of men, women often feel impelled to assert themselves by launching the first salvo. But far more effective, says Huber, an army officer who at age twenty-one had forty-five soldiers in her command, is holding off until others have fired off their best shot. "I learned a lot about military tactics from my father, who was a two-star general," she explains. "Even so, when it came time to do sandtable exercises of moving units around and practicing tactics, I was careful to wait, step back, and let others go first before offering up my solution." Having watched "a lot of cocky West Point types mess up," she adds, she realizes that "sometimes it's best to sit back and listen, first."

Just make sure, when all eyes are upon you, that you do, in fact, offer a solution. A health-care leader described to me how, early in her tenure, she tried to get a team of scientists and engineers to agree on a way forward by eliciting everyone's opinion. Instead of reaching consensus, the room devolved into chaos. "Now I step up and say, 'Okay, we're not going to talk about this anymore,'" she explained. "'Here's the decision I've come to, and here's why we're going with it.' It could be the wrong decision—I've made those, every leader does. But at least I'm making it."

And *that*, she adds, is what marks you as someone others will follow.

ABILITY TO READ A ROOM

A couple of years ago, I was invited by Tulane University's Newcomb College Institute to be its annual Alberto-Culver Speaker, an endowed lecture series that invites high-profile women leaders to campus to talk about cutting-edge issues facing women in business. Given the publicity and branding around this event, I went to New Orleans expecting to address a sizable crowd. And in fact the venue was an auditorium at Newcomb College that easily held four hundred. But minutes before I took the stage I looked out and realized, to my dismay, that given the paltry trickle of students entering the lecture hall I'd be lucky to have fifty attendees.

In fact, there were thirty-eight—I counted them.

For any public speaker—politician or executive, professor or celebrity author—this is a sickening challenge. It's hard to exude executive presence and engage a crowd when, having prepared a speech for the National Mall in Washington, D.C., you arrive on the Capitol steps to find that one earnest busload has shown up. Here I was, armed with a razzle-dazzle deck and a sizzling speech rehearsed for hundreds. What to do? I had minutes to decide.

My host, oblivious to the size of the turnout, walked slowly to the podium, donned her glasses, and read a lengthy introduction of me from a script she'd prepared. Some of those in the back of the auditorium got up and headed for the doors. Realizing that the rest of the audience might well slip away, I walked resolutely to the front of the stage and invited everyone to gather in the first few rows. I asked for a chair, and sat myself down directly in front of them. Abandoning my PowerPoint, I addressed myself to them directly, communicating the essence of my data but relying mostly on narrative to pass the hour. I told many more stories than I'd intended, and at each natural break, I invited the students to ask questions—which they did, with eager energy. By the time we concluded the session, I felt a powerful connection. They felt it, too, because the evaluations they turned in were uniformly hyperbolic with praise. To this day I recall that event at Tulane as one of my most effective presentations, not despite my extemporizing, but because of it.

To command a room, you've first got to *read it*. Sensing the mood, absorbing the cultural cues, and adjusting your language, content, and presentation style accordingly are vital to your success as a communicator, and succeeding as a communicator is vital to your executive presence. Deploying your emotional intelligence and then acting on what it tells you absolutely boosts your EP—especially if you're a woman. Indeed, 39 percent of respondents told us this emotional-intelligence skill mattered for women, whereas 33 percent said it mattered for men.

Being oblivious to the needs of your audience will undermine perceptions of your authority. Here's why: First, it intimates you're a closed circuit, someone who can't or won't take in new information (the woman who introduced me at Newcomb College being a prime example). Second, it implies you don't care about your audience, destroying any chance of connection, which is after all the foundation of any successful communication. Finally, and most damning, it implies you're simply not nimble enough to adapt to rapidly changing circumstances. Agility in a leader is increasingly prized in a global economy characterized by relentless change and persistent volatility.

What does it take to effectively read a room? You've got to tune yourself out in order to tune in to the needs and wants of others, and then course-correct on the spot to establish connection. Demonstrating that willingness impresses people: It shows you have absolute command of your subject matter, and it signals to your audience that you're so invested in the importance of your message that you'll scuttle your carefully prepared speech to make sure they grasp it. That's a recipe for engagement.

Sodexo's Rohini Anand recalls a particularly high-pressure meeting when she had one shot to convince the firm's top leaders to let outside experts advise the company on an extremely sensitive workforce issue. She entered the boardroom prepared to share the evidence she'd amassed, but in the end she elected to make her pitch with a short summary of the benefits, as she sensed the room wasn't interested in how she'd arrived at her insight. It was the right instinct: She made a convincing case, and within months Sodexo announced a new board of external advisors. "The tipping point in my career at this firm was when I figured out how to put myself in my audience's shoes and to paint a picture balancing facts and stories in ways that were powerful for that particular audience," says this seasoned executive.

In this regard, professionals of color may hold an edge. In focus groups we conducted, countless participants confirmed that being a minority is itself a relentless exercise in reading others in order to anticipate and overcome reflexive bias or unconscious resistance. In an interview, Joel Tealer, an African-American senior executive at Chubb Group of Insurance Companies, told me that in order to maintain his EP, he adapts his speech to the culture of his listener and takes care to neutralize his political views, lest his mostly Republican colleagues take offense. "What you have to always do, as a Black executive, is make sure that you use the appropriate language for the appropriate situation," he says. "And during tough discussions, you have to be a bit more balanced because your audience can become uncomfortable if they see you as too left of center or overly passionate."

That's not to say you compromise your views to pander to your audience, Tealer clarifies. "It's about winning their confidence," he says. "Reading your audience is all about making them comfortable so that when you speak, they really hear what you have to say."

HUMOR AND BANTER

When Sallie Krawcheck offers up her analysis of what ails Wall Street, she pulls no punches. Whether it's the lack of oversight on money-market funds, the exorbitant executive compensation, or the absence of women in boardrooms, she serves up criticism heedless of blowback.

Yet precisely because she is blunt and dead serious, Krawcheck takes special care to leaven her critiques with humor. If women are stalled in their careers and need a leg up, for instance, it's because they're worn-out—exhausted by all the demands, professional and personal, placed upon them. "Do the math," Krawcheck exhorts her audiences. "Women spend so much more time on personal grooming than guys do. Take me. This is an underestimation, but let's assume fifteen minutes a day, an hour and fifteen minutes a week, five hours a month, sixty hours a year, on hair and makeup, and I have not shaved my legs yet! I've not yet dyed my hair, there is no mani-pedi, the brows have not been waxed, I have not gone to yoga, I have not run, I have done nothing but my friggin' hair and makeup."[43]

I've heard this shtick from Krawcheck on numerous occasions, and I can attest that it never fails to break up the room in gales of laughter. However brutal her message—in fact, especially when her message is brutal—Krawcheck's reliance on humor endears her to her listeners, who then become open to some inconvenient truths.

Not everyone can pull off a funny story at the lectern, but everyone can learn to banter at the watercooler. Many of our focus group participants affirmed the importance of mastering the art of small talk. "It's the conversation *before* the meeting that establishes whether or not you're worth listening to *in* the meeting," one senior executive pointed out—a skill she refers to as "mastering the banter." It shows, she explained, that you're part of the larger conversation, someone who's "one of the tribe."

To be sure, because the language and interests of the dominant tribe tend to dominate casual conversations, women and multicultural executives often find themselves at a disadvantage. In the words of one African-American focus group participant, "I don't watch the same television shows as my colleagues. That makes it hard to chime in about the most recent episode of *Survivor* or *Succession*."

Well, watching *Survivor* isn't enough to boost your EP. Yet as I found at Cambridge, it's critical you strive to be conversant on a host of topics, if only because you'll then have the confidence to insert yourself into the casual conversations of your superiors. "You don't have to claim you're a diehard Giants fan or a Democrat or a scratch golfer; you just need to know enough to add to the conversation," says Deb Elam, a vice president at GE. "It's all about forging a bond with people—one that you may need to lean on down the road."

BODY LANGUAGE AND POSTURE

On her second day working for a leading insurance firm, one female focus group participant recalls how she was taken aside after a staff meeting and chided for doodling and slouching in her chair. "I don't want to ever see that again," her new boss told her. "You should be sitting up straight, pulled up to the table, making eye contact, and taking notes. You should be paying attention!" She tried to assure him she had been listening. "It doesn't matter," he said, waving a hand impatiently. "What matters is that your behavior told everyone that you weren't."

Never underestimate the communicative power of body language. While 21 percent of senior executives we surveyed recognize that how you hold and carry yourself affects your EP, anecdotally the evidence around body language suggests a much greater impact. "People gauge your EP the second you enter a room: how confidently you walk in, how firmly you shake hands, how quickly you make eye contact, how confidently you stand," observes Deloitte's Adachi. "In those initial seconds, you're going to be judged on what they see, not what they hear, and your body language and poise are what they often see first."

Consider how the U.S. presidential candidates conducted themselves while facing off during nationally televised debates. Indeed, executive coach and body-language expert Carol Kinsey Goman actually called the 2012 election on the basis of President Obama's body language alone, especially during the third debate. "He looked more comfortable and sure of himself," she observed, "using the definitive palm-down gestures and wide 'steepling' gestures that show certainty. And he has a great genuine smile (a big likability cue) that he flashed a couple of times tonight." Governor Romney did well, too, Goman noted. "But he perspired, swallowed frequently, licked his lips, stammered, and (about 58 minutes into the debate) gave a slight shudder that showed in his shoulders and upper chest—all indicators that he was under a high level of stress."[44]

Since people will be "reading you" the moment they lay eyes on you, take care to enter a room or take the stage with aplomb. Is your head up, your gaze focused straight ahead? Shoulders back but relaxed? Do you stride or shuffle? And do you look happy at this opportunity to engage? Or do you look like you're nursing an ulcer?

When Catherine, a corporate senior executive, enters a room, people don't even need to know she spent more than twenty years in federal law enforcement to accord her awed respect.[45] Tall and elegantly dressed, this African-American woman radiates gravitas in her posture, stride, and stance. "I've been told I don't demand respect, that my presence expects it," she says. "Some of that came from growing up in the South and having to fight and wrestle with a lot of challenges. When you are the first Black person in a school classroom or at a company meeting, you learn to walk in with Michelle Obama's confidence and poise. That conditions everything. Because I walk into every meeting with that attitude, holding my head high, I leave a positive impression behind. People want me at their table."

An erect bearing also conveys respect for others. That's why your mother told you to sit up straight at the dining room table: to show deference to those around you. In the film *The Social Network*, Mark Zuckerberg, slumped at the deposition table, telegraphs volumes to the attorneys assembled around him. I saw the movie with a young law firm associate, who told me, "It's hard to root for someone who makes you feel as though you don't warrant his attention."

A number of recent studies find, however, that the most important benefit good posture confers is chemical: When you stand tall, feet planted solidly and somewhat apart, chest out and shoulders back, you actually trigger a hormonal response that boosts testosterone and lowers cortisol, the steroid released from your adrenal glands in times of stress, from your bloodstream. Amy Cuddy, a social psychologist at Harvard Business School, discovered this through a series of controlled experiments she conducted on her colleagues (findings she shared as a TED speaker).[46] While the hormones last only about fifteen to twenty minutes, the rush of well-being and confidence may trigger "a physiological cascade that lasts all day," says Dana Carney, a social psychologist at the University of California, Berkeley's Haas School of Business.[47]

While standing at attention bolsters your own self-confidence, it also signals to others that you are paying attention—which, as we've discussed, is perhaps the keystone of all effective communication. To radiate presence you have to radiate that you *are* present. And as Brady Dougan pointed out to me in an interview, that's where many a would-be executive stumbles. Indeed, virtually every executive I interviewed talked about accomplished, ambitious men and women who sabotaged their chances at a top job by conveying in gestures large and small an inability to remain present when it mattered most. Kent Gardiner, chided early in his career for checking his watch too often during meetings, says he's become a stickler about ensuring his colleagues don't commit similar blunders of inattention, including pen-clicking, foot-tapping, paper-rustling, and device-checking. Jane Shaw told me one of the rudest things she ever witnessed was a board member turning his back on the meeting in order to deal with some emails. Indeed, tuning out to consult your smartphone elicited some of the most heated discourse in our focus groups and interviews. Sara, an executive in the structured finance division at Moody's, told me, "I really get annoyed when

I interact with colleagues who are so distracted they don't hear what I am saying after I've spent weeks preparing a presentation. This behavior really undermines their executive presence in my mind. How can you trust a colleague to keep his eye on the big picture if he can't keep his eye off his iPhone?" A final word on the body language front: As we shall see in chapter 9, one consequence of the #MeToo movement is that body language has become a double-edge sword. Sure, the skillful use of movement, gesture, and posture can greatly increase a leader's ability to reach and hold an audience, but it can also backfire—big time! In the spring of 2020, when Joe Biden's bid for the presidency was heating up, eight women came forward and accused him of inappropriate touching. One talked about being "creeped out" by his habit of patting her head, another complained about the distressing frequency of his squeezes and hugs. Biden weathered this storm but in the contemporary world, managers and executives are well-advised not to invade a colleague's personal space. Experts in the field tell us that coworkers should keep their distance, recommending at least eighteen inches.

BLUNDERS

During her twenty-four years in Congress, Colorado representative Patricia Schroeder was lauded for her stalwart advocacy of work-family issues (she sponsored and guided through Congress the landmark 1993 Family and Medical Leave Act) and her tough stance on congressional reform. However, for many her name will forever be linked with bursting into tears on national television when she announced she would not seek the Democratic nomination for president. "Women across the country reacted with embarrassment, sympathy and disgust," wrote the *Chicago Tri-*

bune a week later.[48] *Saturday Night Live* lampooned her in a skit on the presidential primary debates.[49] More than a decade later, Schroeder told *USA Today*, she was still catching flak about it.[50] The verdict: Wiping away those tears erased the perception that Schroeder might have been fit to be the country's chief executive.

Interestingly, as we shall see in chapter 9, in 2023, crying is not such a big deal. Not that anyone would recommend that an up-and-comer on the fast track make a habit of crying, but when faced with calamity or tragedy, modern leaders, whether they are male or female, are allowed to cry. Ukrainian president Volodymyr Zelenskyy allows tears to run down his face when attending yet another funeral for one of his brave fighters, and Michelle Obama openly sobs at memorial services for fifteen-year-olds mowed down in yet another senseless shootout in Chicago. On these rare occasions we all applaud. Showing emotion is no longer an EP blunder.

Other communication errors identified in our focus groups include breathlessness or any other sign of nerves, constantly checking your iPhone for the latest messages, being obviously bored, being long-winded instead of getting right to the point, and relying too heavily on notes and other props. These flaws damage your brand and your prospects. Which brings us back to the important question of feedback.

Without honest feedback from others, how can you tell whether you've buried your point in an avalanche of self-inflicted communications mistakes? In the moment, there are easy indicators: Listen for the "cough count." How many times does your audience feel compelled to cough or clear their throats? Similarly, check the "fidget factor." Are you spotting people shifting in their seats, crossing and uncrossing their legs, examining their fingernails, or adjusting their arm positions on tables and chairs? All of these things are dead giveaways that your presentation is making them wish they were elsewhere.

Communication Blunders 2012
From focus groups and interviews

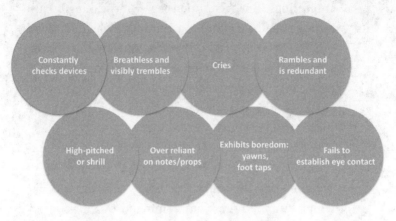

Figure 5. Communication blunders

THREE PIECES OF ADVICE FROM EXECUTIVES WHO HAVE TANGLED WITH COMMUNICATION CHALLENGES

✓ *Overprepare.* Barbara Adachi finds that meticulous preparation allows her to overcome her inclination not to speak unless spoken to. "I used to go to meetings and not say a word," she recalls. "People wondered why I was even there. Perhaps it's my upbringing (Adachi is Japanese-American) but speaking up has always been hard for me. The good news is that I've found a way to push myself in new situations. I do a ton of work beforehand and go in with some dynamite comments and responses already planted in my head. This way, I find it easier to speak up and not retreat to my cocoon."

✓ *Less can be more.* Jane Shaw, former chairman of Intel's board, affirms that you can't afford to be a wallflower at meetings. But she cautions against speaking up just for the sake of it. "Inject a comment when you have something fresh to add. If you're asked for an update, stick to new items. Invite others to add their opinion rather than babble on. If someone has not weighed in, you might throw a question to them when you finish," she advises.

✓ *"Do not allow challenges to your authority to go unanswered,"* says Dwight Robinson, chief of diversity of Freddie Mac. In some situations, hecklers will attempt to undermine your command of the room by getting under your skin. No matter how hostile they are or how loud they shout, don't let them. Parrying these attacks with humor is your best defense, as it demonstrates that your confidence can't be shaken and makes the hecklers look small and petty. Sometimes, however, humor won't work and you need to go full frontal. Robinson then described a tense situation when his boss nominated him as his deputy running the state housing authority committee. Robinson knew he was totally qualified to win the position, but as both he and his boss were African-American, he anticipated his appointment would come under fire. And indeed it did. But Robinson's boss did not flinch. To the builders, the developers, and the mayor who questioned his choice, he countered, "You've got twenty-seven other departments with two people of the same race in charge. In these cases they're white. They're doing their jobs. So what is wrong with the picture when two white people are running twenty-seven agencies and two Black people are running one?" Robinson says his boss's response was a "life lesson" for him in exercising courage and asserting authority.

4

When we first met—at a wedding anniversary celebration for mutual friends—I was impressed and intrigued by D'Army Bailey. He radiated vigor and charisma. A few weeks later we got together for coffee and I learned much more about him. A Memphis-based lawyer and former judge, Bailey started out as an activist in the civil rights movement. He's had a remarkable career litigating and adjudicating landmark cases, writing two books, and ultimately founding the National Civil Rights Museum in Memphis.

But as we chatted and sipped on a second round of lattes, I couldn't help but marvel at his appearance. Fit, toned, and impeccably dressed, he looked impossibly young. I was perplexed. "How is it that you, a man who marched with Martin Luther King, looks not a day over forty-nine?" I asked him.

"I've had three plastic surgeries," he confessed nonchalantly. "I've had a forehead lift, a facelift, and had the bags removed from under my eyes."

My mouth fell open and I spilled some coffee.

Seeing my astonishment, he burst out laughing. "Why shouldn't I look my best?" he exclaimed, not in the least defensive. "I'm not ready to throw in the towel. I don't want to retire."

He then went on to explain that he'd long understood the connection between looking good and looking capable. "Facelifts and good dental work convey a more youthful appearance, but they also signal confidence and credibility. To my clients I'm more trustworthy. To a jury I'm more believable. Now, don't get me wrong, my appearance isn't what wins me a case, but when I look in control I feel in control—and that's how others perceive me."

Keisha Smith-Jeremie, managing director and co-head of talent management at Morgan Stanley when I interviewed her, now chief people officer at Tory Burch, told me that it was quite by accident that she came by her signature look. After a dye job went wrong, she had a barber shave off her hair—and liked the result. In the years since, as she has moved up the corporate ladder into roles of ever greater visibility and responsibility, she has perfected her stand-out look.

Tall, with wide-set eyes and a dazzling smile, she's an executive you'd notice anyway; but as a bald Afro-Caribbean woman who holds a senior position at a Fortune 500 firm, she's a leader you'll never forget. It's not the shaved head so much as the statement it makes: that she's utterly at ease in her skin.

Smith-Jeremie is conscious that her appearance can "widen the gap" between herself and those she meets for the first time. In her words, "I'm aware that my aesthetic is unusual, and can be intimidating, which is why I take pains to close that gap by seeking out personal connections and establishing common ground with my colleagues." However, she explains, it's a style she enjoys, one that she intends to keep even if it does mean feeling self-conscious at every meeting with new clients. "I do what I need to do to make it work in my work environment, because having a style that I'm comfortable in breeds the inner confidence which helps me be successful." She adds, "I really wouldn't have it any other way."

D'Army Bailey and Keisha Smith-Jeremie underscore the complexities of the appearance challenge today. A seventy-year-old male jurist can talk openly about how plastic surgery has enhanced his ability to stay in the game, and a forty-year-old female executive can choose to be bald and have it contribute to her gravitas. But do these voices signal new freedoms or new constraints? We've learned to value authenticity—and this is good—but at the same time standards have risen and we're judged on many more fronts—wrinkles and waistlines as well as a well-cut skirt or suit.

As we wrestle with the thorny—and often annoying—issue of looks, three things are uppermost in our minds: What marks us for success? What exactly are bosses and colleagues looking for these days? And how much does this superficial stuff matter anyhow?

At first glance, CTI survey data seems to show that appearance isn't that important. Sixty-seven percent of the senior executives we surveyed told us that gravitas was the core characteristic of executive presence; 28 percent said that communication skills comprised the core; and a mere 5 percent said appearance was at the heart of the matter. However, from our qualitative data we found that appearance was typically the *filter* through which gravitas and communication skills were evaluated. That explains why high-performing junior employees oftentimes get knocked out of contention for key roles and promotions: they simply don't look the part. In other words, get this appearance thing wrong and you're struck off the list. No one even bothers to assess your gravitas or communication skills if your appearance telegraphs you're clueless.

Over the long haul, the way you look may not be nearly as important as what you say or how you act, but it's incredibly important in the short run. Cracking the appearance code opens doors and puts you in play.

So what are senior leaders looking for? What are their top picks?

According to Senior Leaders

Appearance Top Traits, 2012

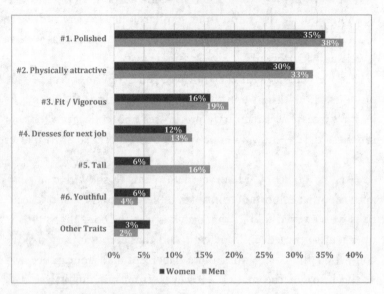

Figure 6. Top aspects of appearance

BEING POLISHED AND GROOMED

I find this top pick extremely comforting because it confers on individuals a great deal of agency and control. More than a third of the senior executives in our survey (men and women) considered "polish and grooming" vital to men's and women's EP, whereas less than a third said that physical attractiveness matters. It turns out that the intrinsic stuff (body type, height) is not what matters most; rather, it's what you do with what you've got. As one leader put it in an interview, "You've got to look as though you tried, that you pulled yourself together." When I present this data, most professionals are relieved to learn that cracking the appearance code is something that can be learned and you're not stuck with what you were born with.

Research conducted by Nancy Etcoff at Harvard Medical School bears this out. In a well-regarded experiment, she showed 268 subjects four different versions of women's faces, flashing images of the faces in front of the subjects for 250 milliseconds. As can be seen in the figure below, the images featured three women of different ethnicities.[51] The *only* difference between the four versions of each woman's face was the amount of cosmetics applied—the range was from no makeup to dramatic makeup.

Subjects were asked to assess each woman's face in terms of how attractive, competent, trustworthy, and likable they judged the woman to be.

First Impressions

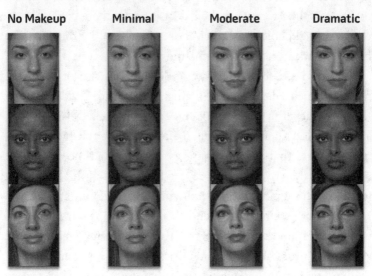

Figure 7. First impressions

What did Etcoff and her team find out? Not surprisingly, judgments about a woman's attractiveness were heavily conditioned by how much makeup she was wearing—the more, the better, it turns out. Number 4 was the top choice. Much more startling, judgments about her competence, likability, and trustworthiness were also deeply affected by cosmetic choices. As though competence is really a function of how much lipstick you wear! Again, the rule of thumb seemed to be the more makeup, the better. The women were judged most competent when they wore dramatic makeup. But, and this is an important but, the top choice for trustworthiness was number 3, not 4. This implies that although dramatic makeup gets the highest marks in most categories of achievement, it's hard to fully trust a woman who looks glamorous.

One eye-catching thing about this study is how quickly these judgments were made (250 milliseconds). And those flash judgments tended to stick. Even after subjects were given unlimited inspection time to review their decisions, they doubled down on their original choices. A quick look, a long look, it didn't matter, highest marks were given to the most adorned faces.[52]

Trying hard really does help. A judicious use of cosmetics, neatly manicured nails, well-fitting jeans (Silicon Valley), a perfectly cut jacket (Wall Street), and carefully coiffed hair all make a difference. When you make an effort to look polished, you signal to others that you see them as worth your time and investment, and that you're even prepared to tolerate mild discomfort (think of those closely fitting shirt collars that rub against your neck or those stylish four-inch heels that cramp your toes). Who wouldn't respond to such efforts! It's a statement of respect, after all—respect for colleagues and clients, respect for yourself.

No one better understands this than my close friend and coauthor Cornel West, the beloved scholar, philosopher, and activist who's much admired for his courage in speaking truth to power. To hear West deliver one of his passionate, powerful speeches is to experience something that rocks you to your core. And appearance is an integral part of it.[53] Sure, there's his body language. He assumes a forward-pitched crouch, which frees up his arms to wave and gesticulate. And there's his delivery, a song that crescendos into a battery of inconvenient truths before resuming its comfort-filled cadence. But then there's West's "uniform," the black three-piece suit, black tie, immaculate white shirt (French cuffs flaring, cuff links glinting), black scarf, and silver-toned watch fob. I have never seen him attired in anything else. He wears this uniform whether he's locking horns with a MAGA Republican on *Real Time with Bill Maher*, debating Newt Gingrich on *Crossfire*, giving an address to the U.K.'s House of Lords on Black Lives Matter, preaching at the Allen Temple Baptist Church in Oakland, or sitting in my backyard on a sultry August afternoon. While this uniform doesn't always help him hail a taxi at night in New York City, West's look does command the attention of heads of state and business titans as well as the loyalty and affection of millions of regular folk.

But there's more to his clothing than distinctiveness. West perceives his attire as his suit of armor, the thing that enables him to face the "bullets and arrows" endemic to his work. "It makes me feel good, to put on my uniform," he says, "because you've got to be ever ready for engagement and combat." If he's rather particular about the details of his uniform—the break of his cuff, the crease in his pants—it's because he cannot permit a crack in his armor; it would breach his self-confidence. "If I walk around without my crease, it's like walking around with my shoes not shined," he says. "I don't feel right."

West wears this uniform because it telegraphs, to himself and others, the seriousness of his mission and the respect he bears for those who launched him on his journey. His suits are akin to Martin Luther King's "cemetery clothes," which, West explains,

MLK wore to remind himself that he was going to live and die for something bigger than he was. "I may be smiling, laughing, fighting, writing, and speaking—with hope, and kindness, and humor," says West, who these days is a professor of religious philosophy and Christian practice at Union Theological Seminary in New York, "but I'm 'coffin-ready' because the tradition that produced me sets the highest standards I could possibly aspire to."

Now, I'm not urging you to wear a three-piece suit or any other uniform. Nor do I wish to imply that polish can only be achieved by wearing black or nailing that crease in your pants. I am suggesting, however, that you take pains to signal, in your appearance, a seriousness of purpose by attending to the details. Casual clothes may be the right choice for your organizational culture, but in their fit and brand and style, they should telegraph that you take your work and those whom you engage in it very seriously. Poor grooming—dandruff on your collar, scuffed shoes, broken nails, runs in your tights, soup on your tie—compromises the ability of other people to see you as someone who's going places because it says that either you don't notice sloppiness or you don't care enough to attend to it. In interview after interview, senior leaders told me that failure to come through on the grooming front signals either poor judgment or lack of discipline. Neither is good.

"If you were making a pitch for a new piece of business, you wouldn't go into that client meeting with hand-scribbled notes," says Mark Stephanz, vice chairman of Bank of America Merrill Lynch. "No: You'd go to no end of trouble to be sure that you had a PowerPoint (or printed deck) at the ready which was polished, powerful, and error-free. And the same rules must apply to your appearance."

Good grooming is not just about making a polished first impression: It's about signaling to colleagues, competitors, and yourself that you're in total control. My lawyer friend D'Army Bailey told me he had his aha! moment about grooming back in high school, when he saw Jackie Gleason and Paul Newman star in *The Hustler*. What impressed him was how Minnesota Fats, the pool shark played by Gleason, maintained his cool throughout a night of fearsome competition by going into the men's room during breaks to wash his face, comb his hair, and straighten his tie. "He wanted his opponent to think he was fresh, and unfazed by the intensity of the challenge," Bailey observes. "I learned from this that in every encounter with an opponent, it's a psychological game you're playing, and no matter how wrought-up or stressed-out you are, you should try not to show it. Don't let them see you sweat; don't allow yourself to look worn or unkempt." So Bailey gets regular facials and manicures, in addition to frequent haircuts. "If I am meeting with someone consequential and look down and see I'm two weeks out from a manicure, I'm going to start worrying about what is showing on my nails, and that's going to distract me," he says. "Tidy nails, a fresh haircut, and a fresh shirt always give me a confidence boost."

Achieving polish comes down to this golden rule: *Minimize distractions from your skill sets and performance.* Have professionals tend to your nails and hair regularly. Invest in well-cut attire that complements your body type. Accessorize, but don't billboard your bling. And unless you're in an industry that prizes physical beauty, don't flaunt your body. For men as well as women, sexuality scrambles the mind. Don't wear shirts that emphasize your build or blouses that emphasize your bust; avoid tight or skimpy trousers or skirts. Clothing that advertises your body steals attention from, say, your laser-sharp analytic skills, your visionary design expertise, or your compelling oratory. All of which underscores one basic principle: Your appearance should focus your audience on your professional competencies, not distract from them.

Minimizing sexual distraction is especially important if you're female. A senior Wall Street executive who's mentored a number of high-flying women told me that oftentimes he's needed to spell out how and why dressing in a sexually suggestive way undermines a woman's EP. "When a female executive walks into a room with three buttons open, a black lacy bra showing under her blouse, and a skirt hiked high, these things are going to distract the men sitting around a conference table . . . and they will take her much less seriously, however big a producer she is," he explained to me. "It's not that I want my protégées to look less feminine, just less provocative." He then went on to speculate, "It's as though at a deep level, some women believe that the power they ultimately wield is their sexuality. But overt sexuality has no place in the executive suite."

Women, it seems, walk a fine line between turning heads and dropping jaws. So another rule of thumb: You should look "appropriate for your environment, and authentic to you," as Kerrie Peraino, chief people officer at Verity, puts it. A tongue stud may be authentic to you, she explains, but it's probably not appropriate to your environment unless you work in an ultrahip environment. Similarly, Dolce & Gabbana suits may be appropriate to your environment, but if glamorous designer wear doesn't speak to who you are, don't don that particular label. "Wearing clothes that feel inauthentic detracts from your internal confidence," says Peraino. "A look that isn't you—that has everyone scratching their heads— can actually sap your executive presence."

That's why the same dress on two different women can telegraph two completely different messages: It's not the clothing per se but *who you are* that determines whether it's appropriate. Peraino told me of an executive vice president at American Express, a woman who wowed everybody with her above-the-knee red dress when she took the podium at a recent women's leadership event. "It totally worked," says Peraino, "because she'd earned it. She was entitled to that red dress. She was hot—not because she was trying to be sexy, but because she really is powerful." Peraino thought for a moment and then added with a smile, "And that red dress had a conservative neckline. A little leg is one thing; cleavage is something else!"

PHYSICALLY ATTRACTIVE, FIT, SLIM

There's a plethora of research proving the point that intrinsically attractive people get a speed pass over life's bumpier transitions: They get hired more often, earn more, and even fare better in court than unattractive people.[54] But thankfully your executive presence doesn't depend on having the looks of a movie star. As I stressed earlier, grooming and polish count way more than conventional good looks (classic features, a well-proportioned body, abundant hair). But even with regard to physical attractiveness, what you do with your God-given gifts counts more than your intrinsic beauty in establishing your credibility as an up-and-comer.

The most important thing you can do, my qualitative data shows, is to signal fitness and wellness. It's not so much what you weigh, but how vigorous and resilient you seem, that enhances or detracts from your executive presence—because leadership is demanding. We tend not to entrust our toughest jobs to people who look like they might keel over from a heart attack. "Being physically fit gives people the confidence that you will take care of what you are asked to do, because you are taking care of yourself," notes GE executive Deb Elam.

As we shall see in chapter 10, Michelle Obama has become the go-to exemplar in this space. Her extraordinary chiseled upper arms and shoulders bolstered her brand as a first lady who both embodied health and fitness and led a successful campaign to create better access to wholesome food and outdoor excercise for America's children. Remember that vegetable garden on the White House grounds? Well, Michelle Obama helped dig it.

There she was, on the evening news, digging, hoeing, and pulling weeds alongside a bunch of telegenic fifth graders from a nearby public school.

The importance of vigor and fitness to any successful brand helps explain why Chris Christie, New Jersey's popular and portly former governor, took the drastic step of undergoing lap band. Irrespective of his political ambition, he told reporters, he had to address his weight; it was a health issue, not an image issue. And yet health *is* the image issue when we're talking about the nation's highest office. Estimated at over three hundred pounds, Christie recognized that his weight might distract voters from his more important attributes and accomplishments.[55] To make a successful presidential run, he cannot be obese. Obama, who is two inches taller than Christie, weighs 180 pounds.[56] He's far more typical of chief executives these days.[57]

Telegraphing fitness is all the more important if you're heavyset and female, because women, our research affirms, suffer more from fat shaming than men. Both men and women with larger waistlines and higher body-mass-index readings tend to be perceived as less effective in terms of both performance and interpersonal relationships,[58] and "lacking in confidence, self-discipline, and emotional stability."[59] But weight is held against women more than it's held against men: 21 percent of the senior executives we surveyed believe that being overweight detracts from a woman's executive presence, while 17 percent believe it detracts from a man's EP. "There's definitely more latitude for overweight men," says one manager I interviewed who struggles with her own weight. "Generously proportioned women are just seen as unprofessional. It's a third-rail kind of thing, so it doesn't ever get mentioned in performance evaluations. But do people with excess weight advance at the same rate as those without? I suspect the answer is no. There is bias." In our focus groups, both male and female executives echoed her point of view. "Women who are overweight are seen as out of control and lazy," one plus-size banker told me, bitterness in her voice.

But unless you're obese, the takeaway here is not to embark on a body makeover campaign. Rather, it's to pay more attention to how well you look after yourself and how healthy you look. Whether you're a size 16 or a 6, get enough exercise to ensure your muscles are toned and your lung power will see you up a flight of stairs without wheezing. Put extra effort into your polish and grooming; make sure your clothing fits your actual size, not the size you're hoping to be. Looking well put together demonstrates respect for yourself and your organization. In the end, that's what matters.

SIMPLE, STYLISH CLOTHES THAT POSITION YOU FOR YOUR NEXT JOB

The platinum pixie, the gauntlet of silver bangles, the Prada dress, the Balenciaga leather leggings—this is Joanna Coles, editor in chief of *Cosmopolitan*. She has an amazing signature look and personal brand, one that totally worked for her in her highly visible role at the helm of the world's most notorious magazine. She's gotten roles playing herself on *Running in Heels* and *Project Runway All Stars*; she's appeared on MSNBC's *Morning Joe* to share her insights on how to interview for a job, and been snapped simply for chatting up Miley Cyrus (and outdressing her) at the Rachel Zoe runway show.

But this wasn't always Coles. It's been a longish journey, figuring out her look. As a young journalist at the *Guardian*, where she had an interview column, her job demanded she be all but invisible. "It really wasn't about me, but rather about the person I was interviewing," she explains. "I would wear black or navy pants and a black or navy jacket; I would try and look as reassuring as possible and ease into the background."

When she left her reporter job for editing roles, Coles experimented with her hair, dyeing it bright red and wearing it long—a trademark look, to be sure, but not one that telegraphed the seriousness of purpose she felt or the ambition that drove her. Only when she became editor in chief of *Marie Claire* and needed to make many public appearances did Coles effectively leverage her fashion smarts to magnify her executive presence. "In my twenties and thirties I worried that if I looked as if I spent time on my appearance I would appear vain and not serious," she says. "But fashion has changed, there are more options for women, and I now realize had I spent more time on it, it might have given me more authority."

We're all on this journey. We're either searching for our signature look, refining it, or reinventing it, because visibility is hard to maintain in our crazy competitive world. To be sure, the older you get and the higher you go, the more latitude you'll have—but it's complicated.

The journey begins by dressing for the job you *want*, not the job you have.

Kalinda, a real-estate analyst, remembers her "uniform" when she was working as a financial analyst for a cable sports channel. Initially, she adopted the sloppy attire typical of staffers who weren't in front of the cameras: jeans, T-shirts, and sweaters. On the advice of a mentor, she traded in her aggressively casual attire for tailored slacks and blazers. "I looked like a grownup, and I felt more confident," she admits. Her superiors agreed. A few months after her makeover, Kalinda was put in charge of a major launch and given oversight of a new hire. "I'd been asking for this sort of thing, and my performance had always been strong," she says. "But only when I started dressing for the part I wanted, instead of the part I had, did others perceive me as ready for that step up."

Appearance

Complement a sophisticated look with a signature piece or accent. For men this might be a pair of colorful socks, a playful tie, vintage cuff links, distinctive shoes, or a bold watch. Women have arguably more options. Margaret Thatcher famously wielded her Launer handbag so vigorously that *handbagging* became the term used for Thatcher-style strong-arming of political opponents. Madeleine Albright adorned every suit with a quirky, oversized brooch. Cornel West leavens his ministerial look with a carefully maintained Afro. The fact is, the more rigorous the dress code, or the more wholeheartedly you embrace it, the more it behooves you to personalize it in some standout way. The most successful look conveys that you know what's expected of you and willingly embrace it—yet have the self-confidence to channel your individuality through it.

It's important to remember that your signature look encompasses not just you but also the physical space you occupy. Your office, like your body, is a vehicle for your brand. Just look at top executives' offices and you'll see how they affirm their image and trumpet their distinctive achievements in their choice of furniture, pictures, books, and objects. For example, black-and-white fashion photographs cover every square inch of wall (and windowsill) in *Vogue* editor Anna Wintour's office, and the understated color scheme (white, glints of gold and silver, a black glass desktop) ensures that the overall effect is, like Wintour herself, sleek, sophisticated, and stunning. In contrast, Nike CEO Mark Parker conducted business in a space that's so crammed with bad-boy posters, toys, prototypes, pop art, and kitschy memorabilia it's a wonder he could work in it. I certainly couldn't. But that's not the point: Parker portrayed himself as an extension of the Nike brand, rather than a contradiction. Interestingly, Parker's bad-boy image became a liability in the wake of #MeToo. Credibly accused of building a culture rife with bullying and sexual harassment, he was pressed to step down from the CEO spot at Nike in early 2020.[60] In very real ways, CEOs *are* the public faces of their companies, and they are well-advised to align their brands with values the outside world respects.

Nowadays, the backdrops managers and executives use for their Zoom and Teams calls is a stand-in for their offices and need to be treated as an extension of their image and look. As we will discover in chapter 9, Princeton professor Eddie Glaude is an exemplar in this space. His go-to backsplash for a video clip is a wall of books. Not any old books, but carefully chosen books that showcase his scholarship's breadth, depth, and inclusiveness. His selections are always beautifully lit. In a recent MSNBC clip, I was able to pick out Roxane Gay, Anton Chekhov, and Orhan Pamuk. This is an intellect to tangle with!

BEING TALL

Michael Dukakis, the Democratic nominee for president in 1988, will go down in history for two things: the infamous tank photo, in which the would-be commander in chief looks like he's been vanquished by a headset, and his height, which was something less than the five feet, eight inches he claimed on his driver's license.[61]

George H. W. Bush, who was six feet one, beat him handily, despite his own image issues ("Our Wimp Can Beat Your Shrimp," declared one Republican bumper sticker), because shortness in a male leader was and is so easily conflated with major shortcomings. "Shortness creates a presumption of weakness," writes Ben Shapiro, author of *Project President: Bad Hair and Botox on the Road to the White House*, noting that Dukakis's diminutive size invited voters to see him as weak on defense and weak on crime.[62]

If women's leadership potential is unreasonably correlated to weight, men's is unfairly correlated to height. Sixteen percent of our respondents said height contributed to men's EP; only 6 percent said it contributed to women's. This bias most visibly plays out in presidential contests: Since Dukakis ran for the office, every man to sit behind the Oval Office desk has been taller than six feet. Over the history of presidential contests, taller candidates have beat out shorter ones 17 to 8.[63]

What to do if you're among the height-challenged? In this regard women have one killer app to help them compensate: high heels. And they use them. Lori Massad, head of human capital at AllianceBernstein, says she's been taken aside and chided for her four-inch-heel designer footwear, which one of her male colleagues had suggested was inappropriate. "It's a good thing I don't dress for you," she countered, explaining to me that the shoes made her feel "powerful and tall" and she wasn't about to give them up.

For men, as the Dukakis campaign discovered, there's not much to be done that doesn't risk exacerbating the image problem. (At one point, his handlers had Dukakis stand on a mound of earth behind a podium, but that only made the height disparity with Bush more apparent when he stepped off the mound.)[64] The best way to make height a nonissue is to take a page out of New York mayor Michael Bloomberg's playbook. Bloomberg's amour Diana Taylor, the former New York State superintendent of banks, is not only a good four inches taller but also inclined to appear by his side in showstopper heels. He "doesn't care" about their height difference, as he enjoys her looking good, Taylor told the *Huffington Post*.[65] A man secure enough to be photographed at the shoulder height of his girlfriend is a man no one will see as weak.

Interestingly, over the last three years Volodymyr Zelenskyy has done much to weaken the bias against short male leaders. As I discovered in the interviews I conducted in 2022, executives selected the Ukrainian as a top pick for executive presence-in-action, despite the fact that he is only five feet seven. His decision to stay rather than flee when Russian tanks encircled

Kiev, telling the world, "I need ammunition, not a ride," was an act of extraordinary bravery. It gave him the moral authority to ask tens of thousands of fellow Ukrainians to put their lives on the line to save their nation.

BEING YOUTHFUL AND VIGOROUS

Looking youthful, our survey respondents confirm, boosts the EP of both men and women because, like fitness, it implies you've got the vitality to contribute 110 percent and not succumb to a health setback. While studies show that the band of "age acceptability" for women is narrower than for men (a topic we'll take up in chapter 6), the popularity of youth-enhancing medical interventions is impressive for both men and women. Like women, men are shelling out on a staggering scale. Hair treatments are a case in point, with men spending $1.8 billion a year on hair implants and other treatments to prevent, or at least ameliorate, baldness. A full head of hair for a man signals youth and vigor. (Consider that Ronald Reagan's ample head of hair helped voters disregard the fact that, at sixty-nine, he was, at that time, the oldest president to take office. Biden, of course, has since overtaken him.)[66] Both men and women are also turning to plastic surgery as a solution to ageism. Data released by the Aesthetic Society show that over the last twenty years plastic surgery has become increasingly popular. Facelifts, browlifts, and liposuction are the most sought-after surgical procedures and the total spent nationwide has reached $14.6 billion. Botox injections are also wildly popular; between 2000 and 2020, the number of annual Botox injections increased by 459 percent.[67] In fact, so many men are opting for Botox injections that there's a slang term for it: Brotox.[68] But it would be wrong to think that men are catching up with women on the cosmetic surgery front. The Aesthetic Society reports that in 2021, a full 94 percent of all cosmetic medical procedures were performed on women. One startling fact is that there was a dramatic uptick in cosmetic surgery during the pandemic. Between 2020 and 2021, facelifts increased by 54 percent and liposuction by 63 percent.[69] Another stunner, a top choice in terms of youth-enhancing interventions, has become the "upper arm lift," a procedure that removes excess skin and fat between the elbow and the shoulder and eliminates "flapping." Arm lifts are up 4,400 percent since 2000, and are particularly sought out by women over forty-five.[70]

As one who launched a new organization and a new career in my fifties, I can affirm that nothing signals vitality in a middle-aged woman more than toned arms with a discreet ripple of muscle. My upper arms are pretty amazing—even if I do say so myself (not quite up to Michelle Obama's standard, but close). However, I acquired them a nonsurgical way. I'm a swimmer and relentless about my daily laps: It soothes my soul as well as tones my body. So these days my professional wardrobe centers on slim-cut dresses—high-necked but bare-armed (Michael Kors has a great selection). As the no-sleeve look isn't always appropriate, I often team these dresses up with a well-cut jacket or a graceful scarf. But it's the rare business event that doesn't allow me to slip off my jacket, unsheathe those biceps, and prove I'm up to the task before me.

If you cannot impress everyone with your obvious vitality, then at least make sure you minimize signs of age and downplay any infirmity. Consider how Franklin Delano Roosevelt managed his disability: Despite being neither young nor vital, he persuaded the country that he was vigorous enough to be a plausible candidate for an unprecedented fourth term. Voters knew he'd been stricken with polio, and some Republicans tried to capitalize on it by suggesting that, as "a cripple," he was unfit for higher office.[71] Yet FDR, who established the March of Dimes during his presidency, "did not conceal his physical limitation except to prevent his opponents from making political capital out of it,"[72] enlisting the press to make sure photographs showed him standing unassisted. As a result, he was perceived as a leader who'd overcome disability to prevail—defeating formidable challenges.

The good news is that you don't need to ace all elements of appearance. If wearing high heels causes such toe-pinching agony that you can't deliver a dynamite presentation, then by all means wear flats and shift attention to your perfectly cut skirt or dress. The crucial point to keep in mind is that your "look" is the medium for your message and, as such, it should neither distract nor detract from what you stand for and what you want to say.

BLUNDERS

Avoiding appearance blunders (which oftentimes involves circumventing prejudice or bias) is critical—almost as important as nailing at least two of those six top appearance picks.

Provocative dressing tops the list of appearance blunders for women (see Figure 8). Senior men find an overtly sexual female colleague tantalizing and terrifying at the same time. And they have reason to be scared. Sex seems to addle the minds of accomplished, ambitious male leaders—they abandon reason and do stupid things. Steve Easterbrook, former CEO of McDonald's, comes to mind. As we shall see in chapter 8, in 2019, he was fired from the top slot and forced to pay a hefty $104 million in clawback money when an internal investigation revealed that he'd had illicit affairs with three junior women, all of whom reported to him. His case was not helped by the fact that he'd attempted a cover-up. In our post-#MeToo world, nothing is a more potent career-ender for senior men than sexual misconduct. Research conducted for my 2020 book, *#MeToo in the Corporate World*, confirms both sexual misconduct and illicit affairs—the actuality of one or the appearance of one—are toxic in corporate cultures and damage sticks to all parties involved.[73] One regrettable result is that fully two-thirds of senior male executives are hesitant to have one-on-one contact with high-performing junior women—out of fear of fomenting perceptions that could lead to career derailment or litigation. Hence the vehement reaction to blouses that feature cleavage, skirts that reveal a stretch of upper thigh, and knit dresses that cling to curvy bodies.[74]

Looking unkempt in ways that aren't cool is a blunder that tops the list for men and comes in second for women. Fully 76 percent of senior executives say that being disheveled detracts from the EP of a man (rumpled jackets, ill-fitting collars, baggy or un-belted pants, scuffed shoes). In interviews they talked about how a disheveled appearance signals laziness or disrespect and distracts attention. As one leader said, "Ketchup on a shirt or gravy on a tie catches the eye and makes it impossible to pay attention to more substantive qualities." So take pains to avoid looking sloppy

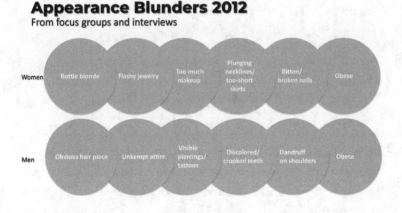

Appearance Blunders 2012
From focus groups and interviews

Women	Bottle blonde	Flashy jewelry	Too much makeup	Plunging necklines/ too-short skirts	Bitten/ broken nails	Obese
Men	Obvious hair piece	Unkempt attire	Visible piercings/ tattoos	Discolored/ crooked teeth	Dandruff on shoulders	Obese

Figure 8. Appearance blunders

and schlumpy—shine your shoes, retire blouses and shirts with underarm stains, repair fallen hems, take up too-long slacks, and iron your clothes. This will telegraph to those around you that you won't tolerate messiness in yourself or your work.

One particularly distressing finding: our survey respondents generated a list of appearance blunders for women that's literally twice as long as the list they generated for men. It would appear that women are judged, and found wanting, on many more appearance issues than men. Take makeup. As we have seen, a professional woman can commit an appearance blunder by wearing either too little or too much. For a man—unless he is a TV anchor—makeup is a nonissue. In addition to the sheer length of the blunder list, women tend to be judged much more harshly than men. On the weight front, for example, a woman can be struck off the list if she's overweight, while a man has to be obese before he's passed over. Later on in this book (chapter 6) we shall explore in detail how and why women are scrutinized so closely and held to higher standards. At this point, suffice it to say that some of this critical attention smacks of gender bias. As Linda Huber of Moody's points out, "There are many more unspoken, unwritten rules for women than men. And while we've made progress, we still have a long way to go."

YOU'RE IN CONTROL

Long before her historic meeting with Mikhail Gorbachev in 1979, Margaret Thatcher, Britain's first female prime minister, demonstrated she was not a woman who would back down. Unwavering in her principles and unfazed by popular discontent, she'd emerged from Edward Heath's cabinet as a new kind of conservative, one who would champion individual empowerment over government assistance even as unemployment rose to record levels on her watch. So when the Soviets, hoping to denigrate her, dubbed her the Iron Lady, Thatcher immediately embraced the moniker publicly, as she saw it paying tribute to both her steely resolve *and* her regal bearing. "I stand before you tonight in my Red Star chiffon evening gown, my face softly made up, and my fair hair gently waved, the Iron Lady of the Western World," she declared in a January 1976 speech to Conservatives in her home constituency of Finchley.[75] Clearly, she relished being seen as a leader of the free world who was female but also feminine *and* instilled fear and respect among strongmen opposed to everything she stood for.

And well she might. Because Maggie Thatcher's image was one she carefully, consciously constructed. She worked on her look as assiduously as she worked on her voice. Long before anyone spoke of "image makeovers," Thatcher turned to Gordon Reece, a known television producer and marketing executive, for advice and guidance. He brilliantly positioned her as a nonthreatening, practical, spirited homemaker to counter a campaign launched by the Labour Party, and then, just as brilliantly, sent her off to luxury clothier Aquascutum when she won the 1979 election. "Gordon was absolutely terrific," Thatcher revealed to her biographer. "He understood that it wasn't enough to have the right policies; one had to have the right message and the right clothes."[76] Thatcher's visit to the Soviet Union is a case in point. Marianne Abrahams, head of the Aquascutum design team, kitted her out with two tailored suits and seven "statement" coats, all teamed up with carefully selected accessories. This was a dream come true for Thatcher since it allowed her to be beautifully dressed each day of her trip without giving it much thought and focus her attention on fixing geopolitics.

The look that Thatcher adopted—the halo of hair, the large

pearl jewelry, the bold, broad-shouldered suits, and formidable handbags—proved so effective that other female leaders have copied her. *Washington Post* publisher Katharine Graham was a dead ringer, as was Liz Truss, the ill-fated British prime minister who, in the fall of 2022, attempted to buttress her failing brand by adopting Thatcher's dress code and mannerisms. It didn't work.

"Thatcher knew the importance of image from the very beginning," says Brenda Maddox, author of *Maggie: The First Lady*. "She put time into the way she dressed, and she got it right. The fact is, Thatcher mastered power dressing before the phrase was even invented."[77] After Thatcher, big hair, big shoulders, and big jewelry were everywhere, and they helped recast women at work as more substantive players.

The making of the Thatcher brand underscores a critical point: Image isn't inborn. Leaders create it, often with help. They diligently work to refine and maintain it. They take pains to avoid blunders that might destroy it.

And to be considered a leader, so must you.

THREE PIECES OF ADVICE FROM EXECUTIVES WHO HAVE TANGLED WITH APPEARANCE CHALLENGES

✓ *Beware of casual/cool cultures.* A couple of years ago, I was invited to keynote a session titled "Beyond Mad Men" at the Cannes Lions Festival—the annual extravaganza of the global advertising community. Michael Roth, the CEO of Interpublic Group, wanted me to help him make the case that Jon Hamm (who played Don Draper, the supermacho Madison Avenue executive in the series) no longer cut the mustard. Roth's view was that the industry needed to rid itself of sexist attitudes and progress more women to senior roles (to this day only 3 percent of creative directors at the top fifty companies are female). I came through for Roth—giving a speech that made a compelling case for why gender smarts around decision-making tables mattered in an industry that needs to be at the leading edge of our culture. But brilliant presentation aside, I must admit I had a great deal of trouble handling the appearance code at Cannes. It's not that the "creatives" at this gathering of Mad Men (and a handful of Mad Women) were drop-dead gorgeous—they were mature professionals in their forties and fifties and had their fair share of wrinkles and paunches. Rather, what was considered cool and chic was decidedly weighted in favor of men. The signature look of the rock stars at this advertising extravaganza comprised two-day-old stubble, designer shorts, flip-flops, and an outrageously expensive watch. As I took in a sea of blithely balding peacocks sprouting impressive amounts of gray facial hair, my stress level rose. The thing is, I couldn't bring any of this off and neither could most of the women at this gathering. Very few middle-aged women look important or leaderly in shorts and flip-flops, but many men can, particularly it seemed when they have copious amounts of gray stubble.

In the end, I went neutral, rejecting both the aggressively casual look (way too unflattering), and the skirted suit and pantyhose look (way too formal and uncomfortable). Instead, I wore a simple sheath dress in white linen, teamed up with bare legs and high heels. Nothing to write home about, but nothing objectionable.

✓ *When in doubt about the dress code, ask and be persistent.* Trevor Phillips, former chair of Great Britain's Equality and Human Rights Commission, describes how he received an invitation from the deputy prime minister to Chevening, the stately country retreat shared by the deputy prime minister and the foreign secretary (this is akin to getting invited to Camp David by an American president). His fiancée, Helen Veale, a savvy film producer/director, asked him what he thought she should wear. Phillips shrugged off her concern, saying, "Just wear what you like, you have a great fashion sense." But Helen persisted. "Don't wave away my question. This is important. I need you to find out what I am supposed to wear, particularly to the evening dinner." So Phillips put a call into the deputy prime minister's secretary, who assured him there was no dress code—guidance he duly passed along to his wife-to-be. "This isn't helpful, and you should have probed deeper," said Helen, showing her frustration. "'No dress code' means, if you don't know the code, you shouldn't be there. I'm an outsider to these circles and need more guidance." Phillips finally got her concern. A British subject of Afro-Caribbean descent, he'd had more than his fair share of being excluded. So, he put in a second call to the deputy PM's secretary and after a few minutes of friendly chitchat found out that the deputy PM's wife would be wearing a sparkling cocktail dress to the evening dinner and the other wives would be similarly dressed up. Helen had her cue.

✓ *Ask for specific feedback—and signal that you're okay with unvarnished feedback.* Giving pointers to someone else about his or her appearance is daunting and difficult, which is why you see so many blunders committed by people who should know better (we'll discuss feedback failures in chapter 5). So make it easy: Ask your sponsor or mentor for feedback on your attire, hairstyle, and grooming. Provide assurance that you will receive their observations and suggestions not as fault-finding but as constructive guidance and a vote of confidence in YOU. Ask for specifics and concrete detail so that you understand how to correct your gaffes. Then, live up to your promise by listening rather than reacting defensively. While it will be painful to hear what you're doing wrong, consider how much more painful it is to learn about your blunders indirectly from a client or customer, when it's too late to reverse first impressions.

5

When Aileen, an executive at a pharmaceutical firm, assumed leadership of its global medical division, she conducted a review of her U.S.-based staff that included 360s, performance evaluations, and one-on-one assessments. As the December holidays approached, she met with all of her direct reports to share what she had learned and discuss either their opportunities to advance or the gaps they needed to close. The meetings went well: Aileen's assessments aligned with feedback her direct reports had already received. But at one meeting, an African-American woman who'd been assured of a promotion by Aileen's predecessor took exception to the news that she wasn't "ready." She hadn't yet acquired the skill sets nor the leadership presence to qualify for a higher role. Not only did she take exception, but she threatened to quit on the spot.

Alarmed and concerned, Aileen urged her to take some time over the holiday break to think about her next steps and come back to her in the New Year to discuss a development plan. "Quite honestly, I was terrified we were veering into EEOC territory," recalls Aileen, referring to the federal Equal Employment Opportunity Commission. "I was prepared to stand by my assessment but wanted time to review it with legal before meeting with her again."

In January, they reconvened in Aileen's office. "I've done some careful thinking," the woman began. "I realized over Christmas that, in all the years I've worked for this firm, not one person has taken issue with my performance or questioned my leadership capabilities. When I've asked for honest feedback on my presentations, the bad and the good, everyone has told me I'm doing just fine. In fact, I've been handed every promotion I've asked for—up until recently, when you arrived."

The woman paused. Aileen held her breath.

"If you would consider it," she continued, "I would very much like to work with you to develop myself as a leader and get to the next level."

With that meeting began an extraordinary alliance. "I talked her up to colleagues who could pull her onto teams where she could get the client exposure and training she needed," Aileen told me. "And she was fiercely loyal to me throughout my own transition here. Today, she's heading up our marketing division."

WHY FEEDBACK FAILS

Think for a minute: When's the last time someone at work gave you honest, critical feedback on some aspect of your EP?

For that matter, when's the last time *you* gave someone at work a critical and specific EP pointer?

Unvarnished, concrete feedback on your appearance, communication skills, and gravitas is hard to come by. It's especially hard if you're female, though your chances improve slightly with a same-sex boss.

It's not hard to see why. Consider the situation Joe Stringer, a partner in EY in London, found himself in when a client told him that they had concerns about the appearance of one of the female members of his project team. Curvy, blond, and inclined to wear inappropriate blouses and short skirts, the woman didn't exude the professionalism, the client told Stringer, that he expected of an EY employee. "The trolley-dolly image makes everyone nervous," the client added. But Stringer couldn't bring himself to confront his team member about her distracting attire. "I couldn't think of a way to point out what was wrong without sounding like I was noticing all the wrong things about her," he explained. He did, however, enlist her in a development course on client interaction, where she was able to make the connection between image and impact and set about transforming herself. "She's a different person now, a real rising star on the team," notes Stringer. He adds, "Thankfully advice worked its way through, but if I'd been confident enough to say something, it might have happened more quickly."

This story goes to show not only how EP feedback can make a critical difference in a woman's career but also why women often don't get it from their (male) superiors. Senior men just can't afford to have their motives misconstrued, especially in the wake of #MeToo.

As every male who's been subjected to sexual-harassment training might conclude, developing female talent by giving women individualized feedback just isn't worth the risk of being accused of sexual misconduct. Indeed, that risk effectively keeps men from helping women develop and advance as leaders, which helps explain why the marzipan layer is thick with highly qualified women (36 percent of senior managers are now female, according to 2022 Lean In research) while the executive band remains thinly populated (a mere 14.3 percent of executives are female).[78] Giving critical EP feedback—one of the key roles an effective sponsor plays—is just so much easier man-to-man.

Men will alert other men to wince-inducing EP gaffes such as bad breath or an unzipped fly, but confronted with a woman in too short a skirt or too tight a top, they'll look away. Better to stay mum about a woman's inappropriate attire than be sued for noticing it.

For similar reasons, people of color don't get the feedback they need to develop their EP: Fearing discomfort as well as discrimination litigation, senior executives told us they would sooner pass over a Black, Latinx, or Asian mananger's lack of executive presence rather than have an honest conversation about shortcomings. In particular, people of color don't get unvarnished feedback about hair and clothing, or grooming, according to our survey results. Participants in our focus groups all had a story to share about tripping over the race issue in giving and getting critical feedback on EP, most particularly when it comes to deficits on the communication and appearance fronts. One Asian executive spoke to me of how she inadvertently unleashed a discrimination suit when she critiqued a Hispanic woman on her team for her shortcomings in failing to prepare adequately for a presentation. Her team member accused her of "fomenting and tolerating a workplace culture that was hostile to Latinas," citing snubs and slights that surfaced bias around Latinas' work ethic and emotional temperament. "It was an outrageous claim, given that the head of our division is part Puerto Rican," this Asian executive explained. "But I've seen it too many times to dismiss it: Nine times out of ten, the aggrieved party will pull the race card. And then the whole workplace takes a step backward. After a messy and costly dismissal every leader privately concludes 'That's the last time I'll hire a fill-in-the-blank.'" She added, "I know we'll have reached real equality when people of color get fired as easily as white people."

People of color likewise spoke of the damage they've suffered—in lost opportunities, mostly, but also in terms of their self-esteem—as a result of white people's perceptions that they'll go nuclear if they're found wanting in any way. As an African-American partner at Deloitte Consulting explained, the insinuation underlying feedback that's restrained or outright withheld is that you're someone "who is actually incapable of hurdling the bar others are held to."

DIFFICULT CONVERSATIONS—BUT EXTRAORDINARILY IMPORTANT

It must be said that some kinds of feedback are intrinsically difficult to give no matter who is on the receiving end. Criticizing someone's appearance, for example, turns out to be emotionally fraught, even woman-to-woman. "You're taking issue with their self-expression," Rohini Anand, global diversity officer for Sodexo, points out. "How can that not be taken personally?"

Indeed, our survey data reveals that, when it comes to appearance, women can be harsher judges of other women than men are. They're more likely than men to consider "poorly maintained clothing" an EP blunder for women, but not for men, and more likely to dock women EP points for wearing too-tight clothing.

Correcting someone on how they speak is also dicey terrain, even when that speech pattern is affecting business outcomes and limiting personal career trajectories. That's because, like appearance, taking issue with grammar, accent, or diction goes straight to ethnic, cultural, or socioeconomic sensitivities.

"I give lots of presentation pointers," says Anand, "but I truly hesitate when it comes to correcting someone on their diction unless we have a genuinely trusting relationship." (Recall Katherine

Blunders and Gender Bias

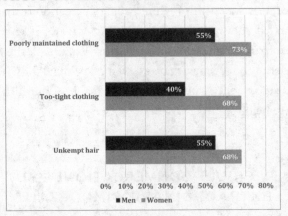

Figure 9. Blunders and gender bias

Phillips's story in chapter 3 about her thesis advisor correcting her pronunciation of "aks" to "ask." This was a bold move indeed.)

Overwhelmingly, however, the consensus among our interviewees is that dispensing unvarnished, concrete feedback across all three EP pillars is a core leadership competency, one that should be developed and evaluated along with other managerial skills. Women and people of color I interviewed who'd been on the receiving end of good EP feedback were adamant about this, as the impact on their own careers had been profound. Receiving such feedback, they acknowledge, can feel like undergoing root canal surgery: Christina, a communications executive, tells of being "stung to her core" when told that her male subordinate had been mistaken for her superior in a meeting because he exuded more leadership presence than she did. And to be sure, giving EP pointers is no picnic: Annalisa Jenkins, nonexecutive director at Geonomics, and former global head of research and development at Merck Serono, has more than once reduced women to tears when delivering constructive criticism. But to shirk the imperative of giving feedback on leadership presence is to throw into question your standing as a leader. "Leadership isn't about being voted Ms. Popular," says Sodexo's Anand. "To be effective, it's more important to be honest, and have those courageous conversations, than to be liked. At the end, that is what will garner the trust and respect so crucial to leadership."

I spoke to one high-flying consultant who actually quit a lucrative job at a bank because she couldn't get her superiors to have those conversations with her. Whenever she asked for explicit feedback on how she handled a presentation or a client encounter, she was told she didn't need any. "You're doing great!" her boss assured her. She attributes this cop-out to two things: an absence of regular, formalized assessments in her division, and a lack of leadership sensibilities among the financial service managers to whom she reported. "They were dealmakers, people who got promoted for hitting the numbers and making money," she explains. "I wasn't impressed with them. They had nothing to teach me, and I wouldn't have wanted to go anywhere they were headed. To develop my own leadership capabilities, I had to leave."

WHAT GREAT FEEDBACK SOUNDS LIKE

If giving EP feedback marks you as a leader, then giving actionable EP feedback marks you as a great one. In our focus groups, consensus emerged on what constitutes truly constructive criticism. A few examples:

- Poised to go into a meeting with someone who reported directly to her CEO, newly promoted Christina was asked to stop by her new boss's office first. "Your extensive knowledge of the business will earn you credibility," the woman told Christina, smiling to reassure her. "But I notice when you're nervous you talk fast, and that can come across as lack of confidence. So take a deep breath. Take a moment to adjust to your audience. Don't be afraid to create some silence."

- On returning from a conference, Tara, a new addition to Rohini Anand's team at Sodexo, got this feedback from Anand's colleague on how to better represent the company: "Look, this job requires a lot of networking. I see, when I take you to events, that you're not mingling except with people on your team. I want you to come back from these gatherings with a stack of business cards. I want you to forge at least five new relationships, and follow up on each of them, because as a senior member of this team it's important that potential clients know you personally."

- "With this particular leader, you've got to cultivate a very different image or you're going to get cut from his team," one chief learning officer recalls hearing from his boss when he was a new hire at a financial services corporation. "This leader values precision and attention to detail, and in your manner and style of dress you're not convincing him that you, too, value these things. Be on time for meetings, not five minutes late. Put in more effort and energy preparing presentations. And your wardrobe needs to be upgraded. The suit you're wearing is substandard and you need better shirts and better shoes. If you'd like I can tell you three places to find them."

Ear-burning stuff, yes? But consider, after the shock wears off, what you will have learned from the leader who delivers such feedback:

✓ *You'll be clear on what the problem is.*
✓ *You'll understand why it must be addressed.*
✓ *You'll know precisely what you need to do to course-correct.*

In short, we know from our qualitative data that great feedback is (1) timely, meaning it's delivered either right before or right after you've blundered; (2) specific to one discrete behavior, as opposed to a global condemnation; and (3) prescriptive, or explicit about what actions need to be taken by you. It should also be framed in the context of the business outcome, whether that outcome is your personal success (for example, exuding gravitas at an important meeting with a superior) or the success of your team (for example, hitting a deadline or winning a new client). There are of course endless variations of this formula, but in essence you follow these guidelines.

All of this makes perfect sense when you consider our survey results on what characterizes *bad* feedback. Feedback is bad when it sets up a very narrow band of acceptability, a phenomenon we'll explore at length in the next chapter: Women, for example, are told they're either too angry or too nice, overly passive or way too aggressive, too young or too old. They're told they need to "dial it back" or "step up to the plate," or "rein in the emotion." Feedback is bad, too, when it's vague: Carolyn Buck Luce, a former head of the global health-care practice at EY, recalls being told as a senior executive that she needed to become "more vulnerable." What was she supposed to do with this comment? Given the ubiquity of bad feedback in the workplace, it comes as no surprise that the majority of our respondents say they haven't been able to act on the feedback they've been given.

Improving feedback will require a two-pronged approach. First, you as a rising star must learn to become better at eliciting, receiving, and acting on criticism. And second, you as a leader must become better at giving criticism while still modeling how to receive it.

TACTICS: HOW TO GET THE EP FEEDBACK YOU NEED

RECOGNIZE YOU NEED IT

In her twenties, as the newly appointed sales manager at a small tech company, Debbie Storey was asked to present her business plan for the coming year. "I'd never created one, let alone seen one delivered," she recalls. But she had lots of ideas—and felt compelled to share them all in her ten-minute slot. "The longer I spoke, the more I realized I had *way* too much material," Storey recalls. "People were squirming in their seats. I saw my boss's face fall, I saw the look of horror on the president's face." After the meeting, Storey sought out her boss and asked for training in public speaking. "No one needed to tell me I had bombed," she says. "I knew it *and* I knew I needed help." Not everybody, however, recognizes they do. On the contrary, says communications exec Christina, "everybody says they welcome feedback, but then persists in thinking they're perfect." She adds, "People I know, probably the smartest people in my group, won't be going anywhere because they don't have EP. And they don't have EP because they don't accept that they need to acquire it."

DEVELOP A THICKER SKIN

Debora Spar, a former president of Barnard College, who now heads up online learning at Harvard Business School, distinguished herself early among a circle of outstanding peers at Harvard University by putting herself repeatedly in the line of fire that emanated from her graduate advisors. "The biggest compliment one of them ever paid me was 'Not bad,'" she says. "But I'd go back for more, because I knew I had a lot to learn." The more Spar demonstrated she could take the heat, the bigger the kitchen she was asked to run. "I'm grateful to have been raised by wolves," she says. "I don't need that pat on the head to excel. I think we're in an era when both women and men are trained up to be overly sensitive to criticism, so that when they finally get out in the real world and they don't get a 5.0 on a performance review, they fall apart. It's so important, early in life, to get that criticism, particularly constructive criticism, is a good thing and toughen up."

ROUTINELY ASK FOR SPECIFIC, TIMELY, PRESCRIPTIVE FEEDBACK

If you make a blanket request, as in "How am I doing?," you may get a blanket answer ("Just fine!"). Better to laser in on a recent encounter that required considerable EP—a meeting with a high-powered client or a leader in the firm—and request that a superior assess you on your body language, speech and delivery, attire, command of the room, and so on. The assessment itself needn't take place immediately, but your request for it should. And if nothing happens, ask again. "Say, 'It's been a while, I'd really like some pointed feedback from you,'" said Lisa Garcia Quiroz, head of corporate social responsibility for Time Warner. "Then put on your iron panties."

IF YOU CAN'T GET ACTIONABLE FEEDBACK FROM YOUR SUPERIORS, ASK FOR A COACH—OR PAY OUT-OF-POCKET YOURSELF

Far from betraying a lack of EP, asking for professional help (if need be on your own dime) signals an impressive level of personal maturity and professional commitment. In some organizations this leadership perk is conferred on "high potentials." Whoever pays for the executive coach, he or she can help you with your image (wardrobe and hair styling), presentation skills, and over-all gravitas—even when you think you've already got a leg up on other people and don't need much help. Elizabeth, now an SVP in the retail sector, worked with an executive coach when she transitioned from a consulting firm to a corporate environment, a process she found eye-opening because she thought she'd learned everything she needed to know working for McKinsey. Through videotaped sessions, she says, she learned to modulate her style to fit her new environment: doing more listening than talking, speaking deliberately and more slowly, instead of selling ideas in a rapid-fire style. "You think you don't use ums and ahs, you think your expression is under control, you think you're concise and hard-hitting," she says. "It's hard to see yourself on video, as others see you, but until you do, you'll never face facts."

CREATE A CIRCLE OF PEERS WITH WHOM YOU CAN SHARE FEEDBACK

Relentless in her desire to improve, Elizabeth also seeks out feedback from both men and women she has come to know and trust—a two-way exchange on what's working and not working that occurs all day, every day. "If a peer asks for an opinion, I'm going to be honest, because I'd expect the same of her or him," she notes. "It comes down to trust." Trust, in turn, is built on a foundation of shared lunches, cups of coffee, drinks after work, or extracurricular activities around charity, sports, or kids, Elizabeth explains. "I always find the time to reach out to people on my team and build these relationships," she says. "I will make sure I'm there to support them when they need my feedback, because at some point I'm going to need theirs."

CULTIVATE A SPONSOR

A sponsor is not just a friendly mentor who gives you advice. A sponsor is a powerful executive who sees potential in you and, provided you give 110 percent of your energies and deliver value, will go out on a limb to make things happen for you.[79] Because sponsors have a vested interest in how you turn out (your reputation now being linked with their own), they will give you the kind of feedback that mentors can't or won't. Tim Melville-Ross, a former CEO of Nationwide and a leader we met in chapter 2, describes how one of the nonexecutive directors on the board sponsored him in his candidacy for the role of chief executive officer—by telling him what he could not otherwise have known about his standing in the race. "You are very agreeable and well liked, and others enjoy your humor," Melville-Ross was told, "but we need to see a tougher, more assertive, more aggressive side in the boardroom." How to do that? "The advice of the nonexecutive director was to single out a senior member of the board and pick a fight with him. Make a challenging remark. Point out something as absolute rubbish." Melville-Ross did precisely that, provoking horror around the table. But a good kind of horror, he says. "When I looked at the nonexecutive director, who was sitting next to this member I'd just attacked," Melville-Ross recalls, "he gave me an enormous wink."

LISTEN FOR THE "RING OF TRUTH"

Not all feedback is accurate or well-intentioned, and occasionally you will be the recipient of off-base, ill-timed, vague feedback. But don't dismiss it out of hand. As Suzi Digby, the British choral conductor, told me, there's no such thing as a bad review—not if you tune your radar for that ping that can help you course-correct. "I've had good reviews and the odd negative one. The reviewer is not always right, but sometimes you recognize the ring of truth in a critical comment, and it's important to allow it to be processed."

DEMONSTRATE YOU WILL ACT ON THE FEEDBACK YOU'VE BEEN GIVEN

It's one thing to nod agreeably to constructive criticism; it's quite another to change your behavior as a result. Yet unless you show superiors that you are willing to course-correct, they might conclude you're not worth the time and energy it takes to impart difficult feedback in the first place. Rohini Anand suggests getting a reality check if you're hesitating to act, as sometimes hearing criticism from peers as well as superiors can bring your next action into sharper focus. With one boss, the feedback Anand received was somewhat oblique: "When I come in with something at a later phase, your mind is already made up," he told her. Only when she got the results of a 360, which pointed out that she tended not to allow other people's ideas to bubble up and gain traction, did Anand understand she needed to do a better job listening to and eliciting late-stage innovations from her team. "I now hold my comments and views until I've heard from everybody," she says. "I want to be sure I model receptivity."

DON'T BURST INTO TEARS

Of course criticism hurts. And yes, you're going to take it personally because some of it is directed at you personally. But put on your best face with your critics, and save your tears for later, because nothing cuts off the spigot of vital feedback more effectively than the loss of emotional control. "Try and remember this is a learning opportunity," advises Time Warner's Lisa Garcia Quiroz. "You have a responsibility to listen, and react appropriately, just as your manager has a responsibility to deliver his or her insight. If you sit there and get angry or emotional, then it will be so much tougher for the two of you to have subsequent conversations. Your manager may feel it's a waste of time, or conclude you're incapable of growing. And then it becomes a self-fulfilling prophecy: If you don't get feedback, you cannot grow."

NEVER BURN A BRIDGE

You may decide, upon hearing negative or critical feedback, that it's time to seek a job elsewhere. This does not entitle you to unleash your anger or give a vindictive response, cautions Garcia Quiroz. Rather, concede the point, even show gratitude, and when you resign, work with your manager to have a seamless and mature transition. You need him or her to be supportive of your transition and may even need a recommendation to secure your next opportunity. "What's important," says Garcia Quiroz, "is that you show dignity and maturity by taking responsibility for your career—by managing the terms of your own exit."

TACTICS: HOW TO GIVE EP FEEDBACK LIKE A TRUE LEADER

GIVE FREQUENT, DISCRETE POINTERS RATHER THAN SEMI-ANNUAL DOWNLOADS

If by the time you sit down to impart feedback you've accumulated a laundry list of criticisms, then you've waited too long. Criticism cannot be constructive when it's too lengthy. Inventorying someone's shortcomings in one sitting is more likely to paralyze and demoralize than incentivize that person to change.

DON'T IMPART FEEDBACK WHEN YOU'RE ANGRY

Wait twenty-four hours, or until you've cooled down, before calling someone to account for a massive blunder. You'll both have gained much-needed perspective on what happened. If you give feedback in the heat of the moment, observes Garcia Quiroz, you risk exposing yourself as someone not in control of your game—and that lapse in leaderlike behavior gives your subordinate license to shift more of the blame to you. "People will blame everybody except themselves when they're hurt or angry," she observes. "For criticism to be constructive, it has to be delivered without the emotion that signals 'personal attack.'"

PUT THE GOOD THINGS OUT THERE FIRST

Recognize what people have achieved or are achieving before pointing out what they haven't delivered. You'll appear to be a more credible critic, one worth heeding, if you demonstrate you've observed the good in measure equal to the bad. One communications expert I interviewed says she always starts a feedback session by soliciting the other person's self-assessment, inviting them to start with the positives. "Tell me the three areas where you think you're doing great," she opens. "Then tell me the three areas where you want to improve."

EMBED CORRECTIVES IN YOUR CRITICISM

In a postmortem with a talented team member who was struggling with communication challenges, AT&T's Debbie Storey detailed not just those aspects of the woman's delivery that needed improvement but also those actions that might improve her delivery. Storey had observed that this individual had several issues. First, she tended to jump straight into data, without any lead-up. Second, she talked too fast. And third, she was hard to hear because she spoke in a low monotone voice. So, Storey couched her feedback in what to do, rather than what to stop doing. "Think about how to get the audience with you before launching into the content," she began. "Let them get to know you, and understand where you're going, before snowing them with data. Then help them keep up: Talk louder and more slowly. Pause more often. Try to inject humor, because this material is dry by nature and you're funny by nature. Let people see there's more to you than boring content, and they'll come back for more."

CATCH PEOPLE WHEN THEY'RE GETTING IT RIGHT

Especially when the wisdom you're trying to impart concerns a person's appearance, pounce on any opportunity to congratulate that person for having made good choices. The communication coach I interviewed, Christina, described one woman whose "completely showstopping, inappropriate attire" had caught the eye of everyone in management, but her immediate supervisor had hesitated to consider her. The expert's advice was to rave about this person's attire on the rare occasions she did dress appropriately. "Pull her into your office and tell her, 'This is a wonderful look for you, a really good look for you as a career professional,'" Christina gushed. It worked: Overnight, the woman, responding to praise, shifted to a more conservative look. The coach's advice to managers: "You want to think about the outcome before you pull someone into your office and say, 'I can see through your dress.' Nobody is going to feel good about that conversation."

PREFACE FEEDBACK WITH THE ASSURANCE THAT YOU HAVE THAT PERSON'S BEST INTERESTS AT HEART AND WISH TO ENSURE THEIR SUCCESS

"This may not be easy to hear," Rohini Anand will begin by saying, "but please depersonalize it. I'm telling you this because I want you to be successful." Better yet, if you're that person's sponsor, establish the ground rules for feedback before you deliver any. Kent Gardiner, senior partner at law firm Crowell & Moring, "struck a deal" with an African-American attorney in whom he saw great promise. He asked him if he wanted feedback on his courtroom manner and style of delivery. Assured that he did, Gardiner further asked if he'd be willing to hear criticism from the chairman of the firm in the spirit in which it was intended, in other words, as an EP tip and not a threat to his standing in the firm. "Feedback works only if there's mutual trust and respect," says Gardiner. "Our agreement convinced him that I had his best interests at heart, and he gave me a green light to dish out unvarnished criticism and constructive advice. Leavened of course by positive feedback. He could listen to what I had to say without taking offense."

DISCUSS APPEARANCE IN THE CONTEXT OF PERSONAL BRANDING

Storey situates any comments she may have about an employee's appearance and wardrobe choices in a larger conversation about that employee's personal brand. "Help them identify that brand first," Storey says. "Then you can afford to point out how their personal style may clash or support that image." For example, talk about their skills and passions, and discuss what distinctive value they add to the team, as in 'You're known for your analytical skills, and your ability to see the trend behind the numbers.' Then stress how every interaction, every verbal and nonverbal message that person sends, including their clothing and overall appearance, should serve to reinforce that image."

ENLIST A THIRD PARTY

If you're concerned in the least that your feedback might be misconstrued as discrimination, share your concerns with an HR or diversity specialist. That third party might refer you to legal counsel, or counsel you directly on ways to handle the conversation so that it doesn't veer into EEOC territory. At the very least, you may find it helpful to role-play with a trained professional to ensure that feedback is received as constructively—and nonlitigiously—as possible.

6

For as long as Hillary Clinton has been part of the zeitgeist—as first lady, as senator, as presidential candidate, and as secretary of state—she has been pilloried for failing to be all things to all people. Too female to be taken seriously (remember that bit of cleavage she revealed on the Senate floor?), she was at the same time considered too aggressive to be considered appropriately feminine (driving health-care reform was seen as unseemly and un-first-lady-like). She was too accomplished to appeal to the electorate (C-student George W. Bush having set the bar) but too politically inexperienced to be seen as "electable." She was perceived as too much "Bill's wife" to run for office, but not enough of a mother to Chelsea (too few cookies baked) to win the soccer mom vote. To her enormous credit, Hillary persevered in the face of this whiplash, and in her mid-seventies is accorded grudging respect as a powerful figure on the global stage and as a joyful, committed grandmother. But it has been a brutal struggle. The mocking, menacing chant "lock her up" has been a feature at MAGA rallies for seven long years. She herself has described her adult life as a fifty-year high wire; one step in the wrong direction could tip her into dangerous territory.

A NARROW BAND OF ACCEPTABILITY

Carolyn Buck Luce, a leader who has negotiated narrow bands of acceptability for decades, calls this the Goldilocks syndrome. "You're never 'just right,'" she explains. "You're too this, you're too that—and you always will be, because what's behind it is hidden bias. If you don't fit the stereotype of a leader, you're not likely to be seen as becoming one."

If you're not straight, or not white, or not male, that is, and you aspire to leadership, you're likely to find yourself up against the impossible expectation that you be someone you're intrinsically not. This expectation is communicated via feedback that's inherently contradictory or paradoxical, and that so many diverse individuals' paths to leadership have had to parse before they can proceed. Consider the impossible demands that met Barack Obama on his first presidential run: He was "too white" for Black voters,[80] but "too Black" for white voters.[81]

Hillary is also a standout example of the Goldilocks syndrome—but many less illustrious women struggle with the perception that they are either too much or too little, never just right. The majority of women being considered as potential "leadership material" hover in that layer just below top management, what's known as the marzipan layer because it's so rich with talent—and so sticky. Women comprise today more than half of the highly qualified talent pipeline (holding some 60 percent of graduate degrees), and the majority (64 percent of senior women, according to CTI research) are eager to be promoted to the next job level.[82] Yet we also find that, at the door to the C-suite, they hesitate to cross the threshold—fearful, we suspect, of having to walk the tightrope between being effective and being likable. Men simply aren't forced to choose, since by dint of being male they're already perceived as leadership material. Since the early 1970s, when social scientist Virginia Schein showed that both male and female managers perceive leadership attributes as more likely to be held by men than by women, studies have repeatedly confirmed that we associate masculine attributes with leadership suitability and feminine attributes with support-role suitability—"taking charge" skills being the province of men, and "taking care" skills being the province of women.[83] Despite research showing that gender is not a reliable predictor of how a person will lead, we persist in vetting leadership candidates on precisely that basis.[84] Women are seen to embody such negative "feminine" traits as being less self-confident, less analytical, and less emotionally stable, traits not associated with capable leaders; whereas men are seen to embody such positive "masculine" traits as being aggressive, dominant, objective, and competitive, traits considered requisite to leadership.[85] Compounding this stereotypical perception of women is men's inability to perceive their own "invisible knapsack" of privileges that grant them access, acceptance, and authority they don't even realize they have and are carrying.[86]

When women do manifest the requisite traits, we're inclined to punish them for it. Research studies repeatedly surface our inclination to fault women for career ambition and entrepreneurial smarts while rewarding it in men. In an experiment conducted at the Stern School of Business at New York University, male and female graduate students who assessed the leadership capabilities of a real-life successful entrepreneur named Heidi were far more inclined to admire this accomplished individual when she was recast as Howard. Students asked to assess Heidi perceived her as "selfish," "out for herself," and "a little political"—in short, not nearly as likable as Howard. When this experiment was replayed several years later, substituting Kathryn and Martin for Heidi and Howard, students actually liked Kathryn slightly better than

Martin (8.0 versus 7.6)—but they didn't *trust* her nearly as much (6.4 for Kathryn, 7.8 for Martin). As the evaluators explained to CNN correspondent Anderson Cooper, who staged the replay, "men seem more genuine," whereas women seem to be "trying too hard," making them less trustworthy.[87]

The likability-versus-competence trade-off is arguably the most tenacious, as well as the most pernicious, double bind that women in leadership confront. First documented in 2004, when Madeline Heilman and others found that successful women, unlike successful men, suffered social rejection and personal derogation (especially when their success was in a male-dominated arena),[88] it continues to be corroborated. A large-scale study of 60,470 men and women conducted more recently found that, while slightly more than half (54 percent) of participants said they had no preference when it came to choosing the gender of their boss, the other 46 percent indicated a strong preference for a male superior—by more than a 2-to-1 ratio, in fact. Those who said they preferred a male boss cited not the positive attributes of male leaders, but rather the negative attributes of female leaders. Comments such as "catty" or "bitchy" cropped up a lot in these discussions. "While not directly addressing the competence of female leaders, these comments attacked the personality of the female leader, indicating that some perceive these abstract female leaders as less likeable than men," the researchers observed.[89]

Every time a woman takes the national or international stage, the likability/effectiveness double bind surfaces. When Michelle Bachelet became Chile's first female president, detractors didn't waste time in taking her to task for being overly "female" in her approach. "She makes commissions," her opponents said, dismissively, "not decisions."[90] She was also referred to as La Gordis ("Fatty"), something that describes Chris Christie but has never been thrown at him in the press. Bachelet was at once "too maternal" (as an inclusive leader who listened to others' input and sought consensus) and "too tough" (she was, after all, a survivor of torture under Pinochet and the country's first female defense minister in 2002).[91]

Eventually Bachelet proved that a female leader could be both effective *and* endearing: She left office with approval ratings of 84 percent.[92] But other high-flying females, according to those who track them, have had to choose. "Women can be powerful. Women can be likeable. Being both is difficult to do," observed Patricia Sellers, the compiler of *Fortune*'s most-powerful-women list.[93] Feminist blogger Jessica Valenti, writing for the *Nation*, noted that "women adjust their behavior to be likable and as a result have less power in the world"—an acceptable trade-off, to her way of thinking, but nonetheless a trade-off.[94] More recently, Sheryl Sandberg, who held the number two position at Facebook (now Meta) for fourteen years, has observed the trade-off and lamented its impact on potentially high-achieving women. "I believe this bias is at the very core of why women hold themselves back," she wrote in her bestselling book, *Lean In*. "It is also at the very core of why women are held back."[95]

NO BANDWIDTH

Has nothing changed? Are women indeed "damned if they do, doomed if they don't"?[96]

Data from CTI's survey research suggests the band of acceptability for women leaders hasn't widened much in the decades since Virginia Schein documented the "think leader, think male" conflation. Across all three pillars of executive presence—gravitas, communication, and appearance—women continue to walk a tightrope.

The Fine Line of Executive Presence
Female leaders have little latitude

> Too self-aggrandizing	Too self-deprecating <
> Too aggressive	Not assertive enough <
> Too opinionated/shrill	Unable to command the room <
> Too blunt/direct	Too nice <
> Bloodless	Hysterical <
> Too provocatively dressed	Too frumpy <
> Looks too young	Looks too old <

Figure 10. The fine line of executive presence

APPEARANCE

Looking like a leader, for women, turns out to be terrain studded with land mines. We found that, while women are as likely as men to believe appearance plays a small part in a leader's executive presence, women are much more likely to be pilloried on the basis of it, whatever they do. Focus group participants told us, for example, that too much makeup undermines a woman's credibility—but then faulted female leaders for looking too frumpy or unpolished (citing, of course, Hillary Clinton). Almost half of our survey respondents said that unkempt nails detract from a woman's EP, yet nearly as many said that "overly done" nails were unleaderlike. The issue of age, which hardly comes up for men, is also fraught with peril for women: Almost the same number of respondents said "looking too young" was a liability as told us "looking too old" undermined a woman's EP. When we pressed managers to identify for us the "sweet spot" for women in terms of looking just the right age, we discovered the band of acceptability was three years (between the ages of thirty-nine and forty-two). Older women fade into the woodwork, they explained, but younger women command "the wrong kind" of visibility. Ageism is just another version, it would seem, of the classic catch-22 for professional women: Either they're too feminine (and therefore incompetent) or not feminine enough (and therefore mannish and inauthentic).

The too feminine/not feminine enough double bind, our interviews made clear, turns out to be as paralyzing to ambitious women today as it was to pioneer feminists of the 1970s. Everyone I spoke to expressed relief that those awful days when women donned mannish suits and bow ties are long gone. But everyone also conceded that "getting it right" across sector and professional environments was as difficult as ever. Suzi Digby, the British choral conductor we've met in earlier chapters of this book, was particularly adamant that women not compromise their femininity. "It's counterproductive to look like a man," she says. "You give up a card." In her profession, however, this presents special difficulties. Conducting demands she put her back to the audience, a pose that features her posterior. This is an EP challenge for men as well as women, but at least men can wear tails to downplay the distraction: "Women tend to have big bums, and that is bad: It has connotations," she points out. So to downplay the distraction of presenting her backside, and to strike the right silhouette (tall, lean, clean-lined), Digby wears heels and "a well-cut trouser suit." She also ties back her long hair (unless she's on stage with the Rolling Stones, where flying hair is in keeping with the show).

"It's important to get it right," she says. Then she sighs and adds, "I just don't know any women who do."

Getting it wrong has potentially dire consequences, as Carol, a global media firm executive, makes clear. As a twenty-four-year-old analyst at a Swiss investment bank, she was constantly seeking new ways to build client relationships. She struck up a tennis friendship with a male client who was, to her way of thinking, "safe"—married, in his fifties, utterly professional in his dealings with her. They played a few Saturdays at his racquet club. On one of these occasions, he showed her some documentation he was looking at to position his firm for a public offering. He wanted Carol's input, and Carol gave it. In exchange, she persuaded him to let her bank handle the offering. "My analytical skills weren't as good as others at the time, but I was young and smart and a good listener," she explains. That IPO turned out to be the biggest piece of business the bank brokered the entire year—an outcome that should have translated into a massive promotion for Carol. But instead her boss threatened to remove her from the account, accusing her of having a sexual affair with the client. His suspicion only grew when the client asked that Carol go to Europe for the road show. "Why do you need to go?" he pressed. "Why does he want you there?"

Carol pointed out the obvious: "I'd won this IPO and this was my client." When her boss refused to let her go to Switzerland, the client sent Carol an airline ticket on the Concorde and arranged for her hotel—a gesture that was in keeping with her accomplishment, but that her boss deemed inappropriate. Carol went on the trip but, in light of the rumors, abstained from the after-hours socializing, to the consternation of her client. "I dressed conservatively; I didn't go out at night," she recalls. "I did not want to be perceived as needing to do anything inappropriate to win my deals." But there was no convincing her boss.

"He just couldn't believe I was capable of building a business relationship on the basis of anything other than sex," Carol remarks. Upon her return from the road show, she contacted a headhunter. "There was no way I could stay at that firm. There were too many barriers to my advancement that had nothing to do with my ability," she told me.

From minority women I heard even more harrowing tales about the impossibility of being perceived as a professional first and as an attractive woman second. Anika, a Pakistani educated in the United States, described a business trip she made to Singapore as a twenty-nine-year-old Big Four consultant. She and two members of her team (white men) were sharing a cab when, to her amazement, they instructed the driver to make a detour to a seedy neighborhood where one of them dipped into a doorway and emerged with two prostitutes. The prostitute started speaking to her in Malay. "She thought I was a prostitute, too," Anika told me. "I felt humiliated but also angry. 'Wow,' I thought to myself, if you're a white guy, even a junior white guy, you're untouchable in this environment, whereas if you're a brown woman with equal or better credentials, you get kicked around."

Even when women succeed at telegraphing professionalism, they can still be penalized for being female. Amy, a former bond broker, described her frustration in competing with male brokers whose client-relationship-building toolkit included not just lavish dinners and tickets to cultural events but also late-night visits to strip clubs. "'Let's get you a car and get you home,' the guys would say after we'd all been out to dinner with a bunch of clients because they were off to the ballet," wink-wink, nod-nod. Amy reflected that the playing field wasn't level because her male colleagues could bond with the client in a way she couldn't. "To avoid dicey situations, to hold on to my professional reputation," she told us, "I always had to leave early."

COMMUNICATION

Women seeking to demonstrate leadership by commanding a room run up against an extremely narrow band of acceptability. Over and over we heard male leaders decry the Shrill Woman—a catch-all descriptor for female leaders whose voice, manner, or body language telegraph intense emotion. Crowell & Moring senior partner Kent Gardiner described one female associate as so shrill he had to take her off the case. "I think she didn't think she was being listened to," he reflected. "And her reaction was to get very heated and pushy without nurturing the client along to where he needed to be. The client came to me and said point-blank, 'I don't want her to run my case anymore.'" Gardiner shook his head, adding, "At any law firm, that's like a death sentence." At the same time, however, this client complained some young women at the firm speak too tentatively and don't seem to have the courage of their convictions. Gardiner then posed the obvious question. "Where, then, is the sweet spot" between too shrill and too tentative?

Many female leaders have yet to find it, our research shows. Recall Margaret Thatcher: She was too shrill, according to her image handlers, yet even after working to modulate her voice she was dogged by harpy imagery, an impression her austere policies fueled. As Bachelet (whom one Chilean described as the "Anti-Thatcher") discovered, there's no getting it right. You're perceived as either hysterical or bloodless; you're seen as either too direct ("ruthless" being a common descriptor) or "too nice," meaning ineffectual. Women who speak confidently about their accomplishments get docked for doing so: 29 percent of our survey respondents identified "tooting your own horn" as a behavior that detracts from a woman's EP. Yet shrugging off kudos or sidestepping well-earned credit isn't considered very leaderlike either: 24 percent said that "self-deprecating" behavior undermines a woman's EP.

Our qualitative research reveals just how fervently women struggle to be heard without alienating their listeners—and the price they pay for not getting it just right. Anna, a planetary geologist with NASA whom I met when we shared a stage at a conference in Bogotá, Colombia, is a scientist nobody's ever heard of. Yet most of us are familiar with the theory that, 65 million years ago, a gigantic asteroid collided with Earth, an impact that effectively wiped out the dinosaurs and allowed mammals to evolve and dominate. While Anna didn't come up with the theory, she did come up with the evidence that confirmed it: Using state-of-the-art satellite imagery, she found the asteroid's impact crater. Despite the significance of her discovery, it took her more than a year to get her findings published, and this enormously undermined her efforts to claim credit. Anna is concerned that the delay in publication had a lot to do with a perceived lack of gravitas (her degrees do not come from elite institutions) and communication challenges—she speaks English with a heavy accent. This double whammy has made it difficult for her to be taken seriously by the interplanetary science community. She still struggles to be heard: At a meeting she called recently to pitch her team on the merits of some pricey technology, it was a male colleague who managed, in the end, to win their buy-in. "I'm pretty good at being clear and compelling when I'm presenting an idea in Spanish," she says, reflecting on this experience. "But in English I get wordy and wishy-washy."

Women who have been more forceful wonder, in turn, if they would have been better off being more restrained. In interviews African-American female executives talked about the need to expose and disprove angry Black woman stereotypes. "In moments of conflict, you can't afford to reinforce those beliefs," says Rosalind Hudnell, a vice president at Intel. "So what does EP look like, or sound like, in those moments? How do you argue a point without being seen as an angry person who is 'not a team player'? If you say 'I don't agree,' or 'I don't want to do that,' as the only Black or only woman in the room, you just serve to remind people you're the outlier. There's often no burden on the group to make you feel a part of it; the burden is on you to show you belong. It is unfair but that is the reality."

The too blunt/too nice bind, a corollary to the too forceful/too circumspect pitfall, also surfaced in CTI's findings. Our survey data shows that both a "failure to convey empathy" and "being too nice" detract from a woman's EP. In addition, just as many (15 percent) believe that "being too nice" and "not being nice enough" detract from a woman's EP. A number of women we interviewed spoke of their frustration in trying to find the space in between. Debbie Maples, a vice president at the Gap, described a typical circumstance: By nature a "very direct, very strong" communicator, she was told by a coach early in her career that "honey attracts more bees than vinegar," so she took pains to rein in her candor and soften her opinions. A few years later, after she'd been promoted at the Gap, her boss told her she was way too nice. "Where's the balance?" she muses. "Do they want me to be harder or softer? It's tricky to figure out."

GRAVITAS

The trickiest EP terrain a woman must navigate is gravitas; here is where the forceful-but-unlikable chasm yawns the widest. A woman who shows teeth, for example—who is decisive, assertive, and willing to hold her ground—risks being perceived as a bitch, abrasive, aggressive, and thoroughly unlikable. Linda, an executive of a global insurance firm, bumped up against this bind early in her career: If she came on strong in an effort to make a point, her (male) superiors viewed her as argumentative and not open to others' input. "They told me I wasn't a change agent, I was too much a naysayer," she recalls, "when I was just trying to get them to see another point of view!" She toughed it out, and today, she says, her gravitas as a leader specifically derives from her extreme candor. "People come to me because they don't want the sugar-coated message that's out there," she explains. "Nine times out of ten, they will say, 'I came to you because I want to hear what is really going on.'" Looking back she still bristles at having been singled out for a criticism that would not have been levied on her male colleagues for exhibiting the same behaviors. "A man is viewed as a strong personality if he is arguing a point, whereas a woman arguing the same point is viewed as a bitch and heartily disliked," she observes.

Michelle Obama learned this, as most women do, the hard way. On the campaign trail in the early months of her husband's presidential campaign in 2008, taking the national stage for the first time, she spoke her mind: She told her audience how she really felt as a Black woman witnessing the nation's revitalized interest in the political process. "For the first time in my adult lifetime, I am really proud of my country," she said. Within hours, the press branded her an Angry Black Woman. The conservative press gleefully took her to task for her lukewarm patriotism, flushing an apology from candidate Obama, who claimed his wife didn't mean what she said. Headlines in both the *New York Times* and the *Los Angeles Times* pegged her as "a potential liability" for the Democratic nominee;[97] one Fox News commentator went so far as to label the fist-bump she shared with her victorious husband "a terrorist fist jab."[98] As discussed in chapter 2, this militant image followed her to the White House, where she switched out challenging topics for lighter issues. As described earlier, Michelle Obama's Get Moving campaign to tackle childhood obesity was chosen in part because it was so very safe. First ladies, she was made to realize, are not allowed to take on anything remotely controversial.

Bottom line? Behaviors that confer gravitas on a man by demonstrating he can "show teeth"—offering candid assessments, interjecting opinions, hammering home a point, banging a fist, showing anger, dropping the F-bomb—come off as aggression in a woman. Consider the flap that erupted when Paula Deen, celebrity chef and the self-described Queen of Butter, admitted to using the N-word. Ballantine canceled her five-book deal, companies yanked away their endorsement contracts, and Deen was left twisting in the wind. Yet when Alec Baldwin, the *30 Rock* star, tweeted to a British reporter some gay-bashing threats ("I'm gonna find you, George Stark, you toxic little queen, and I'm gonna fuck . . . you . . . up," followed by, "I'd put my foot up your fucking ass, George Stark, but I'm sure you'd dig it too much"), the backlash was virtually nonexistent.[99] Baldwin apologized, as he has done in the past, for his hotheadedness (this is a man who left a voice mail with his eleven-year-old daughter calling her a "thoughtless little pig").[100] The incidents and his response have, if anything, burnished his image as an alpha male.

Making this worse, of course, is that men don't see the double standard even as they apply it. In our focus groups male managers delighted in inventorying for us female leaders whom the public had vilified for abrasiveness (Yahoo's Marissa Mayer as well as HP's former CEO Carly Fiorina). But these same managers detected no irony in likewise complaining about female subordinates who embarrassed them in important meetings by being overly deferential or not making their points forcefully enough. Our survey results captured it perfectly: 31 percent of our respondents said that being "too bossy" undermines a woman's EP, and 31 percent said being "too passive" undermines a woman's EP. Go figure.

Speaking truth to power and showing teeth aren't the only gravitas-building behaviors that women can't seem to get right. Reputation, too, turns out to be a double-edged sword for women. Consider that of Christine Lagarde, president of the European Central Bank. Lagarde's credentials, track record, and experience are impeccable, as even her detractors concede. "Altogether, she conforms to a profile common to women who project a steady hand and a cool head and are therefore acceptable to men as leaders of male-dominated organizations," observed Diane Johnson in *Vogue*, noting that "Lagarde is five foot ten, handsome, poised, perfect, exuding confidence and charm, like a glamorous headmistress her students half fall in love with, half fear."[101] Yet for these charms, Lagarde is likewise held in contempt. When she took the reins of the IMF from the scandal-plagued Dominique Strauss-Kahn in July 2011, she was criticized for being "an upper-class woman cut off from common people and more preoccupied with her look than their welfare, the way such elegant, chic people are."[102] In other words, because she positively radiated executive presence, Lagarde wasn't *populist* enough as a person.

Debbie Storey, who led talent development for AT&T for more than a decade, notes a difference in people's reaction to books on leadership authored by men and women—in part because women authors tend to include stories about how they've had to balance their roles as caregivers with their careers as they climbed the corporate ladder. "When powerful men write books about leadership, they tend to leave out the support systems that played a big role in making their success possible," she explained. "You don't read about the stay-at-home spouse who enabled them to move up the ladder more quickly than their female peers.

"Women authors, on the other hand, usually tackle these issues head-on, which makes them vulnerable and frequently triggers harsh judgment. Too often, they're held to a higher and more complex standard. In addition to being an accomplished leader, they also have to be near perfect as mothers, wives, friends, volunteers, et cetera."

HOW TO WIN GREATER LATITUDE: INSIGHTS AND STRATEGIES

WHEN YOU SHOW TEETH, SHOW THAT YOU HAVE THE BEST INTERESTS OF THE TEAM AT HEART

Assert your difference of opinion, but take the "I" out of your argument, advises Intel's Rosalind Hudnell, a leader who's perfected the art of "arguing with grace." Too often, she says, women and people of color set themselves up to be branded "not a team player" by framing their argument in terms of what's bugging them personally. "Don't make it about yourself, because that only underscores your status as the outsider," says Hudnell. "Remember, when you're working for a company, you're responsible to that company. Whatever you're going to argue, whatever decision you don't like or want to push back on, you need to come from a position of not what's good for you but of what's best for the company. Be deliberate with your language. Be careful about your tone and your body language. Consider the perspective of the majority. You'll be far more effective if before taking a stand you consider, 'How will this idea be heard by those in power?'"

WHEN SPEAKING TRUTH TO POWER, WIDEN YOUR BAND OF RECEPTIVITY WITH A JUDICIOUS USE OF HUMOR

Stella, a senior executive at Genpact, a global professional services firm, tells of a boss she had whom she admired tremendously for his intelligence, his knowledge of the business, and his ability to analyze a situation and render a decision. She did not, however, admire his leadership style, which was so abrasive that he effectively preempted any and all pushback. "He'd pound the table, curse, and denigrate anyone who took issue with his analysis," she says, "and it worked: He was so intimidating no one dared to challenge him." But Stella isn't a person who keeps her thoughts to herself when she knows she's right, so when her boss gathered his team to discuss implementing a new sales strategy, one that he believed would drive revenue, Stella refused to be intimidated. "I believed his approach would have a negative impact on customer satisfaction, and therefore on revenue," she recalls, "so I countered his position, not confrontationally, but objectively." He went nuclear. "Goddammit!" he shouted, striking the table with his fist and glaring at everyone around the table. "Does anyone want a piece of Stella before I get mine?" For two heartbeats, Stella remembers, the room went absolutely silent. Then she said, "No, Bob, they're waiting to see you do it." Bob burst out laughing.

Stella did another thing to ensure her remarks enhanced rather than detracted from her gravitas: After the meeting concluded, she sought out her boss to explain that she hadn't been contradicting him but rather ensuring he had the knowledge he needed to render the right decision. "I just want to make sure you had the whole picture," she told him. "If you go in a different direction, okay, but it's my responsibility to put the facts on the table so that your decisions rest on full information." He told her he appreciated her intent, and admired her for her courage. "His respect for me probably tripled as a result of that encounter," Stella says.

HIT THE MARK BY TAKING MORE CAREFUL AIM

Too often, says AllianceBernstein's Lori Massad, women take a broad-spectrum approach to communication that leaves them open to crossfire. Instead of listening to others' views, they blurt out their own first; instead of sharing their best insight, they download everything that's occurred to them; and instead of waiting for an opening that might maximize receptivity, they stream consciousness. Better to be a sniper, says Massad: Pick your target, pick your moment, and fire your best shot. "If I am participating in a meeting, my first communication cannot be meek," she explains. "I do not speak up unless I have a really good point to make or insight to add. I usually wait to speak until I am prepared to make a counterpoint, or ask a dynamite question." The opposite applies, she stresses, if she's leading the meeting. "I take charge immediately by offering a bold statement. I do not do small talk or ask about people's weekends or their family. 'Here is what I need. Here is my objective. Let's get started.'"

BUILD A PERSONAL BRAND THAT GRANTS YOU LOTS OF LATITUDE TO BE YOU—AND BE RELENTLESS IN PROJECTING IT

Take a page out of Richard Branson's playbook. The CEO of all things Virgin cast himself early on as an iconoclast, someone who delighted in taking on challenges and doing things differently. That brand has inoculated him from criticism on a number of fronts; indeed, Branson generates as much revenue from his failures as he does from his successes because his brand—embracing challenge, doing things differently—celebrates the attempt, not the outcome. Consider the bet he made with rival airline owner Tony Fernandes: Depending on whose Formula One racing team finished lower in the standings, the loser had to serve as a cabin steward on the other's airline. Branson lost the bet but reinvigorated his brand by dressing up as a stewardess and putting in a full shift on AirAsia. The stunt endeared him to his public (and apparently to passenger Desmond Tutu, who told him he was "voluptuous"), boosted both airlines' revenues, and raised three hundred thousand dollars for the Starlight Children's Foundation.[103] I'm not saying you need go to such extremes, of course. But a consciously built and confidently maintained brand that positions you outside the box goes a long way in ensuring that others won't dare box you in.

SHOW YOU CARE

For women in particular, winning more latitude in the public's eye depends on showcasing activities that demonstrate you care about the disenfranchised and the disadvantaged. This works wonders on the likability front. Indeed, you won't find a female leader out there who *hasn't* come to embrace this tactic. Kirsten Gillibrand, Hillary Clinton's replacement as the junior senator from New York State, has become a powerful advocate for victims of sexual harassment and assault in the military;[104] Elizabeth Warren, in her run-up to winning a Massachusetts U.S. senatorial seat, recorded a powerful message for the "It Gets Better" video campaign to help bullied LGBT teenagers.[105] For both women, supporting a good cause raised their profile and their popularity.

Feedback can be helpful in pointing out which paths to take—and which pitfalls to avoid—but at a certain point, many up-and-comers feel challenged by the tradeoffs that face them. Yet walking that fine line between courage and conformity is the ultimate test of executive presence.

7

AUTHENTICITY VS. CONFORMITY

A few years ago, I had a conversation over breakfast with Trevor Phillips, the former chair of the Equality and Human Rights Commission (EHRC), at the Covent Garden Hotel, London.

"The most extraordinary thing just happened," he said, sinking into the purple upholstery across from me. He then proceeded to tell me how, a block from the hotel, he'd been approached on the street by a total stranger, a man who'd recognized him as the former host of *The London Programme* but also as the producer of *Windrush*, the 1998 BBC television series documenting the rise of multiracial Britain.

"He wanted me to know that, as a young Black Brit, *Windrush* had changed his life," Phillips continued. "He'd gotten the DVDs and shared them with his children, because he knew they'd come away just as inspired." Phillips shook his head, marveling at the encounter. "Making that series was probably the riskiest move I ever made, but also the most important and the one for which I'll be ever grateful. It returned me to myself."

Outspoken about LGBT rights, a vehement defender of free speech, yet vocal in his opposition to multiculturalism, Phillips had just stepped down from the top slot at the EHRC, which he'd formed in 2006 from the ashes of the Commission for Racial Equality, which he had also chaired. I remember being wowed by his sheer presence. A tall, impeccably dressed, extremely well-spoken Afro-Caribbean man blessed with both an Imperial College British accent and a broadcaster's deep voice, Phillips emanates authority and credibility, and talks eloquently and easily about the complexity of multiracial Britain. Knowing something of his political career—he'd been friends with Tony Blair, a London mayoral candidate in 1999, and chair of the London Assembly until 2003—I assumed that he'd constructed his brand around his heritage and identity.

But in fact, not until he was thirty-eight years old did Phillips come to embrace, as he puts it, his "first language." Born in London to parents who'd emigrated from Guyana, Phillips readily adapted to British ways of speaking, dressing, and socializing, becoming so fluent in this "second language" that, after graduating with a chemistry degree from Imperial College London, he had few qualms about forsaking his origins. Embarking on a career in television, he quickly rose in the ranks, becoming head of current affairs for London Weekend Television (LWT) in 1994. To have gotten so far by his late thirties was an extraordinary achievement. He seemed poised for a top leadership role. Instead, he turned away.

"As you climb the ladder as a Black professional, you get to a place where you're confronted with a choice," he explained to me. "You can either resurrect that first language, give it weight and heft in your new high-profile life—a risky business—or you can play it safe, and continue to speak your second language so that you can survive and thrive in a white world.

"I'd reached that fork in the road," he continued. "At that point in time, I was burning to make this documentary on *Windrush*, the troops ship that brought the first West Indian immigrants to Britain in 1948, but I knew ITV [then LWT] wasn't about to sign on. They didn't see it as an important project. I'd have to leave to produce it, and I knew once I stepped off track there was no coming back."

But step off he did, forming his own production company. He then went on to create a partnership with the BBC, producing his documentary as a four-part television series. When it garnered rave reviews, he teamed up with his brother Michael, a novelist born in Guyana, to write the underlying story, which Harper-Collins published to great critical acclaim.

"*Windrush* was a huge success," he reflected. "And transformative for me. Firstly, its impact gave me enormous satisfaction. But it also made me into a public figure and put me on the map in ways I couldn't possibly have anticipated. It was a turning point, no question about it. Because by embracing what was most meaningful to me," Phillips added, "I forged a career path where my suppressed identity could flourish."

BLEACHED-OUT PROFESSIONALS

In late 2011 and early 2012, when CTI first probed the topic of executive presence with focus groups at Moody's, the Gap, EY, and Freddie Mac, we uncovered a potent source of anguish for up-and-coming professionals of color. While EP for some was a set of unwritten rules that no one had bothered to share with them, for others it was a terrain they felt they couldn't navigate without sacrificing core aspects of their identity. To use the metaphor that Trevor Phillips shared with me, they were all "bilingual," high-performing managers who grew up with a distinct heritage and a "first language" but learned to survive and thrive in a white world by adopting the conventions of that world—in effect a second language. Indeed, they had the track record, credentials, and experience to get to the next level, and understood they were being scrutinized for their EP. But they also feared becoming "bleached-out professionals," to invoke an older metaphor: individuals who in order to be perceived as up-and-comers in their work environments had effectively scrubbed themselves of all ethnic, religious, racial, socioeconomic, and educational identifiers.[106] And they weren't happy about it. Like Phillips, they had reached that place on the ladder where looking and acting like a leader at work suddenly didn't seem to be worth the sacrifice of that "other" identity, of their first language. They resented the pressure to conform. They couldn't justify bleaching out aspects of themselves in order to fit in. In short, they were at a crossroads: Would they plow forward by suppressing their difference—or by asserting it? By fitting in—or standing out? By conforming to the culture in which they found themselves—or owning their authenticity?

The results of our nationally representative survey brought this conflict into sharper focus. Forty-one percent of professionals of color said they had felt the need to compromise their authenticity in order to conform to EP standards at their company. A small minority of white respondents also conceded they felt the need to conform, of course, but people of color were significantly more likely than whites to feel this tension; indeed, a majority of African-American, Hispanic, and Asian professionals reported that they felt held to a stricter code of EP than their Caucasian peers. Overwhelmingly, the EP code they feel impelled to fit into is that embodied by white men.

This should come as no surprise. Everywhere you look—on magazine covers, websites, online journals, industry reports—you will find that corporate leaders in America are nearly always depicted as white men. A quick sampling of the magazines in my office archive reveals just how easy it is to conflate "the right stuff" of leadership with a certain phenotype. Above headlines such as "The Tests of a Leader" (*Harvard Business Review*) or "The Four Types of CEOs" (*Strategy + Business*) you'll find someone who looks like Mitt Romney.

Authenticity vs. Conformity

What does conforming to this standard entail? For people of color, it means expending energy to repress ethnic identifiers in appearance, speech, behavior, and background. In our survey, a majority of Asian, African-American, and Hispanic respondents agreed with the statement "I have deliberately changed the way I tell my personal story in order to bolster my professional image." Alarmingly, the more senior the respondent, the more likely he or she was to agree with that statement. This choice might reflect the realities confronted by an older generation. Then again, it might mean that the pathway to the top imposes increasingly heavy sacrifices for professionals of color.

Invisible Lives, a report CTI published in late 2005, was among the first to document the nature and extent of this sacrifice.[107] Co-authored by myself and Cornel West, the report quantifies not only the terrible cost to minority professionals who feel obliged to cordon off their church, their community, and their family lives in order to succeed at work, but also the cost to their employers, who miss out on the leadership skills minority professionals develop outside of work because they leave much of who they are at home. For two years, Stephanie, an African-American manager I interviewed who worked for a major fashion brand, illustrates perfectly the lose-lose of bleached-out professionalism. Stephanie had poured her heart into a weekend tutoring program she ran at a homeless shelter in Newark, New Jersey, a commitment that meant she had to leave her Manhattan office at 4:30 p.m. on Fridays. Even though she arrived at 7 a.m. on that day, she was acutely aware that, to her boss, her early departure signaled a lack of commitment. Yet she would not speak to him about her community involvement because she was fearful that if he knew he would see her through a new lens—not as an accomplished professional but as a Black girl from the projects. So Stephanie kept quiet about her volunteer role, despite the fact that her work with homeless children won her a Future Leader Today award in a ceremony at the White House. Her lack of candor wasn't good for her or the company. She was passed over for a promotion (her boss continued to see her as disengaged). Shortly thereafter she left the company.

Like so many other minority professionals we interviewed, Stephanie saw herself as two people operating in two irreconcilable spheres: the highly effective and committed leader in her community, and the bleached-out professional on the job. To reveal one aspect of her identity in the community sphere would be to provide her employer with "ammunition," or evidence that could be used against her to the degree that it reinforced racial stereotypes—a distrust that more than half of minority women we surveyed owned up to feeling.[108]

Our focus groups and interviews confirmed the prevalence of Stephanie's defensive behavior: Non-Caucasians expend an awful lot of energy cordoning off aspects of their personal lives. They don't share, because they don't feel comfortable sharing what they care most about, lest details about their children, political leanings, or community involvement undermine the impression they're like everybody else at the firm. "For a long time I have left a large part of 'me' at home—the 'me' who has strong opinions on cultural and political issues—and adopted a persona at work that is more conservative, and less forthcoming, than I would otherwise be," an Asian-American financial analyst explained. "The problem is the longer you do that, the more alienated you become because you are shutting off whole parts of yourself—and the more of yourself you risk losing."

Walling off parts of your life will cost you not just emotionally but also professionally. Ray, an accountant, was for years two people: the person at work who conformed to the way everybody else looked and acted and sounded, and the person outside work who had southern roots, a southern drawl, and strong ties to his church and his African-American community. Recently he's taken steps to reconcile those two personas, having taken a lead role in his firm's Black affinity group. But his decision to no longer "hide his full identity" is due more to resignation, he says, than a change in the cultural climate at work. "I've gotten to the point where I no longer care," Ray explains. "I'm not going to rise up the ladder at this company; I can't even get on the teams or the projects where I could contribute valuable skills, even though I have twice the experience of some of my colleagues. It's a case of the invisible man: the less you get to be yourself, the less likely others are to see your value, the fewer opportunities you will be given, and the less visible you will indeed become."

The experience of minority professionals parallels that of another group: LGBT professionals who feel obliged to pass for straight at work. Nearly half of the gay professionals we surveyed for our report entitled *The Power of "Out": LGBT in the Workplace*, said they remained closeted at work for fear of being ostracized by their colleagues and penalized by their superiors.[109] One-third of them literally live double lives, out to friends and family, but not to their coworkers and superiors. However, whether partially or fully closeted, these individuals expend considerable energy on remaining "off the gaydar" of their colleagues, watching their pronouns, lying about their significant others, or just not volunteering personal information at gatherings at the watercooler or lunch table. And as with minority professionals, that low profile costs them both personally and professionally. More than half of closeted LGBT workers told us they feel stalled in their careers, compared with the 36 percent of gay employees who are out at work. They're more disengaged, too: They were 73 percent more likely than their out counterparts to say they intended to leave their firm within three years. Like bleached-out professionals of color, closeted gays become masters of neutrality and control and increasingly isolated and expendable.

African-Americans in particular spoke to us of their struggle to conform to EP standards at work in terms of their communication. They're careful to modulate their voice, tone, and language lest they affirm "historically embedded notions of being aggressive, angry people, people who will blow up," as one interviewee put it. Joel Tealer, senior vice president of human resources, Strategic Business Units at Chubb Insurance Groups, says he's learned to be "very careful" about the language he uses in any emotionally charged or fraught discussion. "As a multicultural manager, I need to be sure I'm balanced, because if I'm not—if I'm loud or animated or left-of-center—my audience, if they're outside my culture, will judge me as less professional. White males have the ability to be further to the left and a little more animated when discussing volatile topics without being viewed negatively."

African-American women likewise told us how carefully they step in order to tamp down the specter of the angry Black woman, behavior that exacts a toll not only on their authenticity, points out Judith Harrison, chief diversity officer at Weber Shandwick, but also on their productivity. "That struggle to muzzle themselves is just a sinkhole in terms of the time and energy it requires," she says. "And that time could be so much better spent."

Given these significant costs, why do professionals of color take such pains to rein in or paper over who they are to accommodate the expectations of their Caucasian peers and superiors? Because when you trumpet your difference, or make no effort to mute it, you are even more likely to become a target of unconscious bias or even overt discrimination.

For people of color as well as LGBTQ+ professionals, the corporate landscape bristles with land mines in the form of slights or snubs that serve as reminders of latent discrimination. Terri Austin, an attorney and chief diversity officer at McGraw-

Hill Financial who previously served as chief compliance officer at AIG, recalls one C-suite meeting where the leading officer turned to her, the only woman and the only African-American in the room, to request that she take the minutes. "He was serious!" she says, still incredulous that, among equals at that table, she would be called out to render a secretary's services. Fortunately her sponsor, who was then general counsel, intervened to insist that someone else be brought in to perform the task, as Austin wasn't to do it. But the incident underscored for her the difficulties faced by executives of color operating in the uppermost tiers of management.

That racism still presses a heavy thumb on qualified minority professionals is affirmed by the results of our nationally representative survey. Hispanics, we found, are nearly three times more likely than their white colleagues to be mistaken for someone's secretary or assistant. Twenty-two percent of African-Americans say they're frequently mistaken for someone else of their own race. Most distressingly, fully 19 percent of African-Americans say their colleagues perceive them as "affirmative-action hires." Across the board, people of color remain skeptical of their chances of success. More than a third of African-American respondents believe that a person of color would never get a top job at their company, a perception echoed by almost as many Asians and Hispanics.

So while the United States has made significant progress in providing equal access to higher education, and equal access to white-collar jobs, progression to the upper echelons of management is still extremely problematic for people of color. Confronted with Trevor Phillips's fork in the road, most opt to continue hiding their difference lest it limit their ascent. Phillips's protégé David, a Brit of Afro-Caribbean heritage, is a case in point: Recently offered the position of chair of the Black executive network at his company, he turned it down, explaining to Phillips that becoming "a poster child" for Black employees was just too risky. "He sees the whole D&I [diversity and inclusiveness] mandate as a burden," Phillips clarified for me. "He feels it will get in the way of him being taken seriously as a professional at the firm."

RESOLVING THE TENSION

So to return to our question: If you're different from most people at work, do you suppress that difference or embrace it in order to be perceived as leadership material?

Everyone we surveyed or spoke to affirmed the importance of authenticity, pointing out that no leader can win or retain followers without it. Everyone also agreed that succeeding in any organizational culture demands that you make accommodations to that culture. Even straight white men are obliged to conform, whether by dressing more formally than they'd like, reining in their happy-hour jokes, or purging their Facebook walls of incriminating photos. And conformity is hardly a corporate phenomenon: Small businesses ask that their employees mold themselves to fit a culture created by the founder/owner; educators operate within the boundaries established by their school boards, which are informed by state laws; public-sector employees answer to officials who answer to the public. For-profit or nonprofit, ultimately every organization operates within a narrow band of customer or shareholder or board approval. Even rule breakers like Groupon's Andrew Mason, who seemingly reinvent the marketplace, must answer to the strictures imposed by that new marketplace—or be shoved aside and forced to reinvent themselves again. No matter who we are and where we work, that is, the workplace imposes norms around appearance, communication, and gravitas that we'd be fools to ignore if our intent is to thrive and not just survive.

Hence it may be helpful to discern where assimilating is tantamount to "playing the game" as opposed to "selling out." Lawrence, an insurance industry senior vice president I interviewed, notes that conforming doesn't necessarily involve a cost, and may even confer a benefit. By way of example, he describes his reasons for taking up golf, a sport that certainly wasn't prevalent in the African-American community where he grew up. But, recognizing its power as a networking tool, he applied himself to the sport—and discovered he absolutely loved it. "Did it compromise me, to assimilate in this way? I don't think so," he reflects. "Ultimately succeeding is about networking and engaging with people. If you're trying to get to know someone, an executive or senior leader, someone you don't know much about or have much in common with, you need to focus on what they do and where their interests lie. And if there's an opportunity to get involved in something that creates common ground, then you'd best take it, because it will give you the venue to share your personality and potential." Reflecting on his rapid ascent within the firm, Lawrence adds, "In assimilating, you may find that you're changing yourself more than they're changing you—and in very positive ways."

Michael, another insurance executive I interviewed, observed that accusing you of selling out can be your peer group's way of ensuring you don't break from their ranks. A small number of African-American colleagues who were great friends with him at the beginning of their careers together later rebuked him, Michael recalls, when he started differentiating himself in terms of seizing stretch opportunities and establishing strategic relationships. "Oh, you're kissing up? You've decided you're going to be white?" they taunted. Michael shrugged it off. "I've had people ever since I started to rise in management accuse me of not being true to myself or my heritage because I was doing what the majority of people in the organization do to get ahead," he explains. "Well, what's selling out? Working extra hours? Volunteering for assignments? Taking on more responsibility? That's doing your job, *plus*—and that is going to get you ahead. I've found that sometimes when a group starts questioning your authenticity, then that's a group trying to hold you back."

The difficulty, of course, is that only *you* can determine what constitutes a compromise to your authenticity, as opposed to just a compromise. To help you make that call, I've amassed strategic and tactical advice from professionals of color who've been down this road.

TACTICS

KNOW YOUR "NON-NEGOTIABLES" AND WALK AWAY

Some cultures simply don't deserve your best efforts. Weber Shandwick's Judith Harrison recalls how early in her career she worked in an Arthur Young office where the office manager, who was also the head of HR, displayed an enormous Confederate flag over her desk. Harrison, who is African-American, labored for several years in this environment until she realized that the stress of working for a leader whom she couldn't respect and who wouldn't perceive her value was taking a toll on her health. "I had to remove myself," she says. "It was making me physically sick, going into that situation every day, knowing that people did not see me the way I knew I deserved to be seen. Nothing is worth that."

In hindsight, however, she's glad to have had such a test at the outset of her career. "I think that it enabled me to develop much clearer convictions about what was important and what wasn't, and to grow confidence in myself."

NEVER TRY TO BE SOMEONE YOU'RE NOT

Barbara Adachi, whom we met in an earlier chapter, was the first woman at Deloitte ever to head up a region, but she didn't set out to be a trailblazer. Indeed, her tactic in the early years of her career was to simply emulate the "very strong" woman who was her first boss, as there were precious few other women to look up to as role models. Adachi, a petite woman of Japanese descent, was surprised at her boss's client approach and style—she was very aggressive and often swore, but nonetheless was very effective with clients. Thinking this might be the path to success, Adachi convinced herself to adopt it on her next prospective client cold call.

She bombed.

"Oh, it was awful," Adachi exclaims, shuddering as she remembers this long-ago incident. "*Who do you think you are, talking to me like that?*" The client on the other end of the phone was incredulous. "*You're not my wife!*" It was a searing lesson for her in the importance of developing a leadership presence within her own style boundaries. "My boss could get away with it, but it just wasn't me," she reflects. "I was never going to be the loudest voice in the room, though I was under pressure to try. I had to accept that wasn't my style and it could never work for me."

Her own style has served her well: she made partner, she retired from Deloitte as national managing director for U.S. Human Capital (HC) Consulting.

PERCEIVE SLIGHTS AS OPPORTUNITIES TO ADDRESS IGNORANCE

Michael, the senior executive we met earlier, describes how, when he moved to San Jose, California, with his company, the branch manager would arrive each week and, moving from one end of the hall to the other, dip in to each leader's office to say hello and chit-chat about the weekend, the kids, and interesting new projects in the pipeline. "Then he'd come to my office," relates Michael. "'Hey, Michael, what's going on?' he'd ask—and he'd move right on to the next person." As the only minority in the company's leadership it was easy, says Michael, to conclude that he was being slighted. And it occurred to him to respond like someone who'd been slighted. "I remember thinking, 'If he doesn't value me enough to want to get to know me, then I am going to some other company,'" Michael explains.

But he quickly realized he'd likely suffer from a career standpoint if he ignored the situation instead of addressing it head-on. So he took the initiative, seeking out the branch manager at every opportunity. "If he came in early, I came in early and found him," says Michael. "I talked to him about things he was interested in. I'd done my homework and knew what activities he was involved with. We also talked about our families. It got to the point where I couldn't get him out of my office and get work done."

He adds, "It's so easy to think that every slight might have something to do with your background or gender. It's not to say there are no real snubs, but I've found that more often than not somebody's coming from a place of ignorance rather than bigotry. If you're overly sensitive to the possibility of intentional slights and withdraw as a result, you freeze yourself rather than move forward."

SEEK AIR COVER BEFORE YOU STEP OUT TO ASSERT YOUR AUTHENTICITY

One of the high points of her career, says Helen Forrester, a former SVP at a Silicon Valley technology firm, was being praised for her executive presence by the firm's CEO—in front of 1,200 of the firm's leaders. "Yesterday was an outstanding day for the women of this firm," said the CEO as he opened the annual directors-and-above meeting, "and I want to personally thank Helen for her standout leadership." He then asked her to stand up and be applauded by the mostly male audience. "I never felt so proud," says Helen, shaking her head in disbelief. "I think sometimes, as women and as people of color, we avoid the spotlight because we're afraid we're going to pay a penalty for standing out and proactively attempting to earn the admiration and praise of executives. But we can't let that fear stop us. We simply have to embrace who we are and learn to both seek and take credit for our successes."

She didn't get to bask in the glow of that success for long, however. Her sudden visibility threatened her then boss, she says, who went out of his way to keep her offstage and out of the CEO's view. "The more presence I developed—I had the CEO's executive coach working with me—the more brutally critical of me he became," says Helen, a Latina with a master's degree in industrial engineering as well as a master's from Stanford in executive education. "'Why are you talking to him?' he'd question me. 'You stay here, I'll go deliver the numbers.'" As a result of the browbeating, she felt her confidence and control dissipate. "I didn't know how to fight, so I did what I shouldn't have: I let my emotions show when he would interrupt me during a presentation. I had no grace under fire."

She might have weathered the assaults had her ally, the head of HR, not left the firm. But in the wake of her departure, Helen says, she was completely sponsorless. "I didn't have a well-placed senior person to help me navigate," she says, "someone looking out for me, someone who would run interference with my boss or secure me the CEO's protection. You've got to have that air cover so that when you finally take the stage, everyone knows not to challenge your claim to it." A few months later a demoralized and dispirited Helen left the company.

DIFFERENTIATE YOURSELF BY WHAT MAKES YOU DIFFERENT

Linda, the retail sector executive we met earlier, learned early in her career that her roots—she grew up in Africa—were going to assert themselves. "I hardly ever sound like anyone else in the room," she says. "People try to piece together where I'm from, because I've spent a lot of time in London, but it's mostly Africa that comes through, and it's just different from anything they've ever heard."

It took her a while to realize, however, that her accent allowed her to stand out and be heard in ways her female colleagues struggled with. "Women are more likely to be screened out and not heard than men," she observes. "I am less likely to be invisible, because I sound different and look different. I decided this was an opportunity to be noticed."

In the end it is these powerful inescapable differences that most distinguish her as a leader. "I have an advantage as a Black woman from Africa," she elaborates, "because by definition, I am the 'only one' at a leadership table and colleagues are constrained to be more tolerant and open. Everyone must be much more intentional about how they express themselves. No one is able to get away with the statement, 'So-and-so may not be capable because she's a woman.' It is pretty clear that that sort of thing will not fly. With regard to perceptions of women and Black people, leaders in my division are shaped by spending time with me. So then, that trickles down to their teams."

The previous year, a diversity magazine named Linda to their list of top executive leaders under age fifty, honoring her for bringing her distinctive brand and values to the teams she manages worldwide. "People are afraid to talk about gender and race," she says. "I'm better able than most to create an environment where it's possible to have an open, honest dialogue—and not hide behind some of the politically correct labels—to get at what the real issues are."

UNDERSTAND THE DIVERSITY DIVIDEND

In figuring out the hows and whys of lifting up your authenticity in the workplace, consider how the landscape for professionals of color is shifting. As our economy grows ever more globalized and competition intensifies, companies are under ever greater pressure to innovate—both to retain market share and capture new markets in underserved populations. CTI research reveals that, by representing some of those underleveraged markets, diverse voices around decision-making tables hold the key to innovating more effectively.[110]

Other CTI research shows that innate diversity on teams—having members who are female, nonwhite, or of non–European origin—boosts the team's innovative potential by providing critical insight into the needs and wants of overlooked or underserved end users.[111]

Marketing teams with just one Hispanic member, for example, are nearly twice as likely to understand—and effectively solve for—the problems inherent to convincing older Latinos to see a doctor about prostate trouble. R&D teams with just one native African member are, again, almost twice as likely to understand, and innovate products and services for, the millions of sub-Saharan consumers who grapple with limited access to reliable power and clean water. In case study after case study, in this CTI research we see that innate difference brings unique understanding and vital insight to solving intractable problems, or to realizing unfulfilled market potential. At Morgan Stanley, one openly gay financial advisor spearheaded an accreditation campaign in domestic-partner estate planning that won the firm some $120 million in client assets because affluent members of the LGBT community preferred to work with financial advisors who understood their unique predicament. At Standard Chartered, one female executive (a native of India) drove the transformation of two bank branches in Kolkata and New Delhi into all-women branches, a move which drove up net sales at these bank branches by an impressive 127 percent and 75 percent, respectively, from 2009 to 2010. (This compared with a paltry 48 percent average among the bank's other ninety-plus Indian branches.)

Our findings underscore that there is a "diversity dividend": When companies and leaders know how to harness and leverage gender, generation, ethnicity, race, sexual orientation, and culture, there is a significant impact on the bottom line.

Innate difference is worth embracing for at least one other important reason: It can help win you a sponsor.[112] A sponsor is a leader who's committed to seeing you succeed and will go out on a limb to make sure you do. Sponsors are more powerful than mentors, because they're more vested in you. They advocate for your next promotion, steer plum assignments your way, and protect you as you move up the learning curve because they see how their star will rise in conjunction with yours. My several studies on "The Sponsor Effect" demonstrate that not only are protégés of color more likely to be satisfied with their rate of advancement when they have a sponsor, but also that *sponsors* with protégés of color are more likely to be satisfied with their career progress (as compared to nonsponsors).[113]

That is to say, it is precisely your difference that your superiors need to burnish their brand, build their team, extend their innovative capabilities, and ultimately succeed as leaders. It is your toolkit—the way you approach problems as a result of coming from a different background—that makes you worth sponsoring. It is your network, your access to clients or markets they might not otherwise be able to access, that makes you valuable in growing their own networks. It is, finally, your insight into end users like yourself that gives them a competitive edge in the relentless competition to innovate. In this brave new world, the organization absolutely needs you to bring your whole self to work.

So don't downplay your difference. Commit to owning it.

PART II

Executive presence is not static. This is particularly true in turbulent times, and the years since *Executive Presence: The Missing Link Between Merit and Success* was published have been marked by a great deal of turbulence. Over the last eight years, companies and organizations have been hit by seismic changes in the external environment, including the Black Lives Matter and #MeToo movements, a global pandemic, and a European war. As a result, what leaders look for in their bench strength of talent has evolved and shifted.

To explore this evolution and update my original research (the survey that underpinned my 2014 book was fielded in 2012), during 2022 and the early months of 2023, I conducted seventy-three interviews with executives across various industries. My goal was twofold: to collect a second round of data and engage in an in-depth conversation with established and up-and-coming corporate leaders operating in a vastly changed world.

These leaders were carefully selected. A third are seasoned executives (in their fifties) who participated in my earlier research on Executive Presence and have developed views on how EP has evolved over the last decade, while two-thirds are younger executives (in their late thirties and early forties) whom I've met through my consulting practice. This latter group is much more diverse—in terms of gender, race, and sexual orientation—and is much more global. I went out of my way to select executives who "sit" in London, Munich, São Paulo, Shanghai, Reykjavík, and New Delhi as well as in New York and Palo Alto. In addition, to ensure I went beyond the usual suspects, I selected a number of executives who lead companies at the cutting edge of the new economy. I wanted insights from leaders at Splunk, DraftKings, Blizzard Entertainment, and Plum Alley Investments, as well as JPMorgan, AIG, and Cisco. Finally, I interviewed executives from the arts. Individuals who curate art exhibitions, lead dance companies, and head up music organizations have a lot to say about the direction of our culture.

These in-depth conversations allowed me to gauge how much leadership models have changed in response to the new circumstances. I found that while many sought-after traits have remained the same—the ability to project confidence or command a room has not gone out of style—others have changed.

In the gravitas bucket, CEOs seek to promote up-and-comers who can telegraph not just EQ but inclusion, which is a much more complex endeavor. In the communication bucket, they're looking to advance individuals who can inspire teams on Zoom and Webex as well as face-to-face. And in the appearance bucket, they're fast-tracking individuals who've nailed the new normal. It's a bewildering world on the professional "look" front. Whether employees are remote, hybrid, or back in the office full-time, they're looking for role models who can help them display leadership chops in business casual. One thing's for sure: Sweats and sloppy sneakers don't cut the mustard in 2023's new normal.

If sought-after EP traits have shifted, so have EP blunders. Mistakes and missteps that landed a manager or an executive in trouble ten years ago (being lightweight or crying are examples), while still problematic, are less damaging. Nowadays, the big whopper of a blunder is sexual misconduct. No matter how exalted or successful you are (think Harvey Weinstein, Andy Rubin, or Steve Easterbrook), there's no coming back from being credibly accused of sexual harassment or assault. There's a great deal of evidence on this front. Longitudinal analysis done by PwC shows that post-#MeToo, sexual misconduct has become the main reason executives fall from grace and are shown the door, displacing financial malfeasance and incompetence.[114] Increasingly, corporate boards are approaching allegations of sexual indiscretions and abuse with a "zero-tolerance" stance. Even associating with a sexual predator can sully a leader's reputation (and potentially their company) irreparably. Leon Black's ouster from Apollo Global Management illustrates this point.[115]

Where do these insights leave our 2012 EP model?

The comforting news is that despite changes and shifts, the core principles of Executive Presence laid out eight years ago remain remarkably constant. Gravitas (how you behave) is still two-thirds of the EP equation and continues to center on projecting confidence, signaling decisiveness, and demonstrating a compelling vision of where you want to take a team or an organization. The new and the old survey data show that confidence, decisiveness, and vision are among the top six picks in both 2022 and 2012.

Communication (how you speak) is still almost a third of the EP equation and continues to center on superior speaking skills, commanding a room, and utilizing body language. The new, as well as the old data, show these three traits to be top picks in both 2012 and 2022. There are, of course, some important tweaks. In 2022, up-and-comers need to demonstrate their ability to command a Zoom as well as a room and are well advised to monitor their body language as well as proactively use it.

Appearance (how you look) is still a distant third, comprising a mere 5 percent of the EP equation. The data reveal that this bucket has changed a great deal over the last ten years, but despite large shifts, there is significant continuity. For example, in 2022 "polish" and "fit/vigorous" remain front and center of the top-picks list.

A final word on a trait that has dropped precipitously. Forcefulness, which used to be the number 3 pick in the communication bucket, has fallen to number 19. Nowadays, the idea that an accomplished, ambitious up-and-comer needs to come over as a tough guy, someone who bites bullets, shows teeth, and kicks tires, doesn't go over well. Those attributes are now seen as sexist and divisive.

Let's dig down into the three buckets of EP—gravitas, communication, and appearance—and explore how EP has stayed the same and how it has moved around and shifted.

8

As we have learned, EP rests on three pillars: how you act (gravitas), how you speak (communication), and how you look (appearance). Gravitas is the heavyweight, comprising two-thirds of the equation in 2012 and 2022. But while gravitas continues to dominate EP, its constituent parts have shifted over the last ten years in response to significant changes in the external environment.[116]

The comforting news is that the two top picks remain the same. As seen from the bar graphs below, confidence and decisiveness came in at number 1 and 2 in both 2012 and 2022. This is reassuring. Despite upheavals wrought by culture shifts, a global pandemic, and a European war, certain core leadership traits endure. Projecting confidence, exhibiting "grace under fire," and signaling that you can and will make tough decisions are qualities that were and are enormously valued.

More challenging are the shifts further down the gravitas top pick list.

One significant change over the last ten years has been the movement from EQ to inclusion. Ever since the 1995 publication of *Emotional Intelligence* by Daniel Goleman, EQ has been a desired trait in a leader.[117] Indeed, for at least a decade, corporative executives have been held to a high standard on the projection-of-empathy front. As a routine matter, they are expected to demonstrate that they are caring people who will go out

Gravitas, 2012 and 2022

Top Traits, 2012

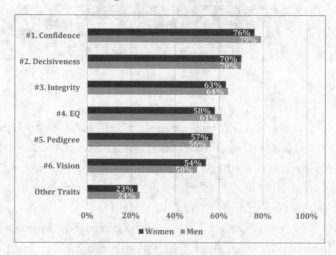

Top Traits, 2022

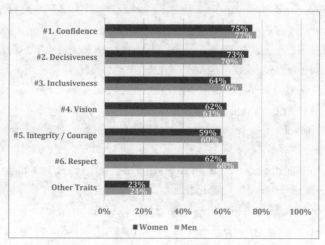

Figure 11. Changes in gravitas top traits between 2012 and 2022

of their way to ensure the well-being of coworkers and constituents. As we saw in chapter 2, BP executive director Bob Dudley got high marks for his EQ when he flew from London to visit the communities devastated by the torrent of crude oil spewing from the wreck of Deepwater Horizon—a BP rig destroyed by a massive underwater explosion. After an extensive tour of the damage, Dudley went on national TV to explain to the American people that he'd walked around Grand Isle and Grand Pass, Louisiana, and seen the massive oil slicks fouling beaches and poisoning marshes. As a result, he totally "got" the scope and scale of the devastation. He then turned directly to the camera, made a heartfelt apology, and pledged that BP would make good on claims for damages brought by individuals and businesses who had suffered losses. "The people of the Gulf will be made whole," he said in a voice freighted with solemnity and conviction.[118]

Dudley's behavior went a long way to restoring BP's reputation in the United States. It contrasted sharply with BP's CEO, Tony Hayward, who hunkered down in London headquarters, releasing statement after statement that downplayed the spill, calling its impact "very, very, modest."[119] A low moment was when he complained peevishly to the press that although he was sorry for people in the Gulf, "there's no one who wants this over more than I do. I'd like my life back."[120] This didn't go down well in the affected communities. Representative Charlie Melancon (D-LA) called for his ouster, and two months later, the BP board of directors did precisely that, showing Hayward the door and replacing him with Dudley, who became BP's new chief executive.

Back in 2010, Dudley's ability to project EQ was both celebrated and richly rewarded. Since then, the bar has risen substantially as an imperative to demonstrate EQ has morphed into a requirement to showcase inclusion—a much more complicated set of behaviors. Nowadays, in addition to displaying empathy and sensitivity, executives are expected to understand the value of inclusion and showcase how they are making a difference by proactively crossing lines of difference to lift up and advance those who have previously been excluded from executive ranks. A key driver on this front is research demonstrating that diversity at the top of the house unlocks innovation and new market growth. One data-rich study shows that when there is diversity at decision-making tables (the requirement is that decision makers should embody at least three forms of difference), companies are much more likely to improve market share and capture a new marketplace.[121]

Over the last several years, Jamie Dimon, the CEO of JPMorgan Chase, has done a splendid job with Advancing Black Pathways (which targets African-American talent), as has Cisco CEO Chuck Robbins with the Multiplier Effect (which targets female talent). These much-admired corporate leaders have added value to their companies and luster to their brands by becoming champions of inclusive leadership. There are a host of less well-known corporate gems. As we shall see, Roger W. Ferguson of TIAA was regarded as a model of inclusive behavior by the executives I interviewed in 2022. The courage and grit with which Ferguson successfully sponsored Thasunda Duckett to succeed him in the CEO spot at TIAA turned him into an instant role model for many up-and-coming leaders.

There have been other minor changes to the list. Vision and integrity remain on the gravitas top pick list, but their positions have changed slightly. Between 2012 and 2022, vision moved up from number 6 to number 4, while integrity moved down from number 3 to number 5. Both shifts are easy to understand. Given the shock waves coming out of the external environment, it makes sense that the "vision thing" has inched up the list. In troubled times business leaders will always seek out up-and-comers who can project an inspiring version of what lies ahead for their team and their company. Integrity has inched down the list, dropping to number 5, but again there's a simple explanation. This minor demotion is due to the ascent of inclusion rather than any loss of faith in the importance of truth-telling. As seen from the meteoric rise and fall of Elizabeth Holmes—featured as a blunder in chapter 9—leaders who build companies on a pack of lies do not survive. Sooner rather than later, they are exposed as fakes and phonies.

When assessing the significance of rank order within the top picks list, it's important to understand that in both 2012 and 2022, the six top picks were chosen from a list of twenty-five leadership traits. In a very real sense all six are prime choices.

The gravitas bucket also features a "dropout" and an "add-in." As can be seen in Figure 11, pedigree is no longer on the gravitas top pick list, having fallen from pick number 5 to pick number 15. In 2022 a high-achieving employee no longer needs to showcase a narrow-gauged pedigree to be considered "leadership material." This idea is considered out-of-date in an age where companies are increasingly committing to acquiring top talent from various backgrounds and identities. For example, to avoid developing an elitist culture, Bloomberg has little interest in hiring Ivy League graduates and proactively seeks out less-advantaged candidates from state schools. DraftKings, as part of a commitment to diversify the company's leadership pipeline, prioritizes recruits from HBCUs such as Howard and Spelman. Indeed, in 2023 there's almost a reverse chic in *not factoring in* old-school notions of pedigree.

While pedigree has been knocked off the top pick list, respect has been added. This trait was number 6 on the gravitas top pick list in 2022—up from number 19 ten years ago. Respect for "the other" has shot up the charts mainly because of the Black Lives Matter and #MeToo movements, which took off in 2014 and 2017 respectively, and dramatically reduced tolerance for harassment and discrimination at work. Until then, abusive and predatory behavior was taken for granted in corporate America, but starting with the ouster of Roger Ailes (Fox News) and Trevor Edwards (Nike), business titans began to be taken down. The data tell us that as late as 2019, a third (34 percent) of white-collar female employees experienced sexual harassment at work, and 7 percent experienced sexual assault. Among those harassed, gay women were more likely targets than straight women, and among those assaulted, Black women were more likely targets than white women.[122]

Senior executives can't get away with this anymore. Many Fortune 500 companies have committed to a zero-tolerance stance on harassment and assault, and as a result, sexual misconduct is now a career-ender. As we shall see later on in this chapter, being a sexual predator has become the number 1 gravitas blunder.

POSTER PEOPLE

Beyond my desire to map and measure changes in "most sought-after" gravitas traits between 2012 and 2022, I also had critical qualitative goals and leaned on my group of carefully selected executives to provide exemplars of gravitas-in-action. Whom do they admire most with regard to their prowess in projecting confidence, decisiveness, and respect for others? Who is their go-to Poster Person for each of the six top picks? In my interviews, I pressed each executive for concrete, detailed reasons why they'd singled out a particular leader, and as a result, I was able to create word portraits of most admired models. Here they are:

CONFIDENCE
Virginia Rometty was voted the most admired Poster Person in confidence and "grace under fire" buckets. Two-thirds of the

seventy-three executives I interviewed singled her out as their number 1 pick.

When Rometty became CEO and executive chairman of IBM in 2012, she faced immense challenges. The company had become dated and clunky and was suffering a steep decline in demand for its legacy products—both software and hardware. To unlock new growth, it desperately needed to transition to next-gen technology, particularly AI and cloud computing.

This was a herculean task. When Rometty took the helm, IBM was a hundred-year-old behemoth with close to half a million employees. Many people had vested interests in keeping the company precisely the way it was. But Rometty, a systems engineer who'd risen through the ranks to lead IBM's global services division, understood the seriousness of her company's problems and was intent on driving a radical agenda. She wanted to meet change head-on rather than be left behind.

There were two parts to her strategy. First, to speed up IBM's transformation, she sold off IBM's legacy businesses while simultaneously going on a buying spree, making a great many acquisitions and forming new partnerships. Her joint venture with A.P. Moller–Maersk is a case in point. A lead player in blockchain innovation, Maersk offered access to a global trade digitization platform that gave IBM the capability of better tracking products within global supply chains.

Second, to support her transformational agenda, she went on the road to publicize IBM's new journey. Rometty has a knack for cutting through jargon and using simple language to inspire audiences with her passion for next-gen technology. At the National Governors Association meeting in 2018, she talked up IBM's partnership with Maersk with such conviction that she got a standing ovation.[123]

"Think cargo," she instructed her audience. "You know those

containers we all see. Well, the paperwork often costs more than what's inside them. With Blockchain, you're able to get rid of all that. Then you go to the rail, trucking, and everything along the way. Blockchain is a great efficiency play."[124]

Despite her credibility and charisma, Rometty ran into intense headwinds. Radical pruning combined with a spending spree led to twenty-two consecutive quarters of revenue decline and slumping share prices (stocks fell from a high of $215 to a low of $116). The low point came in winter of 2017 when Warren Buffett, IBM's biggest shareholder, dumped his stock. He'd lost faith in Rometty's leadership and didn't believe she had what it takes to turn this ocean liner around.

This was the moment when Rometty showed her mettle. She didn't retreat. Instead, she doubled down on radical change. How did she stay the course?

First, she dug deep into the resilience and grit she had developed as a child and young woman. Rometty's early years weren't easy. Her mother, a spunky single mom, held down two jobs and leaned on food stamps to support four children, and put herself through community college. "My mother taught me a lot about how to react to challenging circumstances," Rometty said in an interview.[125]

But Rometty didn't rely solely on inner resources; she made other strategic plays: She deepened her commitment to IBM Watson AI-enhanced technology, rolling it out over several new growth platforms; she diversified IBM's talent pipeline with recruitment and training programs that targeted high school graduates; and she redoubled her efforts to sell IBM as successful "incumbent disruptor" on the world stage, speaking at the World Economic Forum at Davos, the Aspen Ideas Festival, the Council on Foreign Relations, and a host of other blue-chip conferences. She made significant progress in turning IBM's image around. The company's stakeholders increasingly saw IBM as cutting-edge rather than clunky.

Several executives I interviewed in 2022 took pains to share their admiration for Rometty's talent initiatives. In the words of a senior executive at Citi, "Rometty's commitment to 'new collar workers' has paid off big-time." P-tech (an IBM initiative that provides high school graduates with the academic and technical skills they need to hold down a STEM job) has both alleviated skill shortages at the company and burnished IBM's reputation as a standout player in diversity and inclusion.

P-tech was an authentic play for Rometty. For years she'd turbocharged the progression of women at IBM so that developing programs that trained less privileged youngsters for well-paid jobs in the tech sector was squarely in her wheelhouse.

In December 2019, the Aspen Institute hosted its 36th Annual Awards Dinner at the Plaza Hotel in New York. I was in the audience. Virginia Rometty was recognized with the Henry Crown Leadership Award for her "courage and grace" in transforming a 108-year-old company and for her "deep humanity" in opening up tech literacy so that everyone can feel they have a great future ahead of them and not just the privileged few. What a tribute![126]

DECISIVENESS

In the decisiveness bucket, Jeff Bezos was voted the most admired Poster Person by nearly half of the executives I interviewed. Many saw his brilliance on the decision-making front as foundational to his staggering success founding and growing Amazon, a company that employs 1.6 million people and ranks number 2 in the world in terms of revenue.

Bezos has been making what he calls "high-quality, high-velocity" decisions ever since 1994, when he made the risky choice to quit his job at investment firm D. E. Shaw and start selling books on the Internet.[127] His gamble paid off for two reasons: his obsession with customer satisfaction and his prioritization of decision-making. In the words of one of my interviewees, a senior executive at Spotify who used to work at Amazon, "for Bezos, every decision was centered on giving customers something that enhanced their lives, either because it was cheaper or a whole lot easier to obtain. At meetings, he'd pull up an empty chair to the table and instruct his team to imagine a consumer sitting in that chair and focus their minds on what might surprise and delight this person."

Executing a vision, and doing it at scale, is, of course, a big lift. How do you select products and services that customers might want or need? How do you build and leverage distribution centers worldwide that allow quick shipment of products? These are just two of a long list of enormous challenges.

In Bezos's view, great execution rests on excellent decision-making, and from the get-go he devoted a ton of time and energy perfecting his ability to make fast, intelligent decisions under pressure. He passed along this wisdom to colleagues and eventually made exceptional decision-making skills a core competency and a "must-have" in the Amazon leadership culture.[128]

During the twenty-five years he ran the company (in 2021, he handed over operational responsibility to Andy Jassy and stepped into the chairman role), Bezos talked noisily about his favorite decision-making principles:

First, a leader needs to assess decisions before making them to determine whether they are easily reversible. Some decisions are one-way doors: They cannot be undone and therefore require a great deal of deliberation and consideration. But other decisions are two-way doors and can be undone without disastrous consequences. These can be made quickly and without complete information.

Second, a leader must take on board what complete information looks like. Two-way-door decisions—which comprise three out of every four decisions executives make—should be made with around 70 percent of the information you wish you had. If an executive waits for 90 percent, he or she will miss out on most opportunities. According to Bezos, when a leader can course-correct, being wrong is less costly than being slow. Tardiness is expensive in today's world.[129]

INCLUSIVENESS

Roger W. Ferguson Jr. was the number 1 pick in the inclusiveness bucket, garnering a third of the votes in my 2022 executive interviews.

Ferguson led TIAA for twelve years (2008–21) and was regarded as a highly successful president and CEO. During his tenure, he added almost a million new clients and doubled the company's assets.[130] However, as pointed out by one of my interviewees (a senior woman at Morgan Stanley), "his pivotal accomplishment, one that will define his legacy, was what he did when he exited the company."

Just before he stepped down in the spring of 2021, Ferguson proudly announced that Thasunda Brown Duckett would succeed him. With that very intentional move, Ferguson ensured two firsts: TIAA would have its first woman CEO, and, for the first time, a Fortune 100 company would appoint two Black CEOs in a row, replacing a Black man with a Black woman.[131]

These wins are extremely difficult to pull off. As I found in a research study I completed in the winter of 2021–22, Black leaders rarely sponsor up-and-coming Black talent—more than a third say that they never support a junior talent who looks like them. It's just way too risky. In an interview, a Black African woman who is a senior executive at a fashion house in New York described her predicament. "I was just a year into my position when a young

Black woman asked me to sponsor her. I liked this person, she's a hard worker and a high performer, and I wanted to help her out. But I worried I did not have enough clout at the company to get her where she wanted to go. I also worried that I would be accused of favoritism and colleagues would whisper that I was only sponsoring this young talent because she was a Black sister. In the end, I said no. I did it with a heavy heart."[132]

If Black up-and-comers can't rely on Black executives for sponsorship, they certainly can't rely on white executives. In *The Sponsor Effect*, I show that Caucasian leaders focus almost exclusively on sponsoring younger versions of themselves.[133] The vast majority share no social networks with Black colleagues and choose to stay within their comfort zone.

Ferguson was determined to do things differently. He was convinced that appointing another Black leader—this time a Black female leader—would be immensely important to TIAA, both practically and symbolically. The company's mission is to help those who teach, heal, and serve in the government sector to build financial security so they can retire with dignity. But who are the teachers and healers of this world? They are disproportionately diverse, and indeed, a significant minority of TIAA's clients are people of color. During his twelve-year tenure, Ferguson had done much to retain and progress Black talent so the company could mirror its marketplace. By 2021 fully a third of TIAA's executives were African-American.[134]

To preserve this legacy, Ferguson put a great deal of thought into choosing a successor. For sure he wanted someone with a stellar track record in the financial world, but he also wanted someone who modeled inclusion and shared his passionate commitment to leveling the playing field for people of color. He found such a person in Thasunda Brown Duckett. In 2021, she was an up-and-comer with an extraordinary reputation. As head of

Chase Consumer Banking at JPMorgan Chase, she'd overseen more than $600 billion in deposits, spearheaded a major expansion of digital services, and kick-started Advancing Black Pathways. This much admired JPMorgan program focuses on building Black wealth and reaching into underserved communities.[135]

Despite Duckett's knock-your-socks-off qualifications, Ferguson found she wasn't a shoo-in for the top slot at TIAA. There were naysayers on the board who felt that the company had "done that, gone there" on the racial equity front and wanted to move on. But Ferguson lobbied long and hard for his candidate and eventually won them over.

Before leaving the inclusiveness bucket, I want to flag the work of Scott Rothkopf, the chief curator of the Whitney Museum of American Art, who has created imaginatively inclusive exhibitions at one of the most high-brow of New York's top-tier galleries.

In a February 2023 interview, Rothkopf told me that it all started with the design of the Whitney's new building. "Unlike our previous gallery on Madison Ave which you accessed by crossing a moat, our new home sits on a modest side street and has huge glass doors and windows which signal openness and transparency."

But the Whitney's expansive energy goes much deeper than the design of its building. Rothkopf has also shaken up how New Yorkers define American Art. In the winter of 2022–23 he oversaw an exhibition of art and artifacts that explored the tragic impact of Hurricane Maria on Puerto Rico and its people. Fierce and intensely personal (the curator Marcela Guerrero was encouraged to incorporate the experience of her own family), this exhibition has drawn enormous crowds and become a magnet for first- and second-generation Puerto Ricans, some of whom had never gone to an art exhibition before. In Rothkopf's opinion, "in a city that has the largest Puerto Rican community outside of Puerto Rico

(1.8 million and counting), it's a crying shame that this is the first major exhibition focused on Puerto Rican art in half a century."

VISION

Marc Benioff was voted the most admired Poster Person in the vision bucket. He was singled out by almost half of the executives I interviewed. From day one, he had lofty expectations for Salesforce. He promised that the company would create "customer magic" by offering a range of powerful software apps that would greatly improve the experience of users. He also promised that his company would be a force for social justice and promote stakeholder capitalism.

Benioff came by his vision for Salesforce after a highly successful decade-long career at Oracle left him burned-out. At the suggestion of his then-mentor, Oracle cofounder Larry Ellison, Benioff took a yearlong sabbatical leave, during which time he meditated in Hawaii and studied with spiritual masters in India. He came back from those trips with a clear vision of how to build a more benevolent business model.[136]

At the heart of his vision was the centrality of trust. He believed that trust was a company's most important asset, much more important than short-term profitability.

How to build that trust? As a first step, Benioff collaborated with his employees to improve the state of the world. In the early days of the company, he launched what he called the 1-1-1 pledge. This committed Salesforce to giving 1 percent of its equity, 1 percent of its product, and 1 percent of employees' time back to the local community. Benioff followed through and then some: Over the last twenty years, his company has given more than $500 million to philanthropic causes in the Bay Area.[137] After seeking employee input, Salesforce has focused on building affordable housing and improving preschool education.

More recently, in 2020, in response to the murder of George Floyd and many other African-Americans, Salesforce established a Racial Equality and Justice Task Force to drive systemic change. Among other measures, Benioff committed to spending $200 million on businesses owned by people of color and pledged to double the number of Black employees at the vice president level and above at Salesforce over the next few years.

A towering six-foot-five person who often sports a Hawaiian shirt, Benioff stands out as a rare "soulful" leader in the grasping, geek culture of Silicon Valley. His values have proven to be good for business. Salesforce has grown into a $26 billion powerhouse and is consistently ranked as one of the ten Best Places to Work by *Fortune* magazine. In addition, the company boasts a 91 percent employee retention rate, a remarkable achievement for tech, a sector that struggles with labor shortages and high attrition rates.[138] Moreover, his vision has made him a high-profile influencer on the world stage. Everyone listens when Benioff gives a speech at Davos, and his annual Dreamforce conference attracts heavyweights from business and politics. All this visibility increases the status and standing of the company he leads.

INTEGRITY/COURAGE

Singled out by two-thirds of the executives I interviewed, a whopping number, Liz Cheney was the most admired Poster Person in the integrity/courage bucket.

Cheney caught national and international attention when she led the charge to hold President Donald Trump accountable for impeding a peaceful transition of power after he lost the 2020 election. The tumultuous events of December 2020 and January 2021 are etched in all our minds: Trump's refusal to concede (to this day, he maintains the election was stolen), his sixty lawsuits (none of which were deemed to have merit), his illegal attempts to put forward "fake" slates of electors, and the outsize role he played in instigating the January 6, 2021, insurrection by sitting on his hands while the U.S. Capitol was trashed are images that will stay with us forever.

If Donald Trump's egregious acts are front and center in our minds, so are Liz Cheney's courage and integrity. This ultraconservative three-term Republican congressperson from Wyoming became a national hero when she stood up to Trump, first voting to impeach him, then, as vice chair of the congressional committee that was set up to investigate the January 6 insurrection, leading the charge to hold him responsible.

Described by a news commentator as the "compelling central character in the ensuing hearings," Cheney displayed steely resolve and fearlessness in her fight to preserve the Constitution.[139] The eight televised committee hearings, which ran in June and July 2022, attracted an estimated 20 million viewers and shifted opinion in the center of the political spectrum (independents and traditional Republicans). Cheney's shrewd strategy (she leaned on Trump's allies and associates to make the case against him), prosecutorial reach (she convinced Trump's family to testify), and insistence on high production value made these hearings enormously substantive as well as riveting. An executive I interviewed in July 2022 (a Bloomberg executive who sits in São Paulo) told me she had become a "fangirl" of Cheney. "I see her as brave and brilliant and steeped in principle. She's a living, walking example of how a leader should behave."

Cheney's bravery and brilliance cost her dearly.[140] Shunned by many fellow Republicans who've elected to kiss the ring of the former president, she was ousted from the conference chairmanship and defeated in a primary. At the end of 2022, Liz Cheney stepped down from Congress, her political career over, at least in the short term.[141]

Yet Cheney is set to inspire young leaders for years to come.

"History is watching," she wrote in the *Washington Post*. "Our children are watching. We must be brave enough to defend the basic principles that underpin and protect our freedom and democratic process. No matter the short-term political consequences. I am committed to doing that."[142]

My Bloomberg interviewee told me that she is thrilled that Cheney won the 2022 "Profile in Courage Award." So am I.

RESPECT

In the respect bucket, Satya Nadella, CEO of Microsoft, was voted the most admired Poster Person by almost half the executives interviewed. One interviewee, a vice president at software firm Splunk, said she loved that Nadella described himself a "mere-mortal CEO." In her words, "he's such a breath of fresh air after his ego-flaunting predecessors Bill Gates and Steve Ballmer."

When Nadella became CEO in 2014 he was concerned that Microsoft had drifted away from its roots and recommitted to the company's original mission to democratize technology and enshrine empathy as a core corporate value. A few months into his tenure, he asked top executives to read *Nonviolent Communication*, by Marshall B. Rosenberg. This book instructs leaders on motivating their teams with encouragement rather than criticism.[143]

Since then, Nadella has attempted to ensure that respect and empathy guide how Microsoft treats employees and conceptualizes new products. "If innovation is about meeting unmet, unarticulated needs," he reasons, "how can you get in touch with those needs? To extrapolate requires empathy. At Microsoft, we've put 'respect' into our parlance because that's where empathy and innovation start."[144]

Nadella and his wife, Anupama, are the parents of a child with cerebral palsy. Seeing the world through his son's eyes has taught Nadella a lot about empathy and the power of technology to improve lives. He's become an enthusiastic proponent of the ways AI can help people with physical challenges and has invested heavily in the development of AI technology that is safe, ethical, and nondiscriminatory. I have been a small part of this effort. In early 2018, I was pulled in as an expert to advise Microsoft on how to infuse gender smarts into AI technology. Microsoft is the front-runner in taking bias out of facial recognition technology.[145]

Another first, under Nadella's leadership, Microsoft has become much more respectful of competitors and is open to working with other lead tech companies to harness the power of technology in doing good. The company's recent partnership with OpenAI is a case in point. Nadella also holds himself accountable for ensuring that all voices are heard within the organization. "We have some amazing women on the team," he said in a recent interview, "but are we making sure we listen to them?" To model how to cross the divides of gender, race, and seniority and access differentiated skill sets and experiences, he's started a practice of encouraging junior engineers in the Microsoft talent pipeline to phone in and talk about their innovations. He is even handing out his cell phone number.

All of this is working. Microsoft stock valuation has risen tenfold on Nadella's watch.[146]

BLUNDERS

SEXUAL PREDATOR

Ten years ago, sexual impropriety was singled out as a serious blunder on the gravitas front, but in the wake of #MeToo, the stakes have risen considerably. My data show that in 2022 sexual misconduct was the number 1 gravitas blunder. Simply put, a credible accusation of sexual harassment or assault cuts you off at the knees. Half of the executives I interviewed singled out the downfall and

Gravitas Blunders 2012
From focus groups and interviews

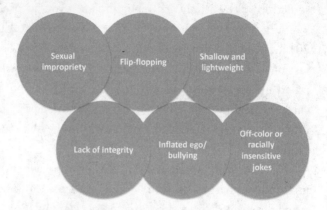

Gravitas Blunders 2022
From focus groups and interviews

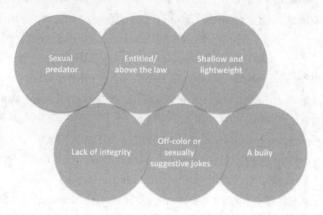

Figure 12. Changes in gravitas blunders between 2012 and 2022

punishment of McDonald's CEO Steve Easterbrook as their go-to cautionary tale. One of my interviewees (a senior executive at Ogilvy) told me, "Steve's ouster was one thing; the 'clawback' was something else entirely. It's enough to keep you up at night."

When Steve Easterbrook became McDonald's CEO in March 2015, the global fast-food chain was in a rut—the company had just posted its worst financial performance in years. Easterbrook rolled up his sleeves and put in place a turnaround strategy focused on technological innovation and third-party delivery platforms. Two years later, McDonald's was in the black and on a new growth path.

None of this success saved Easterbrook when two sexual misconduct charges hit him.[147] The first time around he was accused of sexting with a subordinate—a clear violation of company policy—and the McDonald's board decided to handle things quietly and by the book. They asked Easterbrook to apologize and acknowledge his mistake. They then showed him the door. He walked away with a golden parachute worth $40 million.[148]

Eight months later, another accusation surfaced: a McDonald's employee stepped forward with the allegation that Easterbrook had engaged in a sexual relationship with a subordinate while he was running the company. This triggered an investigation and a high-profile lawsuit in which McDonald's accused Easterbrook of concealing evidence about three sexual relationships he'd had with junior colleagues in his line of command. Evidence included sexually explicit photos and videos. Things grew much uglier after this evidence was found. McDonald's accused Easterbrook of lying in the first investigation and claimed the right to recoup the severance package they had paid.

The case was settled, and in 2020 Easterbrook was forced to make McDonald's whole—paying back $105 million in cash, stock, and penalties, one of the largest clawbacks in history.[149]

ENTITLED/ABOVE THE LAW

The other gravitas blunder highlighted in my 2022 interviews was projecting arrogance and entitlement. A quarter of the executives I talked to singled out Boris Johnson (British prime minister, 2019–22) as an example of a leader who was thrown out of office for ignoring rules and regulations that he believed applied to ordinary citizens but not exalted individuals such as himself.[150] It didn't help that Johnson, an upper-class chap who had attended Eton College and Oxford University, chose to flaunt the law (laws he had put in place!) by throwing parties during a particularly punishing phase of the Covid-19 pandemic.

Johnson, who himself suffered a severe case of coronavirus in the early days of the pandemic, enacted draconian rules and regulations as British hospital admissions and death rates rose precipitously in 2020 and 2021. For anyone who wasn't an essential worker, it became a criminal offense to leave your home for anything except food shopping, crucial medical appointments, or outside exercise, which could last no longer than one hour. Indoor social gatherings were banned, while outdoor get-togethers were limited to groups of six. Many people, including members of my UK-based family, experienced despair as they were prevented from visiting sick and dying loved ones. My sister Enid, who lives in North Wales, was distraught that she wasn't allowed to sit by the bedside of a close friend struggling with stage 4 cancer. "Grainy Zoom footage just didn't do it," she told me. "The poor dab was far gone and just wanted to hold my hand. I felt sick to my soul that I was barred from doing this small thing for her. She died on her own."

Meanwhile, Boris Johnson was partying. Months later, it came to light that on November 13, 2020, Johnson hosted a BYOB party for senior staffers in his backyard at 10 Downing Street. Alcohol consumption was excessive, and there was at least some vandalism. A subsequent investigation of what is now called

"Party Gate" revealed that Johnson hosted at least seventeen raucous parties during the pandemic.[151]

All of this was too much for the British public. Even Tory stalwarts seethed with righteous anger, feeling that Johnson had taken his constituents for fools. Boris was pushed out.

KEY TAKEAWAYS

A final piece of wisdom on the gravitas front. What was the most practical advice from my 2022 executive interviews?

I've interviewed Roz Hudnell, a former VP at Intel, president of the Intel Foundation, several times over the last ten years, and she's contributed much to my work on both Executive Presence 1.0 and Executive Presence 2.0. Hudnell is an exemplar of gravitas in action and has compelling pieces of guidance for up-and-comers.

In an interview, Karen Lynch, president and CEO of CVS Health, added weight and color to Roz Hudnell's guidance.

Lead with Your Authentic Strengths

- Pick two traits from the top picks list that reflect what you're best at and polish THOSE up—no one—not Bezos, Benioff, not Cheney—aces all six.
- Ask for an executive coach—to work on your strengths, not your skill gaps. It's a competitive, pointy world out there, and you need to be golden—a bright shiny star—in your chosen domains.
- Don't self-destruct by going anywhere near serious blunders. This isn't rocket science. Everyone knows that hitting on a junior colleague or lying through your teeth are career-enders. So, use common sense.

These three pointers will ratchet up and secure your gravitas, giving you a shot at the C-suite.

Figure 13. Lead with your authentic strengths

"I totally support Roz's 'leading with your strengths' piece of advice. Mine are empathy/inclusion (which for me are inextricably linked) and vision. For me, learning how to wear these attributes on my sleeve has been key to my success in my chosen field."

Lynch has become a great storyteller and leans on her own formative experiences—her mom committing suicide when she was twelve years old, her aunt-guardian dying from cancer when she was twenty-two years old—to fire up her team. She's become a master at making the connection between her early struggles dealing with death and dying and her fierce commitment to creating compassionate, consumer-focused solutions in the healthcare sector. "These people that rely on us when their health is threatened are mothers, daughters, sons, and fathers just like us, so let's make sure that we're treating them that way." During the Covid-19 pandemic, Lynch could often be found inside the doors of a CVS outlet to personally welcome a long line of masked, frightened people seeking care and precious vaccinations.[152]

9

COMMUNICATION 2.0

As we learned in chapter 3, communication encompasses much more than formal presentation skills. Every verbal or written exchange, every movement or gesture in the actual or virtual world, presents an opportunity to create and nurture a standout brand. Whether it's a quick email to your boss, your comportment and body language at a company retreat, or your most recent post on Instagram, you're conveying who you are and what authority you are due. The breadth and depth of your communication skills are enormously important in winning you the attention and mindshare of stakeholders in your professional life.

In recent years, we've all had to lift our game on the virtual front. This was made clear to me in the summer of 2021 when I attempted to apply for membership at Soho House. I knew my track record as a book author made me a plausible candidate, and I was eager to become part of this sought-after creative community. But how to get in? The application process flummoxed me. First, it was entirely online—there was no interviewing process, either in person or via Zoom. Second, there were strict guidelines regarding what was and was not wanted—no need for a résumé or letters of recommendation (those were passé). You were asked to respond to a couple of questions about your "fit" with the club's mission (max fifty words), but the main things Soho House wanted were my tweets and Instagram posts. Duh! The assumption of the young, hip, media-savvy admissions committee at Soho House is that if you want to find out what a person is doing in the world, all you need to do is look at that person's social media. In their opinion, this is the quickest and most revealing way of finding out how substantial and influential a candidate for admission is.

Well, was I stumped. I did indeed tweet—very occasionally—but I didn't even have an Instagram account. Being a woman of a certain age, I hadn't made these communication platforms a top priority. That clearly needed to change. So in the fall of 2021, I set to work to remedy the matter, and under the tutelage of my twenty-five-year-old daughter, I ramped up my activity on Twitter and got busy on Instagram. Three months later, I was ready to apply. I got in.

During the pandemic, when most white-collar professionals were constrained to work remotely from home, there was a veritable explosion in virtual tools and platforms. Taking advantage of these new technologies is now a must for both up-and-coming and seasoned leaders. This adaptation is easy for twenty- and thirty-year-olds (who are digital natives) and difficult for fifty- and sixty-year-olds, but as I discovered when I wrestled with my application to Soho House, even the most tech-phobic among us can rustle up the new skill sets when we're supermotivated.

Despite the burgeoning importance of virtual presence, the comforting news on the communication front is that three of the six core competencies central to the EP equation ten years ago remain the same. Sure, they've morphed at the edges as these competencies now need to show up online as well as in person, but in 2012 and 2022, "Superior Speaking Skills" came in as the number 1 pick, "Commands a Room" at number 2, "Reads an Audience/Market" at number 4, and "Masters Body Language" at number 6. This is a remarkable degree of continuity.

Within this stable frame, there have been two significant

Communication, 2012 and 2022
Top Traits, 2012

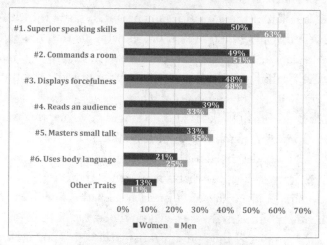

Top Traits, 2022

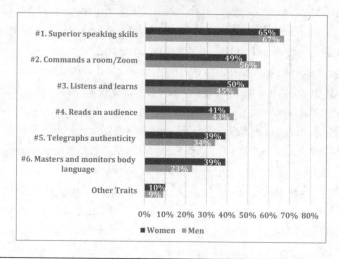

Figure 14. Changes in communication top traits between 2012 and 2022

shifts in what communication traits are most valued. Between 2012 and 2022, "Displays Forcefulness" dropped off the top pick list, falling from pick number 3 to pick number 13. In a world where inclusivity and respect for others are much admired (see the discussion of these qualities in chapter 8), there is little room for overt displays of aggression or "showing teeth." This is good news for female executives, who, as we saw in chapter 3, often feel they are "walking a tightrope" as they attempt to be forceful and assertive without being labeled a bitch.

"Masters Small Talk" is also no longer in vogue; this trait has fallen from pick number 5 to pick number 11. This "small-bore skill," as it was described to me in one of my executive interviews, has been crowded out by what is now seen as more urgent communication imperatives such as "Listens and Learns" and "Telegraphs Authenticity." These traits are newly on the six top picks list at number 3 and number 5. Their prominence reflects a new appreciation of the value of difference and a move toward more inclusive leadership cultures. As we saw in chapter 8, in 2022, much-admired CEOs such as Virginia Rometty and Roger W. Ferguson see diversity and inclusion as central to the competitive strength of their enterprises as well as the right thing to do from an ethical vantage point. Listening to and learning from others and telegraphing authenticity are critical pieces of the inclusion journey.

Body language (a version of which was the number 6 pick in both 2012 and 2022) exhibits its own distinctive dynamic and, in the last few years, has morphed into a double-edged sword. Back in 2012, up-and-comers were expected to use body language to lift their communication game. It was seen as an extra dimension, something of a superpower. As we saw from the research presented in chapter 3, good posture can be powerful. Standing tall with feet planted solidly, chest out, and shoulders back can trigger a "rush of confidence" that is measurable and lasts all day.

Communication 2.0

In recent years, celebrity conductor Gustavo Dudamel has turned body language into an art form. His ability to signal open-heartedness, convey gratitude, and foster collaboration with gestures and movement has won hearts and minds and inspired leaders in business and politics as well as in the music world.[153] In 2023, influential people across sectors and disciplines understand that mastery of body language is enormously additive to their ability to reach and hold audiences.

But if body language can significantly enhance your personal brand, it can also threaten it. This is particularly true since the #MeToo movement changed our culture.

President Joe Biden is a case in point. In the spring of 2020, when his bid for the presidency was heating up and he was under intense scrutiny, eight women came forward to accuse him of inappropriate touching. One talked about Biden's off-putting habit of patting her head. Another complained about the frequency of his squeezes and hugs—how they made her feel uncomfortable. Yet another pointed to his distressing tendency to comment on the physical appearance of young girls he met on the campaign trail. Seven of those eight women went out of their way to say that Biden's behavior, while problematic, did not amount to sexual harassment or assault. The one exception was Tara Reade, a former Biden staffer, who leveled the charge that back in 1993 Biden had seriously hit on her. This charge was eventually discredited.[154]

There's a fine line between inappropriate touching and sexual harassment, and if Joe Biden fell on one side of it, Al Franken fell on the other. In late 2017, a photo of the senator fondling and pretend-kissing a sleeping colleague on a plane returning from a performance gig surfaced and went viral. Although this photo was eleven years old, the fallout was brutal. Leeann Tweeden (the colleague in question) rather belatedly accused Franken of sexual harassment, and Sean Hannity (one of the loudest voices on Fox

News) took up her cause, calling for Franken's ouster from the Senate. Within days, Franken was being hounded by senators on both sides of the aisle. His defense, that he was not hitting on Tweeden, merely hamming it up for the cameras (at the time he made his living as a comedian), went over like a lead balloon. In the fevered atmosphere of December 2017, when many influential people were weaponizing the nascent #MeToo movement, Franken was toast. A few days after that photo ricocheted around the world, he resigned from the Senate. His political career was over.[155]

The bottom line here is that post-#MeToo, both seasoned and up-and-coming leaders need to keep their hands to themselves. It's a slippery slope and encroaching on a colleague's personal space is not a smart thing to do even if you have nothing salacious in mind. Experts in the field tell us that colleagues and coworkers should keep their distance, recommending at least eighteen inches.

A word on communication blunders. As we shall see toward the end of this chapter, the list of significant mistakes—ones that tarnish your brand or get you demoted—changed markedly between 2012 and 2022. Ten years ago, the blunders list was dominated by what might be called "misdemeanors": talking in a shrill voice or constantly checking your devices. In 2023, these transgressions will get in your way and undermine your brand but won't cost you your job. The communication blunders list features much more serious offenses. Coming over as fake and phony or groping a coworker or an underage girl are the current career-enders.

POSTER PEOPLE

As with gravitas, a central goal of my 2022 interviews was to uncover exemplars of communication-in-action. What traits do executives admire most? It's time to turn to their top picks.

Communication 2.0

SUPERIOR SPEAKING SKILLS

Although he's been dead for more than a decade, Steve Jobs was voted the number 1 Poster Person in the speaking skills category by more than half of the leaders I interviewed. Many saw his mastery of communication as the not-so-secret sauce that allowed him to inspire his engineers and stir the souls of millions of new technology consumers. Jobs convinced tech nerds and technophobes alike that his computing devices would delight their senses and turbocharge what they could accomplish on any given day.

One leader I interviewed, a senior executive at Splunk who'd worked with Jobs, told me that his former boss was "a perfectionist who devoted a ton of time to figuring out how to best communicate his passionate belief in the machines he made." Whether holding a face-to-face meeting with his design team, presenting via video to Wall Street's money managers, or staging a global launch of a new product on the Apple campus, Jobs deployed the following techniques and tactics:

- A direct style of speaking which was clear, crisp, and concise
- A singular emphasis on eye contact—whether appearing in person or on camera, Jobs always looked individuals in his audience directly in the eye
- A focus on one big, bold breakthrough idea
- The use of stories to make "the new thing" real. Rather than snow you with big data or fancy graphics, he'd talk about a grad student in Chad or a retiree in Cheltenham tapping into scholarly research or gardening tips on their iPads
- A blank backdrop that used primary colors but

otherwise didn't draw attention away from what he
was saying

- A pared-back minimalist outfit that signaled edgy
elegance but didn't distract
- And most importantly, no props. Jobs avoided
lecterns, notes, flip charts, and PowerPoints packed
with data. He called them security blankets and
thought they got in the way. His advice to others:
"know your stuff cold and then just wing it."

These seven elements account for Steve Jobs's enormous success
as a communicator and explains why in 2023 he's still regarded
as the gold standard. But we should always remember that Jobs's
"gift of the gab" wasn't some kind of God-given gift or talent. As
my Splunk interviewee pointed out, though he appeared relaxed
and conversational, Jobs's communication prowess, like everything
else he did, was highly intentional and required a great deal of
hard work. He considered every public presentation a performance
and would spend hours, even days, preparing.[156] In short, he came
across with a simplicity that belied painstaking preparation.

Steve Jobs's belief that you cannot be convincing and utterly
compelling without intense preparation reminds me of a life lesson the celebrated economist John Kenneth Galbraith taught me
when I was his advisee at Harvard in the late 1970s. "Remember,
my dear," he said, wagging his finger at me, "becoming a good
writer is all about elbow grease and midnight oil. My books are
bestsellers because I put every chapter through endless drafts. The
first six drafts are about getting new ideas down on paper, building
a rigorous case and constructing the arc of an argument. The second
six are all about connecting to the real world. Stuffing each chapter
with just the right amount of interview material to bring my whole
argument to life. Then in the thirteenth draft, I let it rip. Hav-

ing nailed the substance, I allow myself the luxury of introducing notes of lightness and spontaneity: some personal stories, a joke or two. Whatever it takes to convince the reader that I just tossed this book off—that I'm a natural born genius. Well, I'm here to tell you I'm not. I'm just disciplined and passionately committed to writing books that are read by hundreds of thousands of people."

Steve Jobs took a similar approach. "It takes much hard work to make something simple," he said in an interview with Walter Isaacson.[157]

A word about the origins of Steve Jobs's style. Jobs was devoted to Zen Buddhism and Japanese aesthetics and these passions show up in virtually everything he did. They account for the minimalist look of Apple computers and Jobs's stark, sparse personal style. The lack of a disk drive or an on/off button on a Mac computer reflects the Zen concept of *ma*, a not-fully-translatable term that refers to how *what isn't there* shapes and conditions *what is there*. Ma also shows up in Jobs's clothing choices. His commitment to wearing Issey Miyake black mock-turtlenecks makes a statement *and* takes a distraction away. Jobs's underlying beliefs were foundational to his unusually coherent band.

COMMANDS A ROOM (VIRTUAL OR PHYSICAL)

Cynthia "Cynt" Marshall was singled out as the most admired Poster Person in the "commands a room" bucket, capturing the votes of a third of the executives I interviewed. Her fans were primarily women.

In one of my 2022 interviews, a senior vice president at Blizzard Entertainment talked about how Marshall had caught her eye when she was appointed CEO of the Dallas Mavericks. "Marshall was the first Black woman to lead an NBA team, so this was a bold move by Mark Cuban [the Mavericks owner]. But he had his reasons: the franchise was in trouble, and Cuban was prepared to go out on a limb for someone like Marshall, who both embodies change and had tremendous communication chops."

The Mavericks were indeed facing serious challenges. *Sports Illustrated* had just published an article exposing "a corrosive workplace culture" within the franchise, with multiple allegations of sexual harassment and assault.[158] Who better than Marshall to stage a turnaround? She'd spent many years heading up the D&I function at AT&T and had a reputation as a stellar communicator who knew how to build and embed a culture of respect and inclusion.

Marshall took command as CEO of the Dallas Mavericks in February 2018. She didn't waste any time. On day one, she signaled the urgency of her mission by holding a press conference, livestreamed to internal stakeholders, in which she made a heartfelt apology to all the female employees who'd experienced sexual harassment over the previous twenty years. She made a big point of thanking them for their courage in coming forward to tell their stories, share their pain, and seek accountability. Locking eyes with the employees, players, and journalists in the room, she expressed deep gratitude for their assist in helping "make us better," and also promised to transform the culture. Parts of Marshall's press conference made the evening news and were extremely well received.

After putting herself on the line, Marshall followed up with substantive action. This happened almost immediately. Within a month, she'd launched a hundred-day plan, the first step of which was seeking guidance from employees and other stakeholders. Over the next several weeks, Marshall held one-on-one conversations with everyone in the organization: secretaries, janitors, the C-suite, and the players. She set up a 24/7 hotline for employees to report concerns about misconduct, instituted mandatory unconscious-bias trainings, and, most importantly, set up a powerful external advisory committee with authority to "hold feet to the fire."[159] Results came quickly. Within a year, women comprised half of the executive leadership team at the Mavericks franchise, and people of color made up 47 percent. Overnight the organization became a much more diverse and inclusive place, which "risk-proofed" it against new outbreaks of predatory or abusive behavior. Recent research shows that organizations with significant diversity at the top of the house have much lower rates of sexual misconduct than is the norm.[160]

LISTENS AND LEARNS

Jørgen Vig Knudstorp came in as the most admired Poster Person in the "listens and learns" bucket, winning more than a third of the votes cast in my interviews. European executives, in particular, saw him as an important role model.

Knudstorp, chairman of the legendary Danish toy maker Lego, took the helm in 2004, a time when the company was losing $1 million daily and fighting for its life. A former kindergarten teacher and McKinsey consultant, Knudstorp was the first outside CEO at Lego, a company that had been in family hands since its founding in 1932.

One of the executives I interviewed in 2022, a vice president at Siemens, told me why he saw Knudstorp as a standout communicator.

"Look," he told me, "Knudstorp had a clear take on what had gone wrong at Lego: the company had strayed too far from its core mission and core strengths." My interviewee went on to explain how the company had diversified into Lego-branded clothing, theme parks, jewelry, and video games, pushing to the sidelines the interlocking building blocks that had delighted so many generations of children. While the diversification efforts had been intended to bring the company into the twenty-first century, they hadn't been profitable, and Knudstorp believed that Lego would do much better if it were to refocus on its signature building blocks, which were designed to help children learn the essential twenty-first-century skill of systematic, creative problem solving.[161]

In the mind of this Siemens executive, the big question was, "How to do this as an outsider? The brilliance of Knudstorp was that he built trust and created buy-in by 'managing at eye level,' and embarking on a collaborative journey."

Managing at eye level is a Danish concept, and no one has deployed it as effectively as Knudstorp. Over the course of a year, he sat down with and listened to every category of worker at Lego: workers on the factory floor, engineers in their design shops, marketing, sales reps, and leaders in the C-suite. He sought information and asked for ideas and guidance. Knudstorp's listening journey didn't stop at employees. He also sat down with external stakeholders: retailers, customers, and scholars in the early childhood education space. To cap it all off, he spent three days at a Lego conference for adult fans held in Washington, D.C. At this conference, he didn't sit on the dais; instead, he mingled with the conferees and listened at eye level to their concerns and engaged in dialogue.

Knudstorp's discovery journeys fundamentally changed how Lego does business. Inviting customers to contribute their ideas to the product design process became embedded in the business and is a large part of why Lego regained strength and got back on a growth path. Over the last fifteen years more than one hundred thousand "volunteer designers" (customers who fancy themselves as product designers) have worked with Lego, ensuring that the company delivers what children and their families want.[162]

Knudstorp himself continues to use his communication chops

in ways that are close and personal. He makes a point of responding personally to at least some of the customer emails that flood into Lego. A couple of years ago, he heard from a sick child who had been saving money to buy a particular Lego set, only to find out that the model was out of production. Knudstorp told the *Washington Post* that he sent the consumer services department scurrying all over the factory asking, " 'Would you happen to have this particular model we no longer manufacture?' "[163] Someone was able to locate an unopened set that Knudstorp gifted to the sick child, sending it immediately along by express mail.

In an interview with the *Harvard Business Review*, Knudstorp described his main problem at Lego as "cutting through distrust." As the first-ever outside CEO, he'd initially been viewed with great suspicion, but a communication strategy that centers on managing at eye level and doing a great deal of listening generated good will and eventually trust. In his view, "trust-building is core in any company dealing with change."[164]

READS AN AUDIENCE/MARKET

On the reads an audience/market front, Martin Waters, the CEO of Victoria's Secret, was the top pick; he was singled out as the most admired Poster Person by just over a quarter of the executives I interviewed in 2022.

According to one interviewee, an executive at Michael Kors, "when he became CEO, Waters didn't make some small adjustment to the Victoria's Secret brand; he led a revolution. This took vision and guts because this was a big lift: He was doing nothing less than turning on its head a brand that for decades had centered on male fantasies and made it woman-centric."

Another interviewee in the retail sector, a vice president at Bloomingdale's, pointed to the headwinds Waters was facing. "In the late teens, revenues at Victoria's Secret were in free fall [they fell from $7.8 to $5.4 billion between 2016 and 2020]. In addition, he was stepping into a corporate culture riddled with accusations of sexual misconduct." The charges were indeed serious, and Waters's first move was to distance himself from the founding CEO, Leslie Wexner, whose ties to Jeffrey Epstein had just become public.

What was the communication strategy that so impressed colleagues in the industry?

Martin Waters went big and bold with his revolutionary vision. He wasn't afraid of calling out Victoria's Secret as tone deaf and stuck in the past, telling the world that under his watch the company would no longer be in the business of pretending that there's only one kind of beautiful body. As he explained to the *New York Times*, "in the post-#MeToo world, women of all shapes and sizes are demanding that society celebrate them for their accomplishments, not their measurements. I for one intend to deliver." [165]

Waters's first concrete step was to ask a diverse group of high-achieving celebrity women to be the new faces of Victoria's Secret. Among the new brand ambassadors were soccer star and LGBTQ activist Megan Rapinoe, biracial plus-size model Paloma Elsesser, Brazilian trans model Valentina Sampaio, and Chinese American freestyle skier Eileen Gu.

With the new ambassadors in place, Waters was ready to redefine what it means for a woman to be "sexy." Down went the ads and in-store photos of G-string "Angel" supermodels, and up went the ads and in-store photos of women who looked like real people. In 2021 Waters launched Victoria's Secret's first-ever Mother's Day campaign, which featured an ad with a pregnant model. Megan Rapinoe was approving, telling a reporter that she was proud to be part of a brand committed to righting wrongs that had been visited on women since the dawn of civilization.

A second concrete step, which Waters kicked off concurrently, centered on seeking input from Victoria's Secret stakeholders, especially its employees.

"We have about twenty-five thousand women working at the company, and we need to consult them," he declared on a retail industry podcast, confessing that this was a first. Never before had employees been invited to weigh in on the company's product lines or marketing messages. To that end he rolled out a series of focus groups and discussion panels so decision makers at the top of the house could absorb the employee vantage point. He also sought guidance from customers, influencers, and financial analysts. After this consultative process, Waters was happy to report to the press that the collective feedback confirmed his belief that Victoria's Secret had the potential "to become the world's biggest and best advocate for women."

Of course, Martin Waters has needed to deal with his fair share of skeptics and critics. As I learned in my 2022 executive interviews, African-American women were particularly skeptical about the authenticity and depth of Waters's commitment. Tai Green Wingfield, who heads up the global inclusion function at the technology firm Unity, told me that she would find it easier to celebrate the Victoria's Secret rebrand if Waters had done a better job acknowledging (and perhaps partnering with) the pioneering firms that have done the real innovation in this space, companies like Savage X Fenty and Nude Barre. "Does Waters really know—or care—about what's actually going on with Black bodies—or trans bodies?" she asked rhetorically.

One key question is whether Martin Waters's extreme makeover has made Victoria's Secret profitable again.

It's early, but the signs are good. In late 2022, financial analysts saw it as a solid stock trading at a bargain, with substantial website traffic and greater upside than some of its closest competitors.[166]

TELEGRAPHS AUTHENTICITY

Eddie Glaude, chair of the Department of African-American Studies at Princeton University and an on-air MSNBC contributor, was the top pick in the "telegraphs authenticity" bucket, garnering the votes of a quarter of the executives I interviewed in 2022. Black executives—both male and female—were particularly admiring. A senior African-American executive in the insurance industry (a vice president at AIG) told me that she found Glaude's short segments on *Morning Joe* to be among the most teachable minutes on television. "Eddie Glaude is just a top-notch communication coach," she noted.

The fact is, Glaude is a master at splicing erudition with authenticity. And he can produce this magic in a couple of minutes—or paragraphs. Whether speaking in person or on camera, he looks his audience in the eye, speaks crisply and concisely, never uses a script or notes, and blends scholarship with stories from his roots in Mississippi.

His talents were displayed in a TV segment that aired on July 4, 2022. Against a backdrop of the U.S. Capitol, Glaude locked eyes with his audience and explained that Independence Day is a challenging holiday for Black Americans because they still struggle with the legacies of slavery. He shared recent as well as fifty-year-old examples of injustices that are routinely visited upon African-Americans—lacing his account with just the right amount of vivid graphic detail—and then, eager to place himself inside the picture he's painting, he reminded his audience that he is deeply embedded in this American tragedy. "My great-grandmom is buried in Moss Point, Mississippi, and so this history is mine: all of its ugliness, beauty, and all of what it can and should become."[167] A pitch-perfect message for Independence Day 2022.

Eddie Glaude has much to work with in his life story. Born

into a close-knit family in rural Mississippi in a community where his dad was the postman, he won a scholarship to Morehouse College and earned a PhD at Princeton. Today he is a revered scholar who holds a named chair at his alma mater and writes courageous, award-winning books about the scourge of racism and how we might come together to build a more perfect union.

Several of the executives I interviewed in 2022, not just this particular fan at AIG, stressed that while they appreciated the heft, depth, and authenticity of what Glaude had to say, his impact on the world had a whole lot to do with how he said it—particularly the visuals.

A high-ranking design engineer at DraftKings pointed to the backdrops he uses. "They are always evocative," she said. "They always add several dimensions to his authenticity."

Indeed, the backdrop to Glaude's Zooms and video clips are carefully crafted and splendidly lit. His go-to backsplash is a wall of books. Not any old books but carefully selected books that showcase his scholarship's breadth, depth, and inclusiveness. His selected authors range from Martin Luther King Jr. to Ta-Nehisi Coates to Roxane Gay to Anton Chekhov and Orhan Pamuk.

Glaude's personal style and choice of attire are also highly intentional. A trim goatee and tightly buzzed haircut are fitting foil for his direct gaze and beautifully executed pronouncements. As are his perfectly cut suits and elegant silk ties. These accoutrements send a message: This scholar is distancing himself from the shabby, tweedy, "head in the clouds" stereotype of an Ivy League professor, and, in so doing, signaling that he's offering fresh, new ways of thinking. It's also no accident that Glaude gravitates to blue: dark blue suits, a blue palette of ties, and vivid blue eyeglass frames. This brilliant communicator knows that blue in the American flag signifies justice, vigilance, and perseverance and wants to be associated with those values.

MASTERS AND MONITORS BODY LANGUAGE

Body language is a powerful communication tool. The way you stand and sit, the way you hold your head, the way you square your shoulders, the way you move your arms and position your hands—all these elements have the potential of enormously enhancing your impact at work and in the larger world.

In December 2021, I attended a concert at Carnegie Hall. The Venezuelan superstar Gustavo Dudamel was conducting, and Carnegie's grand auditorium was packed to the gills. At 7:55 p.m., the orchestra filed onto the stage, and a hush settled on the crowd. A few minutes later, the conductor, a slight, middle-aged man with a mop of pepper-and-salt curls, entered stage left. The audience went wild, stomping their feet and cheering through cupped hands. I was startled. *This isn't normal*, I thought. Carnegie Hall draws a sedate, buttoned-up crowd.

I'd done my homework and knew that Dudamel was a big deal. As a twentysomething-year-old wunderkind from Caracas, he'd won an ECHO Award for his recording of Beethoven's *Fifth* and a Grammy for his performance of Brahms's *Symphony No. 4*. I also knew that Dudamel didn't limit himself to classical music. He'd conducted the rock band Coldplay at the Super Bowl and appeared on *Sesame Street*.

I'd gone to this concert to find out *what exactly* makes Dudamel so charismatic, especially to such a wide range of fans. After watching him in action, I can say that his body language has a lot to do with it.

From the moment he appeared onstage, Dudamel showed that he was a different kind of maestro. Unlike other famous conductors (think Leonard Bernstein, Arturo Toscanini, or Pierre Boulez), he didn't strut his stuff or preen and puff. Instead, Dudamel's demeanor and deportment conveyed his belief that a conductor's role is to collaborate with and celebrate the onstage musicians, not control them.[168] He was intent on bringing joy and gratitude, not pride and arrogance.

To that end, he eschewed formalwear (white or black tie and coattails), which would have set him apart from ordinary mortals in the orchestra; instead he wore a simple black linen jacket. He'd also done away with a conductor's podium, not wanting to tower over the orchestra. Instead he stood on the stage, on the same level and just a few feet away from his musicians. In addition, he'd eliminated the conductor stand and orchestral score. Not wanting to be distracted by the need to read a score, Dudamel had gone to the trouble of committing an entire symphony and concerto to memory so that he could look his musicians in the eye, cue them, encourage them, and nod approval. They were his focus and had his complete attention.[169]

I was most impressed that at the end of the concert, Dudamel did not turn to the audience and take credit for a splendid performance by indulging in a sweeping, regal bow. Instead he walked around the stage, embracing the principal player in each section of the orchestra; he then stepped back and started applauding the musicians. The audience caught on, and as the applause grew thunderous, he gathered his players around him. With Dudamel setting an example, they all touched their hearts and blew kisses into the crowd.

Dudamel didn't speak a word that evening. Still, his every move and action communicated his conviction that music is a universal language that crosses cultural divides and brings people together on an equal playing field. For two and a half hours, this incredibly impressive maestro had, in fact, "mimed inclusivity." It took my breath away.

Given my exposure to Dudamel, I wasn't surprised that almost a quarter of the executives I interviewed in 2022 selected him as their Poster Person in the "body language" bucket. European and Asian executives were particularly enthusiastic, seeing his mastery of inclusive stances and gestures as eminently transferable to the business world. A senior executive at Nokia explained, "A high-ranking executive who's just landed a new client or hit a stretch goal is well-advised not to preen and puff. Instead, borrow from Dudamel's playbook: Gather the people around you who did the work, take a collective bow, and touch your heart." Using your whole body to share credit, foster collaboration, and express appreciation marks you as a leader in 2023.

BLUNDERS

In the communications bucket, the list of significant mistakes—ones that tarnish your brand or get you demoted—changed markedly between 2012 and 2022. Ten years ago, the blunders list was dominated by small-bore stuff, what might be called "misdemeanors." But, while talking in a shrill voice or constantly checking your iPhone will get in your way and undermine your brand, these transgressions won't cost you your job. In 2022, the communication blunders list features much more serious offenses, like appearing fake and phony or groping a coworker or an underage girl, both of which can be career-enders.

FAKE AND PHONY

At a time when the business world has deep appreciation of authenticity, it's no big surprise that in 2022 the top communication blunder is lying through your teeth and coming over as "fake and phony." Almost half the executives I interviewed in 2022 singled out Elizabeth Holmes as the most glaring example of a leader

Communication Blunders 2012

From focus groups and interviews

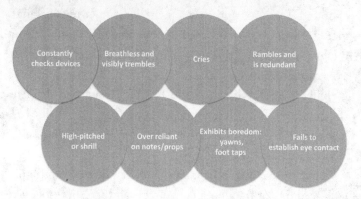

Communication Blunders 2022

From focus groups and interviews

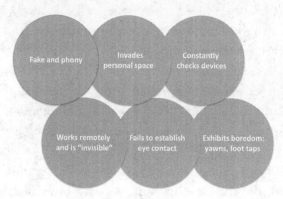

Figure 15. Changes in communication blunders between 2012 and 2022

who hid behind borrowed identities and buried herself under a pile of egregious lies.

The outlines of her meteoric rise and fall are well known. At the tender age of nineteen, Holmes dropped out of Stanford to found Theranos and develop the Edison, a revolutionary device she promised would make it possible to diagnose a hundred medical conditions through a small pinprick of blood. She was a passionate and appealing salesperson. First-round investors included Rupert Murdoch and Larry Ellison, and she attracted the likes of Henry Kissinger and the CEO of Wells Fargo to her board. In the early 2000s, she was the youngest self-made billionaire in the world.

Twenty years later, in January 2022, she was found guilty on four accounts of fraud and conspiracy, and in November, she was sentenced to eleven years in prison, a sentence that is being appealed. What happened?

It turns out that her company was built on lies.[170] Edison never worked. Holmes swore by her miracle machine and relentlessly talked up its virtues, even forming a partnership with Walgreens to roll out testing clinics around the country. But behind the scenes, Theranos was secretly testing blood samples on third-party commercial machines made by Siemens. Eventually her bluff was called, and she was tried and found guilty of defrauding investors of $9 billion, and endangering patients with inaccurate results.

Holmes's phoniness wasn't limited to her gigantic fraud. To impress powerful male investors, she adopted weird macho affectations: dressing like a Steve Jobs look-alike, speaking in a baritone voice, claiming that her husky dog was a wolf, and encouraging her employees to chant obscenities in team meetings.[171]

The surprising thing is that this entirely fake person lasted as long as she did.

INVADES PERSONAL SPACE

In 2022 the second-most-serious communication blunder was invading another person's personal space. Way too many male leaders seem unable to keep their hands to themselves. Such transgressive behavior has gone on for generations, but in our post-#MeToo world, touching, groping, or forcibly kissing a coworker is no longer tolerated. This is particularly damaging if you're accused by a coworker who is junior to you and in your line of command. Then you're cut off at the knees. Examples abound: Andrew Cuomo (governor of New York), Leslie Wexner (founding CEO of Victoria's Secret), Les Moonves (CEO, CBS), and Andy Rubin (Google) were all shown the door after hitting on one or more junior colleagues.

REMOTE AND INVISIBLE

This "mistake" is new to the communication blunder list. During the pandemic nearly two-thirds of white-collar workers were constrained to work from home and whatever disadvantage incurred by remote working was spread across all cohorts. As we now know, remote working did not end with the pandemic; almost half of all professionals, their market power boosted by labor shortages, are electing either hybrid or fully remote work arrangements going forward. These choices are highly gendered; a 10–15 percentage point spread is emerging between the number of female and male managers electing to work exclusively from home. This opens up a new gender gap since being "out of sight and out of mind" impedes progression. In a 2022 interview, Catherine Mann, a member of the Monetary Policy Committee of the Bank of England and a former chief economist at Citi, sounded a warning: "There are professionals on the virtual track and professionals on the physical track. Going forward, I fear that most people on the virtual track will be women, and they will be seriously disadvantaged. Human contact and professional rapport are vital components of business success."[172] The research backs her up; when professionals elect to work exclusively from home, they lose out on networking opportunities and lose traction in their career. It is in-person contact, not emails, LinkedIn, or TikTok, that allows up-and-comers to build trust and rapport with senior executives who can open doors.[173]

KEY TAKEAWAYS

What was the most practical piece of advice to come out of my 2022 executive interviews?

Rosa Gudmundsdottir, whom I talked to in March 2022, is the CFO of Reginn HF, a global estate firm headquartered in Reykjavík, Iceland. Since almost none of Reginn's investors or clients "sit" in Iceland, Rosa has become a whiz at staging virtual meetings. Here is the framework she's perfected.

Staging a High-Impact Virtual Meeting

- Oversee a brief tech check to ensure NO SNAFUS.
- Distribute materials at least SIX HOURS IN ADVANCE. If this can't happen, conduct meeting as though no one has pre-read.
- Introduce new team members and TALK UP HIS/HER VALUE and track record.
- Task a team member to SUMMARIZE DECISIONS MADE at meeting. Rotate this job.
  These four steps ensure efficiency and signal inclusion.

Figure 16. Staging a high-impact virtual meeting

In January 2023, I interviewed Tiger Tyagarajan, president and CEO of Genpact, a 115,000-person professional services firm. He had important thoughts on how to best stage virtual meetings now that companies have put Covid-19 behind them. In addition to Gudmundsdottir's basic frame (which Tyagarajan agrees with), he described two communication tactics he was rolling out across Genpact.

- *Virtual Watercooler Conversations.* Sixty percent of Genpact's employees now work remotely compared to 40 percent pre-pandemic. To make sure that virtual hires have a way of getting to know colleagues and building an internal network, Tyagarajan and his senior team make room on their calendars to meet up with junior talent when they travel. They share their itineraries and calendars, and employees can sign up for breakfast, lunch, or dinner. This new practice has been a huge hit, particularly among women, who tend to opt for fully remote work arrangements.
- *In-Office Mini-Retreats.* As the pandemic wound down Tyagarajan started to pull together his fifteen-person C-suite for two full days every five to six weeks. They don't meet in luxury resorts but in Genpact facilities close to wherever Tyagarajan happens to be. Sometimes it's a factory site in Asia, and sometimes an office suite in Europe. These mini-retreats have cascaded down the ranks, the majority of executives and managers at Genpact now hold them, and they're a resounding success. They've become innovation incubators: team members share many new ideas and spark one another. According

to Tyagarajan you can tell when a team has just had a mini-retreat because you can feel "electricity in the air." They're also turning into great relationships and trust-builders. Tyagarajan's rule that mini-retreat participants "break bread together" and make time for long dinners at nice restaurants is paying off.

10

APPEARANCE 2.0

Appearance is the EP bucket that changed most between 2012 and 2022. The Black Lives Matter and #MeToo movements together with the coronavirus pandemic have radically shifted dress codes as professional attire has become more casual. Your look also now needs to reflect the authentic you. In addition, how you monitor your online presence has become an urgent challenge. Nowadays, video clips and photographs are all-powerful, and a click or a swipe can destroy reputations. In an interview, Brad Hu, the chief risk officer of State Street, told me that the speed with which a damaging photo can zip around the world keeps him up at night. "In the space of a few hours," he said, "billions can be knocked off a company's brand."

As can be seen in Figure 17, while much has changed, two traits that were top picks in 2012 have retained their luster.

Polish (number 1 pick in both 2012 and 2022) continues to be enormously prized. Impeccable grooming and camera-readiness are particularly valued on the global stage. Shinzo Abe was an exemplar of this, and he was singled out by the executives I interviewed in 2022.

Being fit and vigorous is also a keeper. This sought-after trait came in at number 3 in both 2012 and 2022. The executives I talked to in 2022 selected Michelle Obama as their top choice in this bucket. Many of her admirers were women. In the opinion of

Appearance, 2012 and 2022

Top Traits, 2012

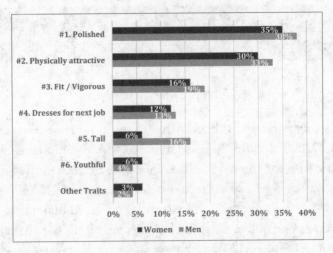

Top Traits, 2022

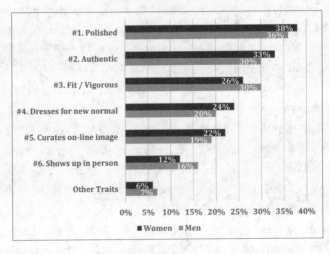

Figure 17. Changes in appearance top traits between 2012 and 2022

Mercedes Abramo (CEO of Cartier North America), "Michelle Obama's muscled arms and toned shoulders contributed enormously to her image as a health-conscious first lady who cares deeply about children's access to wholesome food and outdoor exercise." A sizable number of men singled out Richard Branson, Virgin's longtime CEO. "It's hard to believe that Branson just turned seventy," said a thirtysomething Pimco executive. "I see him as a man in his prime, fit, vigorous, and hell-bent on adventure."

On the "what has changed" front, the list is longer.

The fact is over the last ten years, both seasoned and newly minted executives have needed to make three pivots.

They're now expected to show up in the world looking authentic. A well-cut suit (for a man) or a helmet of straightened, lacquered hair (for a woman) no longer does it. To be seen as "leadership material," to attract a following, and to create buy-in from colleagues and customers, executives are newly required to reveal who they are in the way they dress and look. Authenticity is now the number 2 most-sought-after trait on the appearance front and has become something of a superpower.

We saw this coming in 2014. Remember Keisha Smith-Jeremie? This up-and-coming Black corporate leader disrupted the EP code when she decided to make the best of a disastrous dye job that resulted in a shaved head and showcase her baldness. She did this with grace and dignity, and it both earned her respectful attention from colleagues *and* permitted her to be "utterly at ease in her skin." In 2014, this degree of authenticity was rare, but not so in 2022. In my interviews, executives pointed to an impressive range of leaders who model authenticity. Among their top choices were Warren Buffett and New York congresswoman Alexandria Ocasio-Cortez.

A second appearance pivot has been driven by the pandemic and the large-scale shift to remote work. We're not talking about Covid-related lockdowns anymore. Still, the truth is, in a post-pandemic world replete with labor shortages, a large percentage of white-collar workers (60–80 percent depending on the industry) have been able to negotiate hybrid schedules that allow them to work from home two or three days a week.[174] As a result of these new arrangements, stiff and starchy dress codes are out, and business casual is in, even for senior executives. Achieving this look is surprisingly challenging since there's no go-to uniform for either men or women. The executives I interviewed in 2022 selected Google CEO Sundar Pichai as their number 1 Poster Person in this bucket. One of my interviewees, a vice president at DraftKings, described him as "showing up looking polished but also convincingly cool and casual."

The third pivot centers on curating and controlling online images. In 2023 this is imperative. In the modern world, everyone wields an iPhone, and a "candid" photo or video clip can be a career-ender. As mentioned earlier, all it takes is one click or swipe. Over the last year, iPhone videos have turned Sanna Marin into "the clubbing prime minister"[175] of Finland and made Rudy Giuliani a laughingstock worldwide. Who can come back from hair dye dripping down sweaty cheeks?

Also, we must remember that online photos and videos can build up brands as well as drag them. In general, corporate leaders have been late to this game, and in 2023 relatively few tap into the power of Instagram or TikTok. But more want to. My executive interviewees singled out Sheryl Sandberg as someone who does a splendid job on Instagram—using this platform to cement her legacy as a champion of women.

Before turning to our Poster People, a word of warning.

In chapter 4, we learned that the business world underestimates the power of appearance. This continues to this day. When gauging whether an up-and-comer is "leadership material," senior executives like to focus on gravitas and communication, not dress or look. In 2022 as well as in 2012, a mere 5 percent of the executives surveyed selected appearance as the essential part of the EP equation. This low number is misleading because it ignores the risks of messing up. In reality, a person gets to make a first impression only once; if you blow it, you don't get a second chance. As I pointed out in chapter 4, "if your appearance telegraphs you're clueless," no one bothers to examine the depth of your gravitas. Even more scary are the risks attached to a digital faux pas. If a photo or a video turns up online showing you engaged in sexual misconduct, you're toast. There is no way you can explain it away, or recover, even if you're a prince of the realm. Remember that picture of Prince Andrew at Jeffrey Epstein's Manhattan town house with his arm around seventeen-year-old Virginia Giuffre? That photo, along with other damning visual evidence, made it impossible for the prince to defend himself against a lawsuit brought against him by Giuffre. Forced to settle, he paid a huge fine, and was stripped of royal rights and privileges.

POLISH

Shinzo Abe was the top choice in the polish bucket. He was singled out by almost half of the executives I interviewed in 2022. Abe, who was assassinated in July 2022, served as Japan's prime minister twice: between 2006 and 2007 and again between 2012 and 2020. A skillful statesman from a prominent political family, he sought to reestablish Japan as an economic and military powerhouse on the world stage. He presented himself as an immensely dignified, impeccably dressed Japanese sensei and a warm, approachable global leader with a keen sense of fashion.

Nowhere was this dual image more on display than at Abe's meeting with President Donald Trump at the latter's Mar-a-Lago resort in Palm Beach, Florida, in April 2018. Abe showed up in a perfectly tailored Italian suit set off by a vibrant violet and gold striped tie. This tie was replete with meaning for the cognoscenti in the press corps.[176] Japanese warriors wear violet; this color signifies nobility and strength, while gold is a stand-in for the sun and symbolizes God's bounty and mercy. One of my 2022 interviewees, a senior-level journalist at *Bloomberg Businessweek*, attended the event at Mar-a-Lago and was super impressed. "Abe knocked it out of the ballpark," he told me. "Gone were the boxy black suit and bowed head favored by other Asian leaders. Instead, Abe showcased his sophistication, heritage, and status as the leader of an ancient and powerful nation."

Abe did a great job in the Q&A. After fielding a few tough questions on trade—in perfect English—he flashed a megawatt smile at the cameras, turned to Trump, and declared that the thing he and the president were in total agreement about was their mutual love for the great game of golf. Knowing something about Trump's outsize ego, Abe was astute enough to be self-deprecating. He described himself as having a "disgraceful" golf handicap in contrast to the president, who "everyone knows is a scratch golfer." These comments delighted Trump, who preened and puffed. The relationship between these two leaders was off to a great start.

Amanda Gorman came in as the number 2 Poster Person on the "polish" front, garnering the votes of just under a quarter of the executives I interviewed. One Black interviewee (a managing director at Citi) talked in awed tones about how Gorman, America's youngest-ever inaugural poet, stole the show at President Joe Biden's inauguration on January 20, 2021.[177] "From the moment Gorman descended the steps of the U.S. Capitol to recite her poem, she captured the nation," she said.

I remember being mesmerized, too. Gorman's striking yellow coat and fire-engine-red headband were bold and brave. They set the stage for the vibrant, confident honesty of her poem "The Hill We Climb."

AUTHENTIC

Displaying authenticity is newly on the appearance top trait list, and the executives I interviewed in 2022 selected two very different Poster People. Top of their list was Warren Buffett, who garnered a third of the votes. Their second choice was Alexandria Ocasio-Cortez, who received a quarter. The Sage of Omaha has been showcasing authenticity for fifty years, AOC for a mere five years. Both do it brilliantly.

An auto executive I interviewed in 2022 (a vice president at GM) told me that he deeply appreciates that Buffett, chairman and CEO of Berkshire Hathaway, "behaves just like a regular guy and doesn't flaunt his wealth." Indeed, Buffett isn't remotely ostentatious. Unlike Jeff Bezos, he doesn't blast himself into space or spend half a billion dollars on a megayacht.

Buffett is a salt-of-the-earth midwesterner who hasn't strayed from his roots. For close to seventy years, he's lived in a modest house in Omaha, Nebraska, that he bought for $31,000 in 1958 and is valued at $650,000 today.[178] He wears off-the-rack, made-in-America suits, and avoids anything bespoke or Italian.

The Buffett "look" bolsters and reflects the vision underlying his business philosophy. He's built Berkshire Hathaway on no-nonsense value investing. His long-held belief is that people should only buy stocks in companies with solid fundamentals and strong earnings growth. He likes to make investing sound like folk wisdom. "Just buy something for less than it's worth," he says.[179]

His appearance reflects his moral compass and his values. Despite his enormous wealth (he's worth over $100 billion), Buffett rails against galloping inequality in America and does his bit to fix it. In 2006 he pledged to give away 99 percent of his fortune to philanthropic causes and for the last eighteen years, that's what he's been doing.[180]

Despite the deep authenticity of the Buffett brand, his down-home avuncularity has been carefully crafted and curated. He might talk about life lessons he learned from his father, but he keeps relatively mum about who his father was. Howard Homan Buffett was a four-term Republican congressman who gave his son Warren a start at his Omaha-based investment banking firm. Although Buffett is a bona fide guy next door, he's not self-made and his is not a "rags to riches" story.[181]

In my 2022 executive interviews, Alexandria Ocasio-Cortez (D-NY) came in as the number 2 Poster Person in the authenticity bucket. Her admirers were primarily women and included right-wing Republicans as well as die-hard lefties. One senior executive I interviewed (a senior vice president at Fox News) said, "I don't share her politics, but I love that she's so unafraid. Here's a woman who's bold enough to *wear* her message. That gown she wore to the Met Gala—suffragette white with blood-red lettering that read 'tax the rich'—was a brilliant media play. Every news platform carried it."

AOC rode into Washington, D.C., in January 2019, intent on making a mark and doing it on her terms. She was a new kind of congressperson—young, Latina, and way out on the left wing. She quickly became a polarizing figure, attacked by the right (Republican congressperson Paul Gosar tweeted a video in which a cartoon version of himself swung a sword at AOC) and feted by the left; she's survived and thrived despite being in the crosshairs of party conflict at an extremely polarized time in American politics. She's grown her base of support and become politically untouchable by wearing her authenticity on her sleeve.[182] In the words of one interviewee, an executive at Ogilvy, the advertising powerhouse, "AOC is the real deal, and she's had the smarts to turn her blue-collar background [born in the Bronx, worked as a bartender] and her Puerto Rican heritage into valuable political assets."

I can't leave this section on authenticity and appearance without mentioning hair. Specifically, African-American textured hair. This topic has threaded through the chapters of this book. Both Katherine Phillips and Keisha Smith-Jeremie tangled with the challenge of whether they needed to commit to a lifetime of chemical treatments to appear leaderly, or whether they could opt out and do their own thing. They both chose the latter route and it worked out splendidly. But that was ten to twenty years ago and back then their choices took courage. Today it's somewhat easier for a Black executive to show up at work with her God-given hair. In a 2022 interview, Tai Green Wingfield, the African-American leader we met in chapter 9, described how changing attitudes had affected the choices she's made. "I'm now in my forties and pretty senior," she told me, "but when I was climbing the ladder in the public relations and think-tank worlds, I never wore my hair natural. It was just one of those unwritten rules that an African-American couldn't turn up at client meetings with braids, or, indeed, any style that displayed her textured hair. So every weekend, I'd spent a huge chunk of time (three to five hours) doing the whole relaxing, straightening, ironing thing." But corporate cultures have changed, and these days Wingfield deliberately mixes it up. To use her words, "At least once or twice a week I'll turn up at work 'au natural'—either in person or on Zoom—and the cool thing is, junior African-American colleagues invariably thank me. That gives me such a kick; there's freedom and power in that."

FIT/VIGOROUS

Michelle Obama was voted number 1 Poster Person in the Fit/ Vigorous bucket, winning a third of the votes in my 2022 executive interviews. As mentioned at the beginning of this chapter, her extraordinarily chiseled upper arms and shoulders bolstered her brand as a first lady who both embodied fitness and led a hands-on campaign to create better access to wholesome food and outdoor exercise for America's children.[183] One of my interviewees (a female executive at DraftKings) had vivid memories of Michelle Obama's garden project: "Remember that huge vegetable patch Michelle Obama dug on the White House lawn? It made the evening news. There she was, digging and hoeing alongside a bunch of telegenic fifth-grade kids from a nearby public school. Bully for her, I say."

Many of us remember that garden project and the nation applauded as the first lady used her toned muscles to inspire young kids. It was a brilliant choice of project. Who could be against swapping out ketchup and fries for homegrown veggies?

Despite her eventual success, Michelle Obama's journey to popularity wasn't simple or easy. She had three strikes against her. She was Black—the first African-American first lady ever. She was a Harvard-trained lawyer and moved in elite circles. And she was a vocal feminist with strong views on pay equity and the right to choose. When she and Barack Obama moved into the White House, many right-of-center Americans feared that the new first lady would be a highfalutin "head in the clouds" troublemaker. These fears were stoked by a *New Yorker* cover featuring the Obamas dressed up like Islamic terrorists, bumping fists. This cover—which was meant to be satirical, not literal—was immediately weaponized and used in ads by Republican candidates running for office.[184]

So, not wanting to be a drag on what her husband could accomplish, Michelle Obama toned down her views and her rhetoric, replacing gritty, divisive causes with bland, nicey-nicey ones. It did wonders for her poll numbers.

Professional women like myself greatly admired the original

Michelle Obama. We wanted her to remain an activist feminist and use her White House platform to push hard for working-women's rights, but it's easy to understand why she avoided getting into the trenches and fighting for hard-core issues. Like her husband, she needed to show that she was a uniter rather than a divider. As a consequence, when she moved into the White House, Michelle Obama branded herself as a devoted mother and a health-conscious woman who worked out, had something to show for it (those chiseled shoulders!), and shared her exercise regime with millions of other not-so-young American women. Her garden project, which morphed into a nationwide "Let's Move" campaign, fit right into her new image. My DraftKings interviewee nailed it: "Bringing health and fitness to families across the country resonated hugely in the heartland as well as in the inner cities and drove her approval rating sky-high." Today Michelle Obama's favorability rating is 20 points higher than either Biden's or Trump's.[185]

Richard Branson, founding CEO of a constellation of companies bearing the Virgin brand name, was voted the number 2 Poster Person in the Fit/Vigorous bucket. He was singled out by a quarter of the executives I interviewed in 2022. Most of his fans were older male executives who saw him as their go-to macho-man role model. One interviewee, a senior vice president at Nokia, told me that Branson was an inspiration to him. "Here's a guy in his seventies who's still the 'forever-fit adventurer.' He takes up challenges at the drop of a hat, whether kick-starting the B-team (which focuses on building net-zero businesses) or breaking the Atlantic crossing record aboard the *Virgin Challenger II*. Now, if I could get even close to that . . ."

In his blog posts, Branson tells the world that the endorphin rush he gets from exercising is central to who he is and what he can do. For decades he's gotten up at 5 a.m. to play tennis, run, kite-surf, or work out at the gym.[186] And it shows. On Instagram, it's hard to find a photo of Branson where he's not radiating super-human energy and grinning ear to ear as if he's just scaled another summit. On some days he has done just that!

DRESSES FOR THE NEW NORMAL

Sundar Pichai, the CEO of Google and its parent company, Alphabet, was voted as the number 1 Poster Person in the "dresses for the new normal" bucket by one-third of the executives I interviewed in 2022. As one interviewee (a principal at McKinsey) told me, "Pichai is one of a handful of tech leaders who is trailed by paparazzi and featured in Silicon Valley fashion spreads. He's seen as having cracked the post-pandemic look."

Whether we call that look "business comfort" or "power casual," figuring out what to wear in the new hybrid workplace is challenging. Most white-collar professionals worked remotely during the pandemic and communicated with coworkers via Zoom or Teams. This resulted in a "casualization of the lower half."[187] Heels dropped lower or disappeared altogether, and pantwaists became elasticized or morphed into comfy sweats or shorts.

What to do now that most of us are back in the office, at least two or three days a week?

As we know from the survey data, "polish" is still the most-sought-after appearance trait. But what does polish look like post-pandemic? Pichai gives us some pointers.

The leather bomber jackets he favors, generally worn with jeans and a simple T-shirt, create a professional, approachable look that conveys that the new normal is a seamless interweaving of work and life.

The richly muted yet decidedly industrial color palette he chooses for his go-to jeans—navy blue, dusky blue charcoal, and olive—hold a subliminal message that technology will enhance the quality of your life as well as push out your production-possibility frontier.

He also manages to conjure up tantalizing glimpses of Google products. When Kara Swisher interviewed Pichai at her Code Conferences in September 2022, he "outed" Google's new watch.[188] Whenever he moved his arm or gestured with his hands, the audience saw the much-heralded but yet-to-be-released Pixel Watch. It was quite the teaser.

In addition, Pichai strives to master visual clues and cues. When he met with Indonesian president Joko Widodo he showed up in a shirt with an earth-tone print resembling Southeast Asian ikat patterns—conveying that he was in the business of bridging cultures.[189]

The problem with using Sundar Pichai as a role model on the appearance front is that most of his attire is very pricey. *Business Insider* went to the trouble of pricing Pichai's favorite low-top sneakers.[190] Designed by Lanvin and fashioned in suede and patent, they sell for $495.

CURATES ONLINE IMAGE

Sheryl Sandberg came in as the number 1 Poster Person in the "curates online image" bucket. She was singled out by almost half of the executives I interviewed in 2022. Most of her supporters were women. She has many fangirls. In the words of one interviewee, a senior vice president at Blizzard Entertainment, "I admire her because she's done more than any other person to change the attitude of women toward ambition. Thanks to her, female up-and-comers worldwide are leaning in and convincing power brokers that they're qualified, credible, and needed at the top."

Despite her enormous celebrity, it's not clear what Sandberg will be remembered for. Will historians see her as a corporate titan? Someone who, in her fourteen-year stint as COO of Facebook, helped build one of the most successful companies in the world?

Or will historians see her as a bestselling author who coached women on how to own ambition and shoot for the stars? Her 2013 book, *Lean In: Women, Work, and the Will to Lead*, was phenomenally successful, selling four million copies in five years and spinning off hundreds of thousands of "listening circles" around the world.[191] Her message was that it was time for women to stop holding themselves back, that they needed to ask for raises, try for promotions, and avoid "baby-tracking" their careers. This resonated deeply with Gen X and millennial women.

Or will she be seen as a female leader who excelled at empathy and touched people's hearts when her husband, Dave Goldberg, was killed in a freak accident, leaving her a grieving widow at age forty-five? Her post on Facebook just a month after his death was the social media equivalent of Edvard Munch's *The Scream*. Searingly honest, this post is a model for what to share and what not to share when a public person lands in such terrible circumstances. Sandberg opened her heart but protected her children; she showed both great grief and great strength. In short, she had perfect pitch.

One thing we can be sure of: Sheryl Sandberg isn't leaving the vital matter of her legacy in the hands of historians; she's shaping it herself. Since stepping down from Facebook (now Meta) in June 2022, Sandberg's social media posts have changed in terms of their tone, timbre, and content. She increasingly focuses on women's issues. As she told Bloomberg's Rebecca Greenfield, "It really feels like a very, very, important moment for women, and I'm putting my focus there."[192]

This is particularly evident on Instagram—a platform she favors. Sandberg's recent photos and videos celebrate the achievements of small-scale women business owners: a Lebanese restaurateur who's opened up a chic café in Montreal; a Black entrepreneur who runs a wildly successful dessert company in Tulsa. She likes to intersperse these impressive but largely unknown entrepreneurs with the high-profile female CEOs and political leaders she has easy access to. Taken together, it seems clear that Sandberg is beginning to put her work on behalf of women at the center of her life story. In the words of my Blizzard Entertainment interviewee, "Sheryl's in the business of using her command of social media to mold and map her legacy so that she can control what historians write about her."

SHOWS UP "IN PERSON"

President Volodymyr Zelenskyy was chosen as Poster Person number 1 in the "shows up in person" bucket by a whopping two-thirds of the executives I interviewed in 2022. One of my interviewees, a London-based Citi executive, told me emphatically, "It's a David-and-Goliath situation, and Zelenskyy's courageous presence—in his Kyiv bunker and on our TV screens—has given Ukraine a shot at beating back the Russians and hanging on to nationhood."

When thousands of Russian tanks rolled into Ukraine in February 2022, everyone expected Zelenskyy and his cabinet to flee the country and set up shop in a haven abroad; the U.S. even offered to help him evacuate. Instead, President Zelenskyy, understanding that leaving the country would be an admission of defeat, stayed in Kyiv, telling the global media, "I need ammunition, not a ride."[193] This was an extraordinarily courageous act. Russian tanks encircled Ukraine's capital, missiles were raining down on the city center, and Zelenskyy was target number one. But there he was, on the streets and in his sandbagged bunker leading his people. Zelenskyy is a communication pro (he was

245

a stand-up comic and entertainer before turning to politics) and knows how to put together words that celebrate resistance and stiffen resolve. But his words—no matter how inspiring—would have fallen flat had he fled the country. His willingness to face danger and show up in person gave him the moral authority to ask tens of thousands of fellow Ukrainians to put their lives on the line to save the nation.[194]

Since the outbreak of the war, Zelenskyy also made considerable efforts to show up in person and on large-scale screens in political forums around the world, including the U.S. Congress, the United Nations, the Israeli Knesset, and nearly every Western European parliament. These appearances allowed him to make an impassioned personal appeal for massive military and financial aid. Looking lawmakers in the eye, he made the case that Ukraine was fighting to oust invaders and regain its territory and sovereignty. But much more was at stake. If world leaders allowed Russia to pull off this brazen heist, democracy and nationhood would be at risk everywhere.

Zelenskyy's brave stance in Kyiv earned him these invitations to speak on the world stage, and without the rollout of a global video-based communication campaign, his face and his voice would not have turned up on the evening news in my living room. He talked to millions of people in ways that felt up close and personal. This got him the goods. The U.S. has sent vast amounts of military aid (tens of billions of dollars' worth), the European Union has imposed draconian sanctions despite its dependence on Russian oil, and the North Atlantic Treaty Organization has rallied behind Ukraine in a show of unity that we haven't seen since World War II.

Although it seems like a detail, Zelenskyy also packs a punch in how he dresses. In his video addresses, he often wears army-green short-sleeved T-shirts that show off his impressive muscles.

He also uses his furrowed brow and hangdog eyes to communicate his heavy heart at the wanton cruelty visited on his country by the Russian invaders. He comes off as a homegrown hero and regular guy, tough enough to stand up to Vladimir Putin but vulnerable enough to elicit sympathy worldwide.

BLUNDERS

In my original research, appearance blunders were gendered. Back in 2012, I broke out the data and created separate story lines for men and women. To make it easier to compare and contrast and track trend lines, I continued this practice in 2022.

The graphics in Figure 18 reveal fascinating shifts between 2012 and 2022. The appearance blunders singled out in 2012 centered almost entirely on the choice of attire, bodily image (think weight and teeth), and grooming. Except for obesity, the list for men and the list for women have no overlap.

Ten years later, appearance blunders are much different. Body image and grooming challenges have receded, courtesy of the pandemic. In a world of remote and hybrid work arrangements, dress codes have relaxed and colleagues allow one another more leeway. Concerns about makeup, dental work, and jewelry have been replaced by more complex issues that oftentimes center on identity, authority, authenticity, and sexuality.

There's also much more overlap between men and women. In 2022 male and female executives tend to make the same mistakes and face the same hurdles. Indeed, four of the six most damaging blunders are now shared by men and women. Is that progress? Well, as I found out in my 2022 executive interviews, it's complicated.

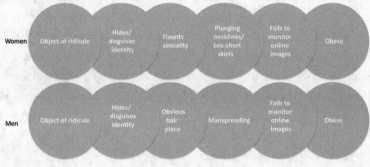

Appearance Blunders 2012
From focus groups and interviews

Women	Bottle blonde	Flashy jewelry	Too much makeup	Plunging necklines/ too-short skirts	Bitten/ broken nails	Obese
Men	Obvious hair piece	Unkempt attire	Visible piercings/ tattoos	Discolored/ crooked teeth	Dandruff on shoulders	Obese

Appearance Blunders 2022
From focus groups and interviews

Women	Object of ridicule	Hides/ disguises identity	Flaunts sexuality	Plunging necklines/ too-short skirts	Fails to monitor online images	Obese
Men	Object of ridicule	Hides/ disguises identity	Obvious hair piece	Manspreading	Fails to monitor online images	Obese

Figure 18. Changes in appearance blunders between 2012 and 2022

Appearance 2.0

More than a third of the executives I interviewed in 2022 singled out Rudy Giuliani as the most egregious example of a leader who's become an object of ridicule. As a vice president at Ogilvy told me, "No leader wants to be the butt of jokes on social media or late-night TV—it's the stuff of nightmares."

Rudy Giuliani used to be highly regarded. In 2001 he was dubbed "America's mayor" for his sterling work pulling New York City back from the edge after the attacks of 9/11. But in recent years, his standing and status have slipped dramatically as he's joined Trump's inner circle and become part of the extreme wing of the Republican Party.[195] His best pals are now conspiracy theorists and insurrectionists.

The coup de grâce in terms of his mainstream brand was Dye Gate. On November 19, 2020, Giuliani held a press conference at the Republican National Committee headquarters in Washington, D.C., to make the case that Joe Biden had not won the presidential election. As he let loose a stream of baseless claims that Dominion, the company that made the voting machines used in crucial battleground states, was controlled by left-wing billionaire George Soros and had deliberately thrown the election, Giuliani grew sweaty. A dark brown liquid (identified as a hair dye) began to drip down both sides of his face. While he wiped his face and forehead, he didn't seem aware of the hair dye situation and wasn't made aware of it by anyone on the stage.

Twitter had a field day. One user tweeted, "Giuliani's dripping hair dye, and he has no idea. I'm crying and laughing at the same time." Another user posted a clever pun: "Rudy Giuliani is an attorney to die for." Anderson Cooper nailed the farcical scene on CNN that evening. "It wasn't a press conference; it was a clown show," he said.

Another new top pick in the appearance blunder bucket was failing to monitor online photos and videos. A third of the executives I interviewed in 2022 singled out Sanna Marin as a leader who's been seriously damaged by losing control of her online image.

Marin, who became the prime minister of Finland at the ripe old age of thirty-four, has always been a hip and fearless politician. She attends rock festivals, wears leather jackets, and talks enthusiastically about "shaking up" the highest office in the land.[196] Despite her youth—or perhaps because of it!—Marin has achieved a great deal. She's credited with Finland's low death rate during the pandemic and, more recently, for galvanizing public support for Finland's bid to join NATO.

In August 2022, her accomplishments were no longer front-page news; they were overshadowed by leaked photos and videos of the prime minister dancing and drinking—with apparent abandon—at late-night parties. Marin had been videoed at nightclubs before, but now resurgent conservative groups were in attack mode and decided to expose what they saw as her freewheeling approach to sex and drugs. A photo surfaced showing two women exposing their breasts and kissing at a party at the prime minister's official residence, and a far-right message board claimed that cocaine use was a regular feature of the PM's clubbing scene. Marin agreed to take a drug test, and it came out negative. But the floodgates had opened.

Marin barely survived the ensuing furor. She has plenty of defenders among the youth of Finland and public figures worldwide. Hillary Clinton tweeted a photo of herself dancing and drinking, as did AOC. But as Finland's prime minister, Marin has no choice but to deal with public opinion in a buttoned-up country where dancing in public was illegal until after World War II. As one of my interviewees, a female executive at Nokia, told me, in somewhat exasperated tones, "If Marin wants to hang on to power, she doesn't need to change her identity; she just needs to do a better job controlling what is shared on social media. This isn't rocket science; entertainers like Beyoncé have monitored their online image for years."

KEY TAKEAWAYS

A final word on the appearance front. What was the most helpful piece of advice offered up in my executive interviews?

In several conversations over the last five years, Shari Slate (chief inclusion and collaboration officer, Cisco) and I discussed the value of full-spectrum diversity—see graphic below. For us, the list displayed is not just practically useful, a tool any HR leader could deploy when recruiting top talent to a team; it's personally empowering, something any ambitious up-and-comer should internalize and put to work. "Don't just read this list," Slate told me firmly, "own it."

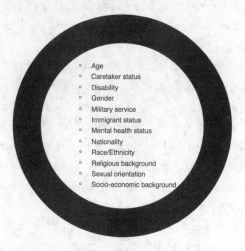

° Age
° Caretaker status
° Disability
° Gender
° Military service
° Immigrant status
° Mental health status
° Nationality
° Race/Ethnicity
° Religious background
° Sexual orientation
° Socio-economic background

Figure 19. Full-spectrum diversity

What does this mean?

Slate's viewpoint is that every high achiever has two or three identities that differentiate them and allow them to bring out-of-the-box insights and skill sets to the table. We've seen this in the pages of this book. Eddie Glaude is a distinguished academician, an African-American, and a person who grew up in modest circumstances in the Deep South. He wears all three identities on his sleeve and uses them to reach an audience that is much wider and deeper than policy wonks and scholars. Similarly, Virginia Rometty has multiple identities. She is a much admired business leader, a female systems engineer who needed to fight for recognition, and the daughter of a single mom who struggled to pay the bills. She's proud of all three of her identities and wears them well. And why not? They gave her the tools to drive transformational change at IBM and become both a radical disruptor and a breath of fresh air at Davos and Aspen.

Shari Slate's advice gives new heft and weight to the simple idea that professionals are much more successful when they bring their whole selves to work. My conversations with her have made me reflect on my journey. Have I done a good job showcasing my own foundational identities?

Over the years, I've done a reasonable job with two of my identities. In my writings, talks, keynotes, and "fireside chats," I've owned the struggles I've faced and the wins I've scored as a female economist and the mother of five. I've been somewhat fearless about this—showing up eight months pregnant at a congressional hearing, and pumping milk in the Xeroxing room at Barnard College (couldn't a women's college come up with something better?).

But I've done much less well owning my blue-collar roots and hardscrabble childhood. This is my most fundamental identity, yet I've played fast and loose with it. From time to time, I mention my working-class origins and tell charming stories about growing up with five siblings in a house with no refrigerator, phone, or heat, as well as my desperate attempts to lose what my Cambridge tutor called a "dreadful" Welsh working-class accent. But I keep it light, doing my level best to avoid my heart of darkness: the ugliness and despair stitched into the bones of my childhood and early womanhood. Fact is, until very recently, I haven't had the courage to own the nasty stuff. Stuff that runs the gamut from the bedbugs that infested our childhood home in the summer months, to the death of a beloved sister from a drug overdose.

I think it's time to take Shari Slate's advice and finally own my most potent identity. After all, my hardscrabble blue-collar background has contributed enormous passion and purpose to the work I've done in the world. My book *When the Bough Breaks* dug into the cost of neglecting our children, and one of my recent talks at the Yale School of Medicine centered on the career costs borne by upstarts and outsiders. I know because I've lived it, that people from the wrong side of the tracks are weighed down by heavy baggage. Whether it is crippling student debt, poor dental care in childhood, or a lack of access to power brokers and door openers, there are myriad ways in which coming from a low-income, struggling family can throw sand in the wheels of a person's progress.

It's high time I put myself more centrally in my stories and cease pretending that I'm just some outside arm's-length expert. It would allow me to touch hearts as well as minds and deepen my impact on the world.

CONCLUSION

Ordinary mortals can crack the EP code. These skills are eminently learnable. You don't have to be a born actor or be endowed with a James Earl Jones voice. I find it painful to remember how bad I was when I started doing public lectures. I used to stand behind large podiums reading from copious notes, determined that my audience hear every last piece of the evidence I had assembled to prove my point. I wince at the thought of how boring I must have been. Oftentimes I was also invisible. At five feet four (with heels) I could barely peer over the podium in many venues.

But I confronted my shortcomings and, by dint of hard work and with help from various coaches, lifted my game. Today I can command most spaces and stages. I have my own checklist: I prepare so thoroughly that the arc of my speech (vivid stories as well as pithy facts) gets beaten into my brain and I'm able to ditch my notes; I call ahead and ask that the podium be moved out of the way; and I use a lavaliere microphone so that I can roam free, making eye contact with as many people in the audience as possible. Over the years I've transformed my ability to engage and inspire an audience.

If EP is learnable, it's also doable. **You don't have to be some kind of genius** and ace all top picks across the three categories of gravitas, communication, and appearance. No need for straight A's. Not even Barack Obama is that good—and neither is his spectacular wife, Michelle Obama. My advice here is to work with your strengths and try to nail three picks in each category. Take my approach to gravitas. My personality and skill sets position me well for number 1 (confidence), number 4 (emotional intelligence), and number 6 (vision). I have therefore sought to develop these natural strengths while making sure I don't totally mess up the other three picks. I also seek to avoid serious blunders.

Figure out what is negotiable—and what is not. In your drive to crack the EP code, don't compromise your authenticity to such an extent that it puts your soul in play. It will make you miserable and will also backfire, because in the end gravitas rests squarely on your true identity.

If you're a woman (or a gay person) working in a testosterone-laced organizational culture, don't put up with off-color or homophobic jokes. Make clear what your values are. If this means you're cut loose and encouraged to find employment elsewhere, so be it. Eventually your integrity and authenticity will win out.

Or if you're passionate about your field and enjoy inspiring others, yet work in an organization where coolness and restraint are admired behaviors, you may need to quit and find a work culture that values your enthusiasm and commitment. It's distressing to be constantly dialing back; it also eats into how much you can contribute to any venture.

A final word: **Commit to the work involved and embrace your EP journey.** It will be enormously empowering. Of course it will require a ton of effort and energy. Learning how to command a room, figuring out how to use silence to punctuate a speech, becoming an adept and agile player on social media to project a distinctive brand, finding the perfect skirt or suit to complement your body type—none of this is easy and it will require hours of painstaking effort. But you can count on the results being transformative. Cracking the EP code will close the gap between merit and success, between where you are right now, and where you could be if you unleashed your full potential and allowed it to fly and soar. And it will make you feel quite wonderful.

Is failure to crack the EP code holding you back from achieving your full potential? Take this assessment and find out.

1. You're making a presentation to twenty senior executives in your organization. Just before stepping into the meeting venue you receive a phone call from your doctor with some disturbing news, which leaves you distressed and distracted. How do you handle this when you are expected to present immediately? Do you . . .

    a) Delay the meeting by ten or more minutes while you pull yourself together

    b) Take several deep breaths, walk into the meeting, and present with as much composure as possible

    c) Cancel the meeting because you feel you're not in a fit state to handle it

2. You are abroad, conducting a workshop in your area of expertise. Most of the participants are engaging and interactive, as they have substantial experience and knowledge of this subject matter. This adds to the productivity of the workshop. However, there are one or two participants who know very little and who are not quite grasping some of the concepts you are introducing.

As a result, they interrupt you often by asking questions and/or requesting that you repeat yourself. Do you . . .
- a) Ignore their questions, hoping they will eventually stop interrupting and catch up with the rest of the group
- b) Become irritated and display a "what do you want now" attitude
- c) Head off future disruptions by calling a short break so that you can talk to the participants who do not seem to be catching on and offer to meet with them after the formal presentation for a fifteen-minute coaching session

3. You've been called into a strategy meeting by your CEO, who wants input from his senior team on recent hits to the bottom line. Some key clients have walked out the door. You know (as do others) that one of the main reasons this is happening is that the CEO has old-fashioned ideas and/or concepts, and does not want to move with the times. He chooses you out of the group and asks for your thoughts. What do you do?
- a) Smile pleasantly and offer reassurance to the CEO.
- b) Stand up and in a confident tone speak "truth to power," telling the CEO that the organization needs to move to next-gen products/services and making sure to offer some concrete suggestions.
- c) Get yourself off the hook by asking the CEO to call on a more senior person who is better in touch with the organization's business strategy.

4. You are a director in a consulting firm and have twelve direct reports. Your team is the top-performing group at the company largely due to two outstanding individuals: a white male and a Black woman, who also has a slight speech impediment. The se-

nior partners at the firm want to promote one of these "stars" and hand over the decision to you. Kind of. "Offline" they express a preference for the Caucasian male, making the case that his communication skills are superior to the Black woman and he's a better "fit" in the culture. What decision do you make?

a) You give the promotion to the Black woman despite her speech impairment because she is the better performer; the previous year she'd brought in twice the new business as the Caucasian male.

b) You promote the Caucasian male because in the end you agree with the senior partners: fit and eloquence are more important than acing the numbers.

c) You ask the partners to make the decision because they are in a better position than you are to gauge the long-run needs of the company.

5. You are attending a business conference that has featured an unusual number of speakers—most of them uninspired if not outright boring. It is late in the afternoon and you're eager to go home when unexpectedly you're asked to make the wrap-up remarks. How do you deal with this EP challenge?

a) You reluctantly agree to do your best—making sure to tell the audience that you're a fill-in and not prepared. Then you make some desultory comments.

b) You decide to put comfort first and request a chair be put on the stage. You know yourself well enough to know that you'll have a better shot at being bright, scintillating, and responsive to questions from the audience if you're not on your feet.

c) You drink a glass of water and walk on with a welcoming smile. You make your closing remarks short and sweet and focus on making eye contact with the weary professionals still in the room.

6. As team leader, you must meet with your team and let them know that despite their hard drive to boost sales in the second half of the quarter, expansion didn't happen—largely due to headwinds from the outside—and the team is being disbanded, with some individuals being let go and others distributed to other divisions. How do you handle the meeting where you communicate the bad news?

    a) You are truthful and direct. Without sugarcoating the situation, you emphasize that this is no one's fault; rather this is a structural thing. You also offer to use your personal network to help those newly out of work to find a next job.

    b) You explain that this is a decision made by senior management and you don't have line of sight on why the team's being broken up. You direct your team to go to HR with any questions.

    c) You use this opportunity to blame the big bosses at the company and shame the poor performers on the team. This will deflect attention from yourself.

7. You are at a dinner reception honoring the leader of your organization. You are seated at a table with executives from other companies whom you do not know. They're focused on talking with one another. Which of the below is a good way to open a conversation that could lead to a substantive connection?

    a) Pick the person sitting next to you or across from you. Turn to that person with a smile and make a lighthearted comment about the food, the venue, or the honoree. This breaks the ice and initiates an interchange and eventually some kind of discussion.

b) Introduce yourself to the most important people at the table, making sure to mention two or three of your accomplishments.

c) Sit quietly and wait for someone to engage you in conversation. If you get bored, you can always scroll on your phone.

8. You have a great track record at the company and have been promoted several times. You're now being considered for a VP slot and have been invited to speak to members of the C-suite about your goals and visions. You find this a terrifying prospect as you're shy and soft-spoken and have a tendency to quiver with nerves when put in the spotlight.

a) Calm your fears by telling yourself that this presentation doesn't matter too much, that the decision of these leaders will hinge on what you've delivered over the years, not your skills as a public speaker.

b) Prepare like crazy and practice in front of a mirror. If you beat your presentation into your brain, muscle memory will take over and "nerves" won't matter.

c) Ask if you can meet with each C-suite executive individually. You know you're much more impressive one-on-one.

9. You're excited because you've been invited to the company's golf retreat this year, despite being a golf "beginner" with a handicap of 130. You go shopping for a new golf outfit and end up buying two. Your enthusiasm is dampened a little when you arrive at the retreat and walk into a wall of male colleagues. Almost all of

the attendees at this event are men; most of them scratch golfers. How do you comport yourself to appear leaderly? How do you avoid humiliation?

a) Play the "good sport" card by tagging along in a foursome and taking whatever knocks come your way. As long as you pick up your ball when lagging behind and don't slow down the pace of play, no one will find fault with you. And the advantage of getting out there and playing is that you'll really get to know some of the male leaders. Golf is a long-winded game. Eighteen holes takes about five hours.

b) Wear the outfits—all look good on you—but ditch the actual golf. As long as you display know-how and enthusiasm for "all things golf" over drinks and dinner, you'll be one of the boys, strengthen your connection to these male leaders, and have a new network going forward.

c) Cut your losses. Realize that you won't cut the mustard with this crowd and therefore can't make this golf retreat work for you. Retreating to your room with a good book is the way to go.

10. Which of these statements accurately describes the elements of executive presence?

a) To be seen as someone who is "leadership material" and has "what it takes," you need to ace all six top traits in the gravitas, communication, and appearance buckets.

b) Appearance is superficial nonsense that only superficial folks pay attention to.

c) How we behave, how we talk, and how we look determine how we are seen in this world and what we can accomplish for ourselves, for others, and for the work we are privileged to do.

Total Your Score: 1. a-2, b-3, c-1; 2. a-2, b-1, c-3; 3. a-2, b-3, c-1; 4. a-3, b-2, c-1; 5. a-1, b-2, c-3; 6. a-3, b-2, c-1; 7. a-3, b-1, c-2; 8. a-2, b-3, c-1; 9. a-1, b-3, c-2; 10. a-1, b-2, c-3

Your score	What it means
Less than 23	Poor to fair. But don't worry, EP can be learned! Utilize mentors, sponsors, role models, and pointers in this book to burnish how you act, how you speak, and how you talk.
24–26	Good. You're on the right track! To bolster your EP, use coaches and other external resources to get a more solid grasp of all three pillars (gravitas, communication, and appearance).
27–30	Excellent. You've nailed EP! You have what it takes to convert your abilities into impact, influence, agency, and a path to a top job.

For a more in-depth diagnostic of your or your colleagues' executive presence, please visit hewlettconsultingpartners.com.

INDEX OF EXHIBITS

Index of Exhibits

NOTES

1. Identities have been disguised.

2. Chia-Jung Tsay, "Sight over Sound in the Judgment of Music Performance," *Proceedings of the National Academy of Sciences in the United States of America* 110, no. 36 (2013): 14580–85, published online before print, August 19, 2013.

3. Kweilin Ellingrud, Alexis Krivkovich, Marie-Claude Nadeau, and Jill Zucker, "Closing the Gender and Race Gaps in North American Financial Services," October 21, 2021, https://www.mckinsey.com /industries/financial-services/our-insights/closing-the-gender-and -race-gaps-in-north-american-financial-services.

4. ABC News, "Top BP Executive Bob Dudley on 'Top Kill' Failure," interview on *This Week with George Stephanopoulos*, uploaded May 30, 2010, http://www.youtube.com/watch?v=kup3nTBo_-A&list=P LC8BBAB0172164E53&index=117.

5. *PBS NewsHour*, "'America Speaks to BP' Full Transcript: Bob Dudley Interview," air date July 1, 2010, http://www.pbs.org/newshour /bb/environment/july-dec10/dudleyfull_07-01.html.

6. The War in Afghanistan began on October 7, 2001, when the armed forces of the United States, the United Kingdom, Australia, France, and the Afghan United Front (Northern Alliance) launched Operation Enduring Freedom. See http://www.washingtonpost.com /wp-srv/nation/specials/attacked/transcripts/bushaddress_100801 .htm.

7. Jack Welch and Suzy Welch, "J.P. Morgan: Jamie Dimon and the

Horse He Fell Off," *Fortune*, May 24, 2012, http://management
.fortune.cnn.com/2012/05/24/j-p-morgan-jamie-dimon-and-the
-horse-he-fell-off/.

8. Hugh Son, "Jamie Dimon says 'This Part of the Crisis Is Over'
    After JPMorgan Chase Buys First Republic," CNBC, May 1,
    2023, https://www.cnbc.com/2023/05/01/jamie-dimon-jpmorgan
    -first-republic.html.

9. "Worst Moments of My Life: Pilot Tells of Ditching in Hudson,"
    Sydney Morning Herald, February 6, 2009, http://www.smh.com.au
    /news/world/audio-reveals-exactly-what-happened--a-hrefhttp
    mediasmhcomaurid45888blistenba/2009/02/06/1233423442580
    .html.

10. Tim Webb, "BP Boss Admits Job on the Line over Gulf Oil
    Spill," *Guardian*, May 13, 2010, http://www.theguardian.com/busi
    ness/2010/may/13/bp-boss-admits-mistakes-gulf-oil-spill.

11. Stanley Reed, "Tony Hayward Gets His Life Back," *New York
    Times*, September 1, 2012, http://www.nytimes.com/2012/09/02
    /business/tony-hayward-former-bp-chief-returns-to-oil.html?page
    wanted=all.

12. Claire Cain Miller and Catherine Rampell, "Yahoo Orders Home
    Workers Back to the Office," *New York Times*, February 25, 2013,
    http://www.nytimes.com/2013/02/26/technology/yahoo-orders
    -home-workers-back-to-the-office.html?pagewanted=all.

13. Kara Swisher, "'Physically Together': Here's the Internal Yahoo
    No-Work-from-Home Memo for Remote Workers and Maybe
    More," All Things D blog, February 22, 2013, http://allthingsd
    .com/20130222/physically-together-heres-the-internal-yahoo-no
    -work-from-home-memo-which-extends-beyond-remote-workers/.

14. Richard Branson, "Give People the Freedom of Where to Work,"
    blog, February 25, 2013, http://www.virgin.com/richard-branson
    /give-people-the-freedom-of-where-to-work.

15. Charles Wallace, "Keep Taking the Testosterone," *Financial Times*,
    February 9, 2012, http://www.ft.com/intl/cms/s/0/68015bb2-51b8
    -11e1-a99d-00144feabdc0.html#axzz2NG4LUhfT.

16. Cenegenics website, http://www.cenegenics-nyc.com/mens-age
-management-new-york-city.

17. Cindy Perman, "Wall Street's Secret Weapon for Getting an Edge,"
CNBC, July 11, 2012, http://www.cnbc.com/id/48149955.

18. Mayo Clinic website, "Testosterone Therapy: Key to Male Vitality?,"
http://www.mayoclinic.com/health/testosterone-therapy/MC00
030/NSECTIONGROUP=2, accessed October 4, 2013.

19. Massimo Calabrisi, "Governor Christie on Sandy, Romney and
Obama," *Time*, October 30, 2012, http://swampland.time.com/2012
/10/30/gov-christie-on-sandy-romney-and-obama/.

20. Kate Zernike, "One Result of Hurricane: Bipartisanship Flows,"
New York Times, October 31, 2012, http://www.nytimes.com
/2012/11/01/nyregion/in-stunning-about-face-chris-christie
-heaps-praise-on-obama.html.

21. Burgess Everett, "Chris Christie on Hurricane Sandy: Holdouts
Are 'Stupid and Selfish,'" *Politico*, October 29, 2012, http://www
.politico.com/news/stories/1012/83007.html.

22. "Chris Christie Criticizes Obama for 'Posing and Preening' as
President," *Star-Ledger*, May 20, 2012, http://www.huffingtonpost
.com/2012/05/20/chris-christie-obama_n_1531471.html; "Gov.
Christie: Obama Is 'Posing and Preening,' Not Resolving Issues
as President," NJ.com, May 20, 2012, http://www.nj.com/news
/index.ssf/2012/05/gov_christie_obama_is_posing_a.html.

23. Christina Rexrode, "Struggling Bank of America Shakes Up Exec
Ranks," AP on Yahoo, September 7, 2011, http://news.yahoo.com
/struggling-bank-america-shakes-exec-ranks-225348682.html;
Halah Touryalai, "Bank of America's Latest Peril: Losing Merrill
Lynch?," *Forbes* blog, September 2, 2013, http://www.forbes.com
/sites/halahtouryalai/2011/09/02/bank-of-americas-latest-peril
-losing-merrill-lynch/.

24. Daniel Goleman, *Emotional Intelligence* (New York: Bantam Books,
1995).

25. Kara Swisher, "Survey Says: Despite Yahoo Ban, Most Tech Companies Support Work-from-Home for Employees," All Things D

blog, February 25, 2013, http://allthingsd.com/20130225/survey
-says-despite-yahoo-ban-most-tech-companies-support-work-from
-home-for-employees/.

26.   Robin J. Ely and Debra E. Meyerson, "An Organizational Approach
to Undoing Gender: The Unlikely Case of Offshore Oil Platforms,"
Research in Organizational Behavior 30 (2010): 3–34.

27.   Andrea Tantaros, "Material Girl Michelle Obama Is a Modern-
Day Marie Antoinette on a Glitzy Spanish Vacation," editorial,
Daily News, August 5, 2010, http://www.nydailynews.com/opin
ion/material-girl-michelle-obama-modern-day-marie-antoinette
-glitzy-spanish-vacation-article-1.200134?pgno=1.

28.   See, for example, Shawna Thomas, "Michelle Obama: 'Hadiya Pendleton Was Me and I Was Her,'" NBC News, April 10,
2013, http://firstread.nbcnews.com/_news/2013/04/10/17692560
-michelle-obama-hadiya-pendleton-was-me-and-i-was-her?lite.

29.   Leah Hope, "Obama Center 'Winter Garden' to Honor Chicago
Teen Killed Days after Performing at Inauguration," *ABC News*,
January 28, 2022, https://abc7chicago.com/obama-presidential-center
-hadiya-pendleton-chicago-shooting-winter-garden/11517110/.

30.   "Angelina Jolie Fact Sheet," UNHCR, http://www.unhcr.org
/pages/49db77906.html, accessed October 4, 2013.

31.   The study, conducted by Quantified Impressions, analyzed financial executives' communication effectiveness by applying a
suite of software tools developed in conjunction with the Kellogg
School of Management at Northwestern University and enlisting
a panel of experts along with one thousand listeners to augment
the digital analysis. The most effective financial spokesperson
turned out to be Richard Davis, CEO of US Bancorp, because
he appeared "genuine, emotionally connected to his audience, and
relaxed in front of the camera," according to Quantified's president, Noah Zandan. http://www.quantifiedimpressions.com/blog
/quantified-impressions-new-scientific-analysis-of-top-financial
-communicators-pinpoints-how-speakers-build-trust-influence
-audiences/.

32. Quantified Impressions study.

33. Cited by Sue Shellenbarger in "Is This How You Really Talk?," *Wall Street Journal*, April 23, 2013, http://online.wsj.com/article/SB1000 14241278873237356045784440851083674898.html.

34. Charles Moore, "The Invincible Mrs. Thatcher," *Vanity Fair*, December 2011, http://www.vanityfair.com/politics/features/2011/12 /margaret-thatcher-201112.

35. David Baker, "Hollywood Vocal Coach Helped Margaret Thatcher Lose Her 'Shrill Tones,'" *Mail Online*, February 5, 2012, http:// www.dailymail.co.uk/news/article-2096785/Hollywood-vocal -coach-helped-Margaret-Thatcher-lose-shrill-tones.html; Moore, "The Invincible Mrs. Thatcher."

36. William J. Mayew, Christopher A. Parsons, and Mohan Venkatachalam, "Voice Pitch and the Labor Market Success of Male Chief Executive Officers," *Evolution and Human Behavior* 34 (2013): 243–48.

37. Melissa Korn, "What Does a Successful CEO Sound Like? Try a Deep Bass," *Wall Street Journal*, April 18, 2013, http://blogs.wsj .com/atwork/2013/04/18/what-does-a-successful-ceo-sound-like -try-a-deep-bass/?blog_id=226&post_id=882&mod=wsj_valet top_email.

38. "Americans Speak Out, Select the 'Best and Worst Voices in America' in Online Polling by the Center for Voice Disorders of Wake Forest University," press release, Wake Forest University Baptist Medical Center, September 10, 2001, http://www.nrcdxas.org/ar ticles/voices.html.

39. William J. Mayew and Mohan Venkatachalam, "Voice Pitch and the Labor Market Success of Male Chief Executive Officers," Sidney Winter Lecture Series, April 12, 2013, http://tippie.uiowa.edu /accounting/mcgladrey/winterpapers/mpv_ehb_accepted%20-%20 mayew.pdf.

40. Sue Shellenbarger, "Is This How You Really Talk?," *Wall Street Journal*, April 23, 2013, http://online.wsj.com/article/SB100014 24127887323735604578440851083674898.html.

Notes

41. Huffingtonpost.com audience measurement, Quantcast, http://www.quantcast.com/huffingtonpost.com, accessed April 4, 2013.

42. Erik Hedegaard, "Beauty and the Blog: *Rolling Stone*'s 2006 Feature on Arianna Huffington," *Rolling Stone*, December 14, 2006, http://www.rollingstone.com/culture/news/beauty-and-the-blog-rolling-stones-2006-feature-on-arianna-huffington-20110207#ixzz2gIpcBwfa.

43. Allen Dodds Frank, "Former Wall Street Executive Sallie Krawcheck Critiques Financial Reform Policy," *Daily Beast*, October 16, 2012, http://www.thedailybeast.com/articles/2012/10/16/former-wall-street-executive-sallie-krawcheck-critiques-financial-reform-policy.html.

44. Carol Kinsey Goman, "The Body Language Winner of the Third Presidential Debate," *Forbes*, October 23, 2012, http://www.forbes.com/sites/carolkinseygoman/2012/10/23/the-body-language-winner-of-the-third-presidential-debate/.

45. When only first names are used they are pseudonyms. Identifying details have been changed to protect confidentiality.

46. See Amy Cuddy's TED talk at http://www.ted.com/talks/amy_cuddy_your_body_language_shapes_who_you_are.html, posted October 2012.

47. Kate Murphy, "The Right Stance Can Be Reassuring," *New York Times*, May 3, 2013, http://www.nytimes.com/2013/05/05/fashion/the-right-stance-can-be-reassuring-studied.html?emc=eta1&_r=0.

48. Elise Hu, "Campaign Trail Tears: The Changing Politics of Crying," NPR, November 25, 2011, http://www.npr.org/2011/11/25/142599676/campaign-trail-tears-the-changing-politics-of-crying.

49. *Saturday Night Live*, "Democratic Debate '88," transcript from Season 13, Episode 10, available at http://snltranscripts.jt.org/87/87jdemocrats.phtml.

50. Nancy Benac, "Has the Political Risk of Emotion, Tears Faded?," *USA Today*, December 19, 2007, http://usatoday30.usatoday.com/news/politics/election2008/2007-12-19-emotion-politics_N.htm.

51.   Photos reprinted with permission. http://www.plosone.org/article; Nancy L. Etcoff, Shannon Stock, Lauren E. Haley, Sarah A. Vickery, and David M. House, "Cosmetics as a Feature of the Extended Human Phenotype: Modulation of the Perception of Biologically Important Facial Signals," *PLoS ONE* 6, no. 10 (2011): e25656, 2011, doi:10.1371/journal.pone.0025656.

52.   Etcoff et al., "Cosmetics as a Feature of the Extended Human Phenotype," 7.

53.   Check out the Occupy Wall Street debate at the Oxford Union Society on YouTube: http://www.youtube.com/watch?v=CoWiV6Q8qME.

54.   Deborah L. Rhode, *The Beauty Bias: The Injustice of Appearance in Life and Law* (New York: Oxford University Press, 2010).

55.   Timothy Noah, "Chris Christie's Crowd-Sourced Weight Is . . . ," *New Republic*, September 30, 2011, http://www.newrepublic.com/blog/timothy-noah/95641/chris-christies-crowd-sourced-weight#.

56.   John Kenney, "The Unbearable Lightness of Leading," *New York Times*, March 6, 2010, http://www.nytimes.com/2010/03/07/opinion/07kenney.html.

57.   OPEN N.Y., "The Measure of a President," *New York Times*, October 6, 2008, http://www.nytimes.com/interactive/2008/10/06/opinion/06opchart.html?_r=0.

58.   Leslie Kwoh, "Want to Be CEO? What's Your BMI?," *Wall Street Journal*, January 16, 2013, http://online.wsj.com/article/SB10001424127887324595704578241573341483946.html.

59.   Rhode, *The Beauty Bias*, 21.

60.   Julie Creswell and Matthew Futterman, "Nike's Chief Executive, Mark Parker, Is Stepping Down," *New York Times*, October 22, 2019, https://www.nytimes.com/2019/10/22/business/nike-ceo-mark-parker.html.

61.   Ben Shapiro, *Project President: Bad Hair and Botox on the Road to the White House* (Nashville, TN: Thomas Nelson, 2007), 53.

62.   Ibid., 54.

63.   OPEN N.Y., "The Measure of a President."

64. Shapiro, *Project President*, 54.

65. "Diana Taylor Addresses Her and Bloomberg's Height Difference," *Huffington Post*, January 10, 2011, updated January 10, 2012, http://www.huffingtonpost.com/2011/01/10/diana-taylor-bloomberg-do_n_807031.html.

66. Chris Woolston, "A Costly Turf War," *Los Angeles Times*, January 29, 2012, http://articles.latimes.com/2012/jan/29/image/la-ig-balding-20120129.

67. Dr. Dominic Castellano, "Botox Statistics You Need to Know in 2023," December 12, 2021, https://www.elitetampa.com/blog/botox-statistics-you-need-to-know/.

68. "Brotox? Cosmetic Procedures Rise, Growing Number of Men Turn to Botox," *ABC Action News*, WXYZ, June 14, 2013, http://www.wxyz.com/dpp/news/brotox-cosmetic-procedures-rises-growing-number-of-men-turn-to-botox.

69. The Aesthetic Society, "Statistics 2020–2021," //efaidnbmnnnibpcajpcglclefindmkaj/https://cdn.theaestheticsociety.org/media/statistics/2021-TheAestheticSocietyStatistics.pdf.

70. Melissa Preddy, "Quicktips: From Upper-Arm Tucks to Up-in-Arms Truckers," Reynolds Center, BusinessJournalism.org, April 30, 2013, http://businessjournalism.org/2013/04/30/quicktips-from-upper-arm-tucks-to-up-in-arms-truckers/.

71. William J. vanden Heuvel, "LETTERS: Another Look at F.D.R.," *New York Times*, January 12, 2010, http://query.nytimes.com/gst/fullpage.html?res=9C02E4DF1F30F931A25752C0A9669D8B63.

72. Ibid.

73. Sylvia Ann Hewlett, *#MeToo in the Corporate World: Power, Privelege, and the Path Forward* (New York: Harper Business, 2020), 23–38.

74. Sylvia Ann Hewlett, *#MeToo in the Corporate World: Power, Privelege and the Path Forward* (New York: Harper Business, 2020), pages 91–113.

75. Margaret Thatcher, "Speech to Finchley Conservatives," January 31, 1976, Margaret Thatcher Foundation, http://www.margaretthatcher.org/document/102947.

76. Michael Cockerell, "How to Be a Tory Leader," *Telegraph*, Decem-

ber 1, 2005, http://www.telegraph.co.uk/culture/3648425/How-to
-be-a-Tory-leader.html.

77. Stephen Moss, "Looking for Maggie," *Guardian*, March 6, 2003,
http://www.theguardian.com/books/2003/mar/07/biography
.media.

78. Women in the Workplace Study, Lean In, 2022, https://leanin.org
/women-in-the-workplace/2022/the-state-of-the-pipeline.

79. Sylvia Ann Hewlett, *Forget a Mentor, Find a Sponsor: The New Way
to Fast-Track Your Career* (Boston, Mass.: Harvard Business Review
Press, 2013), 27–50.

80. "Jesse Jackson Slams Obama for 'Acting Like He's White' in Jena 6
Case," ABC News, September 19, 2007, http://abcnews.go.com
/blogs/headlines/2007/09/jesse-jackson-s/.

81. Stanley Crouch, "What Obama Isn't: Black Like Me on Race," *New
York Daily News*, November 2, 2006, http://www.nydailynews.com
/Archives/Opinions/Obama-Isnt-Black-Race-Article-1.585922.

82. Sylvia Hewlett, Kerrie Peraino, Laura Sherbin, and Karen Sumberg,
"The Sponsor Effect: Breaking Through the Last Glass Ceiling,"
Harvard Business Review Research Report, December 2010, 26.

83. Virginia E. Schein, "The Relationship Between Sex Role Stereo-
types and Requisite Management Characteristics," *Journal of Applied
Psychology* 57 (1973): 95–100; Virginia E. Schein, "The Relationship
Between Sex Role Stereotypes and Requisite Management Char-
acteristics Among Female Managers," *Journal of Applied Psychology*
60 (1975): 340–44; Virginia E. Schein, "Managerial Sex Typing:
A Persistent and Pervasive Barrier to Women's Opportunities," in
M. Davidson and R. Burke, eds., *Women in Management: Current
Research Issues* (London: Paul Chapman, 1994).

84. "Women 'Take Care,' Men 'Take Charge': Stereotyping of U.S.
Business Leaders Exposed," Catalyst, 2005, http://www.catalyst
.org/knowledge/women-take-care-men-take-charge-stereotyping
-us-business-leaders-exposed.

85. See Veronica F. Nieva and Barbara A. Gutek, "Sex Effects on Eval-
uation," *Academy of Management Review* 5, no. 2 (1980).

86. Peggy McIntosh, "White Privilege: Unpacking the Invisible Knapsack," *Peace and Freedom*, July/August 1989.

87. "How Are Powerful Women Perceived," *Anderson Cooper 360*, CNN, March 12, 2013, http://www.cnn.com/video/data/2.0/video /bestoftv/2013/03/13/ac-powerful-women-experiment.cnn.html.

88. Madeline E. Heilman, Aaron S. Wallen, Daniella Fuchs, and Melinda M. Tamkins, "Penalties for Success: Reactions to Women Who Succeed at Male Gender-Typed Tasks," *Journal of Applied Psychology* 89, no. 3 (2004): 416–27.

89. Kim M. Elsesser and Janet Lever, "Does Gender Bias Against Female Leaders Persist? Quantitative and Qualitative Data from a Large-Scale Survey," *Human Relations* 64, no. 12 (2011): 1555–78, http://hum.sagepub.com/content/64/12/1555.

90. Oliver Balch, "The Bachelet Factor: The Cultural Legacy of Chile's First Female President," *Guardian*, December 13, 2009, http:// www.guardian.co.uk/world/2009/dec/13/michelle-bachelet-chile -president-legacy.

91. Ibid.

92. Katrin Bennhold, "Taking the Gender Fight Worldwide," *New York Times*, March 29, 2011, http://www.nytimes.com/2011/03/30 /world/europe/30iht-letter30.html?page-wanted=2&ref=michelle bachelet.

93. Patricia Sellers, "Facing Up to the Female Power Conundrum," CNN Money, January 31, 2011, http://postcards.blogs.fortune.cnn .com/2011/01/31/facing-up-to-the-female-power-conundrum/.

94. Jessica Valenti, "She Who Dies with the Most 'Likes' Wins?," *Nation*, November 29, 2012, http://www.thenation.com/blog/171520 /she-who-dies-most-likes-wins.

95. Sheryl Sandberg, *Lean In: Women, Work, and the Will to Lead* (New York: Alfred A. Knopf, 2013), 40.

96. "The Double-Bind Dilemma for Women in Leadership: Damned If You Do, Doomed If You Don't," Catalyst, 2007, http://www.catalyst .org/knowledge/double-bind-dilemma-women-leadership-damned -if-you-do-doomed-if-you-dont-0.

97. David Mattingly, "Michelle Obama Likely Target of Conservative Attacks," CNN.com, June 12, 2008, http://www.cnn.com/2008/POLITICS/06/12/michelle.obama/.

98. Jeremy Holden, "Fox News' E. D. Hill Teased Discussion of Obama Dap: 'A Fist Bump? A Pound? A Terrorist Fist Jab?,'" June 6, 2008, cited on Media Matters for America, http://mediamatters.org/video/2008/06/06/fox-news-ed-hill-teased-discussion-of-obama-dap/143674.

99. Avery Stone, "What If Paula Deen Had Called Someone a Fag?," HuffPost Blog, July 1, 2013, http://www.huffingtonpost.com/avery-stone/what-if-paula-deen-had-called-someone-a-fag_b_3526186.html.

100. "Ireland Baldwin Talks About Father Alec Baldwin's Infamous 'Pig' Voicemail," *Huffington Post*, September 6, 2012, http://www.huffingtonpost.com/2012/09/06/ireland-baldwin-alec-baldwin-pig-call_n_1861892.html.

101. Diane Johnson, "Christine Lagarde: Changing of the Guard," *Vogue*, September 2011, 706, http://www.vogue.com/magazine/article/christine-lagarde-changing-of-the-guard/#1.

102. Ibid.

103. Richard Branson, "Richard Branson on Taking Risks," *Entrepreneur*, June 10, 2013, http://www.entrepreneur.com/article/226942.

104. Eleanor Clift, "Kirsten Gillibrand's Moment: Women's Champion vs. Military Assaults," *Daily Beast*, May 10, 2013, http://www.thedailybeast.com/articles/2013/05/10/kirsten-gillibrand-s-moment-women-s-champion-vs-military-assaults.html.

105. Steve Williams, "Elizabeth Warren: It Gets Better," Care2, January 27, 2012, http://www.care2.com/causes/elizabeth-warren-it-gets-better-video.html.

106. Sanford Levinson, "Identifying the Jewish Lawyer: Reflections on the Construction of Professional Identity," *Cardozo Law Review* 14, no. 1577 (1993): 1578–79. Interestingly, Levinson also used the multilingual metaphor to describe his spheres of identity as a Jewish lawyer.

107. Sylvia Ann Hewlett, Carolyn Buck Luce, Cornel West, Helen Chernikoff, Danielle Samalin, and Peggy Shiller, *Invisible Lives: Celebrating and Leveraging Diversity Talent in the Executive Suite* (New York: Center for Work-Life Policy, 2005). The Center for Work-Life Policy changed its name to the Center for Talent Innovation in 2012.

108. Ibid.

109. Sylvia Ann Hewlett and Karen Sumberg, *The Power of "Out": LGBT in the Workplace* (New York: Center for Work-Life Policy, 2011).

110. Sylvia Ann Hewlett, Melinda Marshall, and Laura Sherbin, with Tara Gonsalves, *Innovation, Diversity, and Market Growth* (New York: Center for Talent Innovation, 2013); Sylvia Ann Hewlett, Melinda Marshall, and Laura Sherbin, "How Diversity Can Drive Innovation," *Harvard Business Review*, December 2013.

111. Ibid.

112. Sylvia Ann Hewlett, *Forget a Mentor, Find a Sponsor: The New Way to Fast-Track Your Career* (Boston, Mass.: Harvard Business Review Press, 2013).

113. Sylvia Ann Hewlett, *The Sponsor Effect* (Boston, Mass.: Harvard Business Review Press, 2019), 21–22.

114. Per-Ola Karlsson, DeAnne Aguirre, and Kristin Rivera, "Are CEOs Less Ethical Than in the Past?," PricewaterhouseCoopers, no. 87, Summer 2017, https://www.pwc.com/ee/et/publications /pub/sb87_17208_Are_CEOs_Less_Ethical_Than_in_the_Past .pdf.

115. Andrew Ross Sorkin et al., "Tracking the Epstein Scandal's Fallout," *New York Times*, May 21, 2021, https://www.nytimes .com/2021/05/21/business/dealbook/jeffrey-epstein-resignations .html.

116. Between January and August 2022, I conducted seventy-three interviews with executives across a range of industries (finance, tech, auto, pharma, law, professional services, media, fashion, and gaming). A third of those I interviewed are established leaders who were involved in the research that fed into my 2014 book, *Execu-*

tive Presence: The Missing Link between Merit and Success. The other two-thirds are up-and-coming leaders whom I've gotten to know in recent years through my consulting practice. These executives are half a generation younger than the established leaders I interviewed and considerably more diverse. They tend to work in the "new" as opposed to the "old" economy. DraftKings, Splunk, Blizzard Entertainment, and TikTok rather than GE, Credit Suisse, or BP.

117. Daniel Goleman, *Emotional Intelligence: Why It Can Matter More Than IQ* (New York: Random House, 2005), https://www.danielgoleman.info/.

118. Ray Suarez, "America Speaks to BP," full transcript, Bob Dudley interview, *PBS NewsHour*, July 1, 2010, https://www.pbs.org/newshour/show/america-speaks-to-bp-full-transcript-bob-dudley-interview.

119. Rowena Mason, "Gulf of Mexico Oil Spill: BP Insists Oil Spill Impact Will Be 'Very Modest,' " *Telegraph*, May 18, 2010, https://www.telegraph.co.uk/finance/newsbysector/energy/oilandgas/7737805/Gulf-of-Mexico-oil-spill-BP-insists-oil-spill-impact-very-modest.html.

120. Gus Lubin, "BP CEO Tony Hayward Apologizes for His Idiotic Statement: 'I'd Like My Life Back,' " *Business Insider*, June 2, 2010, https://www.businessinsider.com/bp-ceo-tony-hayward-apologizes-for-saying-id-like-my-life-back-2010-6.

121. Sylvia Ann Hewlett, Melinda Marshall, and Laura Sherbin, with Tara Gonsalves, *Innovation, Diversity, and Market Growth* (New York: Center for Talent Innovation, 2013).

122. Sylvia Ann Hewlett, *#MeToo in the Corporate World: Power, Privilege, and the Path Forward* (New York: Harper Business, 2020), 22–36.

123. "National Governors Association Winter Meeting, Innovation and Workforce Skills," C-SPAN, February 25, 2018, https://www.c-span.org/video/?441465-3/national-governors-association-winter-meeting-innovation-workforce-skills.

124. Ibid.

125. Member Profile, 2016 Horatio Alger Award Recipient, Virginia M.

Rometty, https://horatioalger.org/members/member-detail/vir
ginia-m-rometty.

126. Sophie Rivera-Silverstein, "IBM's Ginni Rometty on Responsibility and Technology," Aspen Institute, December 16, 2019, https://
www.aspeninstitute.org/blog-posts/ibms-ginni-rometty-on-re
sponsibility-and-technology/.

127. Benson Buster, "Ex-Amazon Manager: Jeff Bezos Is 'Obsessed'
with This Decision-Making Style—'It's His Key to Success,'"
CNBC, November 14, 2019, https://www.cnbc.com/2019/11/14
/how-billionaire-jeff-bezos-makes-fast-smart-decisions-under
-pressure-says-ex-amazon-manager.html.

128. Peter Economy, "Amazon's 14 Leadership Principles Can Lead
You and Your Business to Remarkable Success," *Inc.*, November 18,
2019, https://www.inc.com/peter-economy/the-14-amazon-leader
ship-principles-that-can-lead-you-your-business-to-tremendous
-success.html.

129. Tom Alberg, "What I've Learned from Watching Jeff Bezos Make
Decisions Up Close," *Fast Company*, November 2, 2021, excerpted
from Tom Alberg, *Flywheels: How Cities Are Creating Their Own
Futures* (New York: Columbia Business School Publishing, 2021),
https://www.fastcompany.com/90691896/what-ive-learned-from
-watching-jeff-bezos-make-decisions-up-close.

130. "Roger Ferguson to Retire as President and CEO of TIAA," press
release, TIAA, November 17, 2020, https://www.tiaa.org/public
/about-tiaa/news-press/press-releases/2020/11-17.

131. Jenna McGregor, "TIAA Is the First Company in Fortune 500
History to Have Two Black CEOs in a Row," *Washington Post*, February 25, 2021, https://www.washingtonpost.com/business/2021
/02/25/tiaa-is-first-company-fortune-500-history-have-two-black
-ceos-row/.

132. Sylvia Ann Hewlett and Kennedy Ihezie, "20% of White Employees Have Sponsors. Only 5% of Black Employees Do," *Harvard
Business Review*, February 10, 2022, https://hbr.org/2022/02/20
-of-white-employees-have-sponsors-only-5-of-black-em

ployees-do#:~:text=Employees%20Have%20Sponsors.-,Only%20
5%25%20of%20Black%20Employees%20Do.,retain%20and%20
advance%20Black%20talent.&text=The%20power%20of%20spon
sorship%20to%20transform%20careers%20is%20now%20well%20
known.

133. Sylvia Ann Hewlett, *The Sponsor Effect* (Boston, Mass.: Harvard Business Review Press, 2019), 57.

134. McGregor, "TIAA Is the First Company in Fortune 500 History to Have Two Black CEOs in a Row."

135. Tanaya Macheel, "Most Powerful Women in Banking: Thasunda Brown Duckett, JPMorgan Chase," *American Banker*, September 29, 2020, https://www.americanbanker.com/news/most-power ful-women-in-banking-for-2020-thasunda-brown-duckett-jpmor gan-chase.

136. David Gelles, "Marc Benioff of Salesforce: 'Are We All Not Connected?,'" *New York Times*, June 15, 2018, https://www.nytimes .com/2018/06/15/business/marc-benioff-salesforce-corner-office .html.

137. Garrett Parker, "10 Things You Didn't Know About Marc Benioff," *Money, Inc.*, September 19, 2016, https://moneyinc.com/things -you-didnt-know-about-marc-benioff/.

138. Michal Lev-Ram, "Force of Nature: How the Unstoppable Marc Benioff Fueled Salesforce's Stratospheric Rise," *Fortune*, June 3, 2021, https://fortune.com/longform/marc-benioff-salesforce-slack-acqui sition-diversity-inclusion-fortune-500/.

139. Margaret Sullivan, "Four Reasons the Jan. 6 Hearings Have Conquered the News Cycle," *Washington Post*, July 22, 2022, https:// www.washingtonpost.com/media/2022/07/22/jan6-hearings -news-cycle-media/.

140. Benjamin Wallace-Wells, "Liz Cheney's Kamikaze Campaign," *New Yorker*, August 10, 2022, https://www.newyorker.com/news /the-political-scene/liz-cheneys-kamikaze-campaign.

141. Paul Kane, "Liz Cheney's Political Life Is Likely Ending— and Just Beginning," *Washington Post*, August 15, 2022, https://

www.washingtonpost.com/politics/2022/08/15/liz-cheneys-politi
cal-life-is-likely-ending-just-beginning/.

142. Liz Cheney, "The GOP Is at a Turning Point. History Is Watching Us," *Washington Post*, May 5, 2021, https://www.washington
post.com/opinions/2021/05/05/liz-cheney-republican-party-turn
ing-point/.

143. Vivek Wadhwa, Ismail Amla, and Alex Salkever, *From Incremental
to Exponential: How Large Companies Can See the Future and Rethink
Innovation* (Oakland, CA: Berrett-Koehler, 2020).

144. Sachin Waikar, "Microsoft CEO Satya Nadella: Be Bold and Be
Right," *Insights*, Stanford Graduate School of Business, November 26, 2019, https://www.gsb.stanford.edu/insights/microsoft-ceo
-satya-nadella-be-bold-be-right.

145. Kashmir Hill, "Microsoft Plans to Eliminate Face Analysis Tools in
Push for 'Responsible A.I.,'" *New York Times*, June 21, 2022, https://
www.nytimes.com/2022/06/21/technology/microsoft-facial-rec
ognition.html#:~:text=the%20main%20story-,Microsoft%20
Plans%20to%20Eliminate%20Face%20Analysis%20Tools%20
in%20Push%20for,of%20its%20facial%20recognition%20tool.

146. Austin Carr and Dina Bass, "The Most Valuable Company (for
Now) Is Having a Nadellaissance," Bloomberg, May 2, 2019,
https://www.bloomberg.com/news/features/2019-05-02/satya-na
della-remade-microsoft-as-world-s-most-valuable-company.

147. Heather Haddon, "McDonald's Fires CEO Steve Easterbrook over
Relationship with Employee," *Wall Street Journal*, November 4, 2019,
https://www.wsj.com/articles/mcdonalds-fires-ceo-steve-easter
brook-over-relationship-with-employee-11572816660.

148. Ibid.

149. David Enrich and Rachel Abrams, "McDonald's Sues Former
C.E.O., Accusing Him of Lying and Fraud," *New York Times*, August 10, 2020, https://www.nytimes.com/2020/08/10/business
/mcdonalds-ceo-steve-easterbrook.html.

150. Stephen Castle and Peter Robins, "How Boris Johnson Fell, and

What Happens Next," *New York Times*, July 19, 2022, https://www
.nytimes.com/article/boris-johnson-prime-minister-explained.html.

151. Ibid.
152. Sylvia Ann Hewlett, *The Sponsor Effect* (Boston, Mass.: Harvard Business Review Press, 2019), pages 72–74.
153. Charles McNulty, "Gustavo Dudamel's Captivating Theatrics Serve the Music," *Los Angeles Times*, October 27, 2012, https://www.la times.com/entertainment/arts/la-xpm-2012-oct-27-la-et-cm-du damel-notebook-20121028-story.html.
154. Lisa Lerer and Sydney Ember, "Examining Tara Reade's Sexual Assault Allegation Against Joe Biden," *New York Times*, September 20, 2020, https://www.nytimes.com/2020/04/12/us/politics/joe-biden -tara-reade-sexual-assault-complaint.html.
155. Jane Mayer, "The Case of Al Franken," *New Yorker*, July 22, 2019, https://www.newyorker.com/magazine/2019/07/29/the-case-of-al -franken.
156. Carmine Gallo, "How Steve Jobs Made Presentations Look Effortless," *Forbes*, March 26, 2015, https://www.forbes.com/sites/car minegallo/2015/03/26/how-steve-jobs-made-presentations-look -effortless/?sh=20d888316bf6.
157. Walter Isaacson, "The Real Leadership Lessons of Steve Jobs," *Harvard Business Review*, April 2012, https://hbr.org/2012/04/the-real -leadership-lessons-of-steve-jobs.
158. Jon Wertheim and Jessica Luther, "Inside the Corrosive Workplace Culture of the Dallas Mavericks," *Sports Illustrated*, February 20, 2018, https://www.si.com/nba/2018/02/21/dallas-mavericks-sexual -misconduct-investigation-mark-cuban-response.
159. Doyle Rader, "Dallas Mavericks Win NBA Inclusion Leadership Award," *Forbes*, January 17, 2020, https://www.forbes.com/sites /doylerader/2020/01/17/dallas-mavericks-win-nba-inclusion-leader ship-award-cynt-marshall/?utm_source=TWITTER&utm_medi um=social&utm_content=3068412047&utm_campaign=sprinklr SportsMoneyTwitter&sh=3d45fd1c2d54.

160. Sylvia Ann Hewlett, *#MeToo in the Corporate World: Power, Privilege, and the Path Forward* (New York: Harper Business, 2020), 117–91.

161. "Jørgen Vig Knudstorp," profile, *EuropeanCEO*, March 15, 2010, https://www.europeanceo.com/profiles/jrgen-vig-knudstorp-lego/.

162. Laura Ross, "Lessons from Leaders: Jørgen Vig Knudstorp," Thomas Insights, September 14, 2021, https://www.thomasnet.com/insights/lessons-from-leaders-j-rgen-vig-knudstorp/.

163. Jenna McGregor, "Brick by Brick: The Man Who Rebuilt the House of Lego Shares His Leadership Secrets," *Washington Post*, December 8, 2016, https://www.washingtonpost.com/news/on-leadership/wp/2016/12/08/brick-by-brick-the-man-who-rebuilt-the-house-of-lego-shares-his-leadership-secrets/.

164. Andrew O'Connell, "Lego CEO Jørgen Vig Knudstorp on Leading Through Growth and Survival," *Harvard Business Review*, January 2009, https://hbr.org/2009/01/lego-ceo-jorgen-vig-knudstorp-on-leading-through-survival-and-growth#:~:text=J%C3%B8rgen%20Vig%20Knudstorp%2C%20a%20former%20McKinsey%20consultant%20who,and%20opened%20it%20to%20ideas%20from%20enthusiastic%20users.

165. Sapna Maheshwari and Vanessa Friedman, "Victoria's Secret Swaps Angels for 'What Women Want.' Will They Buy It?," *New York Times*, June 16, 2021, https://www.nytimes.com/2021/06/16/business/victorias-secret-collective-megan-rapinoe.html.

166. Cavenagh Research, "Victoria's Secret: Market Is Mispricing the Company's Value," Seeking Alpha, July 14, 2022, https://seekingalpha.com/article/4523323-victorias-secret-market-mispricing-company-value.

167. Tyler Stone, "Eddie Glaude: July 4th 'Has Always Been an Incredibly Vexed Holiday for Me,'" RealClear Politics, July 1, 2022, https://www.realclearpolitics.com/video/2022/07/01/eddie_glaude_july_4th_has_always_been_an_incredibly_vexed_holiday_for_me.html.

168. Brian Phillips, "What Makes Superstar Conductor Gustavo Dudamel So Good?," *New York Times*, November 1, 2018, https://www

.nytimes.com/2018/11/01/magazine/gustavo-dudamel-los-angeles
-philharmonic.html.

169.   Ibid.

170.   Katie Thomas and Reed Abelson, "Elizabeth Holmes, Theranos
C.E.O. and Silicon Valley Star, Accused of Fraud," *New York Times*,
March 14, 2018, https://www.nytimes.com/2018/03/14/health/ther
anos-elizabeth-holmes-fraud.html.

171.   Avery Hartmans, Sarah Jackson, Aline Cain, and Azmi Haroun, "The
Rise and Fall of Elizabeth Holmes, the Former Theranos CEO Found
Guilty of Wire Fraud and Conspiracy, Whose Sentencing Has Now
Been Delayed," *Business Insider*, updated January 20, 2023, https://
www.businessinsider.com/theranos-founder-ceo-elizabeth-holmes
-life-story-bio-2018-4.

172.   Emma Powell, "Women Who Work Remotely Will Hurt Their Careers Says Bank of England's Catherine Mann," *Times* (London),
November 11, 2021, https://www.thetimes.co.uk/article/women
-who-work-remotely-could-damage-their-careers-says-bank-of-en
gland-s-catherine-mann-cfvc7qgxx.

173.   Callum Borchers, "Think Working from Home Won't Hurt Your
Career? Don't Be So Sure," *Wall Street Journal*, June 9, 2022,
https://www.wsj.com/articles/think-working-from-home-wont
-hurt-your-career-dont-be-so-sure-11654725511.

174.   Lydia Saad and Ben Wigert, "Remote Work Persisting and Trend-
ing Permanent," Gallup, October 13, 2021, https://news.gallup
.com/poll/355907/remote-work-persisting-trending-permanent
.aspx.

175.   Katrin Bennhold, "In Finland, a Partying Prime Minister Draws
Tuts and Cheers," *New York Times*, August 27, 2022, https://www
.nytimes.com/2022/08/27/world/europe/sanna-marin-finland-pm
-party.html.

176.   David Nakamura, "Trump, Japan's Abe Work on Strengthen-
ing Ties—but Also, Change Them After Awkward Coincidence,"
Washington Post, April 18, 2018, https://www.washingtonpost.com
/news/post-politics/wp/2018/04/18/trump-japans-abe-work-on

-strengthening-ties-but-also-change-them-after-awkward-coinci
dence/.

177. Alexandra Alter, "Amanda Gorman Captures the Moment,
in Verse," *New York Times*, January 19, 2021, https://www.ny
times.com/2021/01/19/books/amanda-gorman-inauguration
-hill-we-climb.html.

178. Katherine Clarke, "The Omaha House Where Warren Buffett
Launched His Business Empire Asks $799,000," *Wall Street Jour-
nal*, April 13, 2022, https://www.wsj.com/articles/warren-buffett
-omaha-house-for-sale-11649865478.

179. "Three Lectures by Warren Buffett to Notre Dame Faculty, MBA
Students and Undergraduate Students," Spring 1991, Whitney Til-
son's Value Investing Website, https://www.tilsonfunds.com/Buf
fettNotreDame.pdf, 15.

180. Nicolas Vega, "Warren Buffett Is 'Halfway' Through Giving Away
His Massive Fortune. Here's Why His Kids Will Get Almost None
of His $100 Billion," CNBC, June 23, 2021, https://www.cnbc
.com/2021/06/23/why-warren-buffett-isnt-leaving-his-100-billion
-dollar-fortune-to-his-kids.html.

181. Debanjali Bose, "Warren Buffett Just Became the Longest-
Serving CEO of an S&P Company. Take a Look Inside His In-
credible Life and Career," *Insider*, February 20, 2020, https://www
.businessinsider.com/warren-buffett-incredible-life-2017-5.

182. Catie Edmondson, "How Alexandria Ocasio-Cortez Learned to
Play by Washington's Rules," *New York Times*, September 18, 2019,
https://www.nytimes.com/2019/09/18/us/politics/alexandria-oca
sio-cortez-washington.html.

183. Liz Robbins, "She's Pumped. Your Turn," *New York Times*, March 18,
2009, https://www.nytimes.com/2009/03/19/fashion/19fitness
.html.

184. "Controversy over the New Yorker's Cover Illustration of Obamas,"
New York Times, July 14, 2008, https://www.nytimes.com/2008/07/14
/world/americas/14iht-york.3.14484322.html.

185. Katherine Fung, "Michelle Obama's Favorability Rating Nearly 20

Points Higher Than Trump, Biden and Pence's: Poll," *Newsweek*, August 18, 2020, https://www.newsweek.com/michelle-obamas -favorability-rating-nearly-20-points-higher-trump-biden-pences -poll-1525850.

186. Staff, "Health Hacks from the World's Favourite Billionaire, Rich- ard Branson," *Australian Men's Health*, May 1, 2021, https://www .menshealth.com.au/richard-branson-workout-routine/.

187. Sapna Maheshwari, "The Office Beckons. Time for Your Sharpest 'Power Casual,'" *New York Times*, April 29, 2022, https://www.ny times.com/2022/04/29/business/casual-workwear-clothes-office .html.

188. Kristijan Lucic, "Pixel Watch Shown by Google CEO During Interview," Android Headlines, September 7, 2022, https://www .androidheadlines.com/2022/09/pixel-watch-shown-by-google-ceo .html.

189. Glynda Alves, "Google CEO Sundar Pichai Masters the Art of Ca- sual Dressing," *Economic Times*, February 5, 2016, https://economic times.indiatimes.com/magazines/panache/google-ceo-sundar -pichai-masters-the-art-of-casual-dressing/articleshow/51133240 .cms?from=mdr.

190. Avery Hartmans, "Silicon Valley's Ultimate Status Symbol Is the Sneaker. Here Are the Rare, Expensive, and Goofy Shoes Worn by the Top Tech CEOs," *Business Insider*, March 15, 2019, https:// www.businessinsider.com/sneakers-worn-by-tech-execs-2017-5#.

191. Emma Goldberg, "What Sheryl Sandberg's 'Lean In' Has Meant to Women," *New York Times*, June 2, 2022, https://www.nytimes .com/2022/06/02/business/sheryl-sandberg-lean-in.html#:~: text=The%20book%20sold%20over%20four,Sandberg's%20ad vice%20as%20a%20guide.

192. Rebecca Greenfield, "Sheryl Sandberg's 'Lean In' Missed What Most Women Needed," Bloomberg, June 3, 2022, https://www.bloomberg .com/news/articles/2022-06-03/sheryl-sandberg-s-lean-in-missed -what-women-wanted#xj4y7vzkg.

193. Glenn Kessler, "Zelensky's Famous Quote of 'Need Ammo, Not

a Ride,' Not Easily Confirmed," *Washington Post*, March 6, 2022, https://www.washingtonpost.com/politics/2022/03/06/zelenskys -famous-quote-need-ammo-not-ride-not-easily-confirmed/.

194. Edward Segal, "As Ukraine Resists Russian Invasion, Zelensky Demonstrates These Leadership Lessons," *Forbes*, March 1, 2022, https://www.forbes.com/sites/edwardsegal/2022/03/01/as-ukr aine-resists-russian-invasion-zelenskyy-demonstrates-these-leader ship-lessons/?sh=4a896b593837.

195. Aatish Taseer, "How Rudy Giuliani Went from 9/11's Hallowed Mayor to 2021's Haunted Ghoul," *Vanity Fair*, September 2021, https://www.vanityfair.com/news/2021/08/how-rudy-giuliani -went-from-911s-hallowed-mayor-to-2021s-haunted-ghoul.

196. Katrin Bennhold, "In Finland, a Partying Prime Minister Draws Tuts, and Cheers," *New York Times*, August 27, 2022, https://www .nytimes.com/2022/08/27/world/europe/sanna-marin-finland-pm -party.html.

INDEX

Italic page numbers indicate illustrations.

Index

Index

292

Index

Index

Index

Index

Index

Morehouse College, 221
Morgan Stanley, 90, 173, 191
Morning Joe (TV show), 101, 220
Motorola, 54
Moynihan, Brian, 40
Multiplier Effect, 184
Munch, Edvard, 244
Murdoch, Rupert, 226
Musk, Elon, 47–48

Nadella, Satya, 197–98
nail care, 78–79, 94, 96, 97, 142
Nation (magazine), 141
National Center for Refugee and
    Immigrant Children, 46
National Civil Rights Museum,
    89
National Enquirer, 6
Nationwide Building Society, 33,
    129
Neale, Margaret, 62
nervousness, 84, *85*
networking, 124, 167
Newman, Paul, 97
New Yorker, 240
New York Review of Books, 6
New York Stock Exchange, 36–37
New York Times, 4–6, 39, 149,
    218
New York University, Stern School
    of Business, 139
Nike, 103–4, 186
"non-negotiables," 168–69
Nonviolent Communication
    (Rosenberg), 197
North Atlantic Treaty Organization
    (NATO), 246
Northwestern University, Kellogg
    School of Management, 26

Obama, Barack, 38–39, 80–81, 100,
    138, 240, 255
Obama, Michelle, 11, 81, 84,
    239–41, 255
  gravitas and walking the tightrope,
    44–45, 149–50
  physical fitness, 99–100, 107, 231,
    233, 239–41
Ocasio-Cortez, Alexandria, 233,
    237, 238–39
office appearance and decor, 47, 103
office mini-retreats, 229–30
Olivier, Laurence, 63
online image, *232,* 243–45, *248,*
    250–51. *See also* social media
  Sheryl Sandberg and, 234, 243–45
Oprah (TV show), 4
Oracle, 51, 194
Othello (movie), 63
Oxford University, 1–2, 7, 201

Pamuk, Orhan, 104, 221
Pandit, Vikram, 40, 68
Parker, Mark, 103–4
Parsons, Dick, 68
pauses (pausing), 67–68
PayPal, 47
pedigree, *29,* 185
Pendleton, Hadiya, 44–45
People (magazine), 4
people of color, 19–21
  "angry Black woman," 147–48,
    149, 164
  appearance and walking the
    tightrope, 145, 233, 239
  authenticity vs. conformity. *See*
    authenticity vs. conformity
  "bleached-out professionals,"
    159–66

Index

Index

Index

SYLVIA ANN HEWLETT is an economist, entrepreneur, and acclaimed author. She is CEO of Hewlett Consulting Partners and founder of Coqual. Her eighteen highly acclaimed books include *When the Bough Breaks* (winner of a RFK Memorial Book Award); *Forget a Mentor, Find a Sponsor* (an Audible bestseller); and *#MeToo in the Corporate World* (a *Financial Times* book of the month). She has been honored by Google with its Global Diversity Award, appeared on *The Oprah Winfrey Show* and *60 Minutes,* and lampooned on *Saturday Night Live.* A Kennedy Scholar and a graduate of Cambridge University, Hewlett earned her PhD in economics at London University. She grew up in the Welsh mining valleys in a family of six daughters and currently lives in New York City.